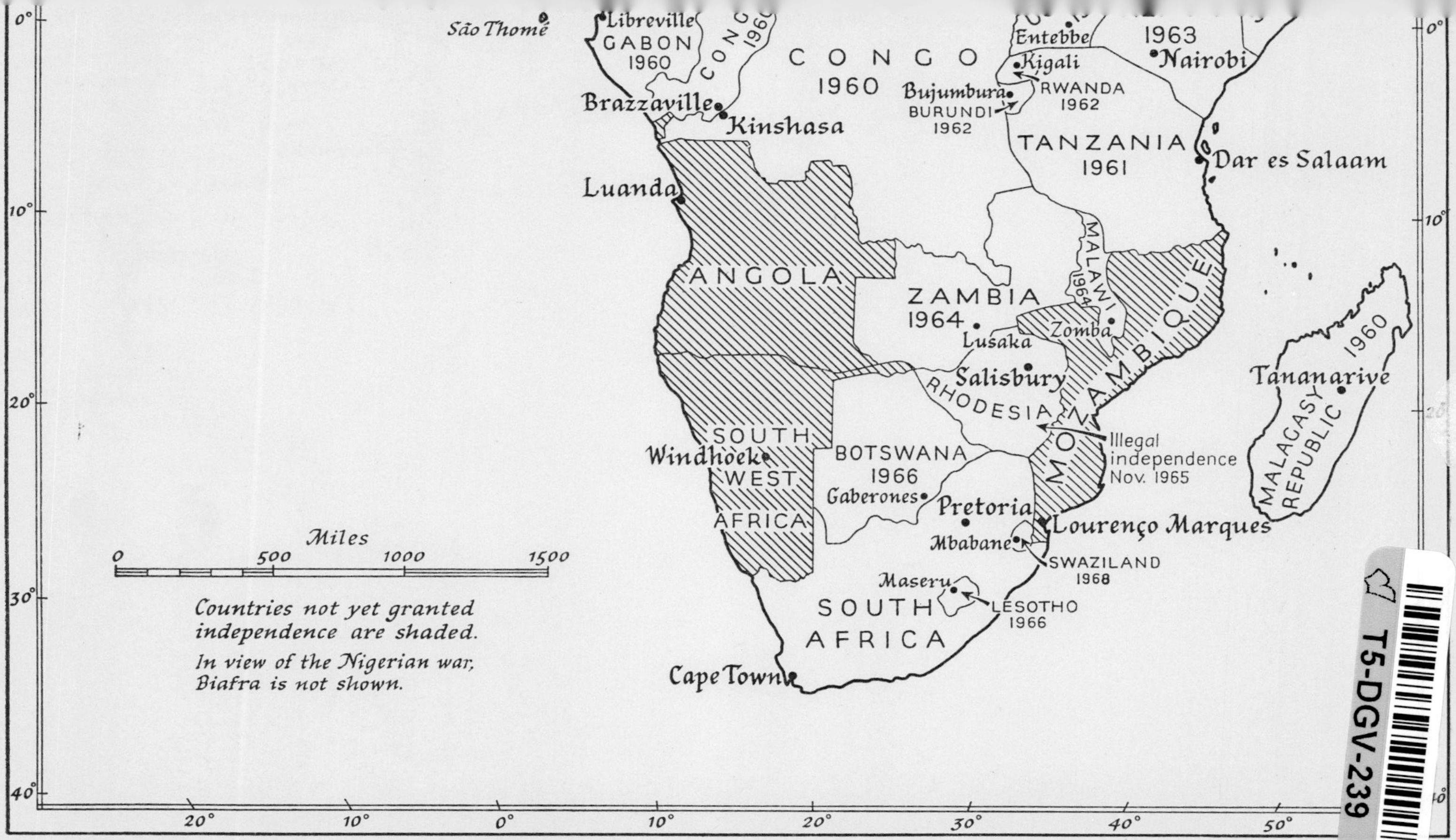
São Thomé
Libreville
GABON
1960
CONGO
1960
CONGO
1960
Brazzaville
Kinshasa
Bujumbura
BURUNDI
1962
Entebbe
Kigali
RWANDA
1962
1963
Nairobi
TANZANIA
1961
Dar es Salaam
Luanda
ANGOLA
ZAMBIA
1964
Lusaka
MALAWI
1964
Zomba
MOZAMBIQUE
Salisbury
RHODESIA
Illegal
independence
Nov. 1965
Tananarive
MALAGASY
REPUBLIC
1960
SOUTH
WEST
AFRICA
Windhoek
BOTSWANA
1966
Gaberones
Pretoria
Lourenço Marques
Mbabane
SWAZILAND
1968
Maseru
LESOTHO
1966
SOUTH
AFRICA
Cape Town
Miles
0
500
1000
1500
Countries not yet granted
independence are shaded.
In view of the Nigerian war,
Biafra is not shown.
0°
10°
20°
30°
40°
50°

AFRICAN RENAISSANCE

AFRICAN RENAISSANCE

by

LEONARD BARNES

LONDON
VICTOR GOLLANCZ LTD
1969

575 00171 2

PRINTED IN GREAT BRITAIN
BY EBENEZER BAYLIS AND SON, LTD.
THE TRINITY PRESS, WORCESTER, AND LONDON

CONTENTS

I. THE CURRENT PHASE

Chapter		Page
1	First Glance	9
2	Who are these Africans?	16
3	The Work there is to do	27
4	The Dark Wood	33
5	Escape	43
6	The Positive Policy: General Idea	57

II. THE POSITIVE POLICY: SPECIAL IDEAS

7	Redundant Men	69
8	Operation Habitat	85
9	The Menace of the Towns	106
10	Trained Minds	114
11	The Race Issue	132
12	Debalkanisation	152
13	Expansion without Growth: Ivory Coast	167
14	Growth without Expansion: Guinea	184

III. THE LONG RUN

15	The Real Priorities	207
16	Peasant Truth	216
17	Sub Specie Evolutionis	222

APPENDICES

A	Figures of Area, Population, Output	234
B	Rhodesia Story	238
C	Nigeria Story	254
D	China Story	280
	Index	295

CONTENTS

Part One. The Cheaper Place

Chapter   *Page*

1. First Sights
2. Who are these people?
3. Black on the Copper Belt
4. The Deep North
5. Labour
6. The Politics of the Urban Divide

Part Two. The Rhodesian Federation

7. Birth of an Idea
8. Opening the Trail
9. Free Enterprise and its Legacy
10. Divided Minds
11. The Reaction
12. Breakdown ...
13. Nationalism on the March Towards Crisis
14. Growth without Expansion — Culture

Part Three. Long Run

15. The Road to Revolution
16. Peasant Lands
17. A Post-War Revolution

APPENDICES

A. Figures and Facts, Input and Output
B. Rhodesia Story
C. Prison Story
D. Gwelo Gaol

Index

I

THE CURRENT PHASE

FIRST GLANCE

AFRICANS ARE AWARE that their newly independent countries
are not greatly esteemed outside Africa, or even inside it. They
do not like this. But they do not react by resolving to deserve
praise through improved performance. They blame the world
for not having a higher opinion of them, and believe that, but
for neo-colonialism and race-prejudice, it would. They ask how
they can improve, not their souls, but their image.

The great year of African Independence was 1960, though
the graduation ceremony began a few years earlier. By 1964
virtually the whole of the continent between the Mediterranean
and the Zambesi was no longer subject to overt political control
from outside. The exceptions were four small enclaves, Spanish
Sahara and Spanish Guinea, Portuguese Guinea, and French
Somaliland.

Probably the non-African world at no stage nursed any extra-
vagant hopes that the general well-being of Africans would take
a great leap forward, merely as a result of a political independence which, with the best will in the world, would have to
remain pretty nominal for some time to come. But there certainly existed a widespread feeling that the old colonial system
ought not to survive as an acknowledged feature of the post-war
world. The new constitutional terms negotiated by the British
and the French with their African dependencies were thought
to open up an interesting and perhaps promising experiment.
They involved at any rate a real increase in the practical
responsibility of Africans for managing their own affairs. The
world, in effect, said to Africa "Good luck to you. Now show
us what you can do."

In the case of the early starters, such as Sudan and Ghana,
ten years or more have gone by; in the case of most of the rest,

1*

seven years. The impression grows that such initial promise as there may have been has not been fulfilled. The surface trends, political and economic, are downward, not upward. What the new African States have demonstrated is a high degree of political instability and administrative incompetence; a reckless squandering of economic resources combined with an absolutely king-size capacity for corruption and graft of all sorts in all social strata including the highest (indeed especially in the highest); a perverse tendency to break up useful political and economic associations into ever less viable smithereens; and finally a morbid relish for meeting their difficulties with violence and savagery.

Each of these counts can be supported by much day-to-day evidence. It is hardly surprising that casual observers often conclude that the grand experiment of African independence has failed and ought never to have been tried; that white supremacy, with or without apartheid, stands on an altogether higher plane of political wisdom; and that, while the independence constitutions cannot now be revoked, it is mere prudence and honesty to admit that basically the running of African affairs must remain in non-African hands for many years still.

In mid-1964 I had an illuminating interview in Kampala with Mr. Jimmy Simpson (J. T. Simpson, C.B.E.), then Chairman of the Uganda Development Corporation, and some of his African colleagues. He enlarged upon the potentialities and charms of Uganda, and then turned smilingly to the African gentlemen present. "We could make a paradise of this country in five years, if only there were no Africans in it." I froze in horror, waiting for the explosion he seemed to be deliberately provoking. Africans can be exceedingly touchy about such taunts, even when made under licence as good-humoured jokes. To my relief and their credit they chuckled with appreciative laughter. Simpson knew his men and how far he could safely go in pulling their legs.

But he had touched on a valid point, which those of us who study the African scene do well to bear in mind as a standard of reference. A great deal of important economic development, for example, is going on in Africa today; almost all of it is conceived, programmed, and executed by, or under the direction of, non-Africans. If it were possible to empty the continent of Africans and to replace them with much smaller numbers of, say, Chinese or Japanese or even Americans, the *mise-en-valeur* of these desperately ill-used territories would proceed at a pace and in a relatively orderly fashion of which there is no current prospect. Africans are inevitably judged today not merely by reference to their own past, but also by comparison with their contemporaries in other parts of the world.

I do not think it can be disputed that the great obstacle to social and economic progress in Africa is the African population itself. The tragic history of the continent over the last five centuries, and the forms of social organisation prevalent at the present time, have resulted in a human medium very recalcitrant to the processes of modernisation of which the best African minds are now beginning to dream, and which will have to be gone through before Africa makes to the global civilisation the contribution it is capable of, and therefore owes. Heaven knows the world cannot do without that contribution. How long must we wait?

While it is true that African independence has in many ways made a shockingly bad start, it has also to be remembered that the mini-states into which the continent has got itself fragmented are, as they stand, ungovernable. Apparent exceptions to this judgment, so far as concerns Mediterranean and tropical Africa, are the Congo, Nigeria, and Egypt. The last is perhaps a real exception, but the Congo and Nigeria are certainly apparent only, since their nominal unity is in fact as thoroughly fragmented as any other part of the continent. So the real failure of the new African rulers is not that they give bad government to meaningless units which cannot be governed well. It is rather that they insist on perpetuating the conditions that make good government impossible; in other words, that they continually shy away from the closer political association with their neighbours which is the sole cure for the chronic unviability of all.

I have been travelling about tropical Africa since the

beginning of 1964. I should have been blind indeed if I had not
been appalled by the destructive social vortices in which African
life is spinning—apparently out of all rational control. But I
should have been blinder still if I had missed a number of
other perspectives which in their aggregate present the continental outlook in a much modified light, and one which in the
long term is more favourable.

The first of these concerns the timing of African independence. It is often said that independence began prematurely and
has been carried through too quickly and too completely. In my
view, this belief is grounded in misunderstanding.

Possibly it is true that, if the colonial powers had set out, from
the time of the great scramble for Africa eighty years ago,
systematically to train the local populations for full autonomy
at the earliest possible date, the new African states of 1960 and
thereabouts would have been better found than they were when
independence actually came. But this was not the policy the
powers adopted. Consequently by 1960 African populations
were 50 years in arrears, so far as concerned real competence
to manage their affairs. What then? Is it suggested that they
ought to have undergone a further 50 years of colonial status
while these arrears were being made up? If so, is it supposed
that by 2100 the crown of sovereignty would be sitting more
easily on their heads in the world then current than their 1960-
sovereignty does in the world of the sixties?

No, the fact is quite simply that by the time 1960 was rung in
the world had reached a point at which the subjection of any
population to direct political control from outside was no longer
workable in ways satisfactory either to controllers or controlled.
I know of no evidence to suggest that the general situation in
any part of Africa would have been either improved in practice
or made effectively more promising, if the 1960 constitutional
developments had been put off to 1970, or 1980, or any other
date. In 1960 the risks of further delay were much more serious
than the risks of going ahead, as Portugal, white Rhodesia, and
white South Africa, for all their blurred vision, have already
begun to perceive.

It has further to be said that the notion of "fitness for self-government" as a principle for determining actual constitutional status is devoid of practical meaning. On what criteria can a country be awarded a certificate of such fitness, if, for example, it also goes about the globe dropping atom bombs? Would not reason urge that countries which so behave are fit only for life-imprisonment?

Or, again, take those nations whose policies landed us in two world wars in twenty years. In the face of so gigantic a failure to adapt to their social habitat, in the face of such brutal un-teachability, can they be adjudged on an objective assessment to possess overall fitness for anything? The truth is that where a nation exercises so-called independence, it is never because it is fit to do so. Always because no agency yet exists in the world which is fit to prevent it. Until such an agency emerges there is no firm ground on which to distinguish between the constitutional entitlements of different human populations.

Along the line of such reflections the student of the contemporary African scene learns his first serious lesson—that there are literally no stones whatever which it is safe, or even decent, for non-Africans to throw at Africans. Of course, the student must note and honestly reckon up the frightful ways in which Africans continually dishonour human life. But he has to grasp equally honestly that African misdemeanours of this sort are matched by counterparts, often graver, often more numerous, in every other part of the world without exception. And not least in his own fatherland. Culturally speaking, Africa is not nearly so far behind the West as the West is behind its own best possibilities.

Just appreciation has only one starting-point. The troubles of Africa's proud and angry dust are a particular aspect of a global phenomenon in which we are all enmeshed, and which with superb impartiality threatens the future of all nations alike. This phenomenon is the A.A.L.A. Gap. A.A.L.A. stands for Asia, Africa, and Latin America. The gap is the widening divergence between living standards in those continents on the one hand

and in North America and Europe on the other. The movement of the overdeveloped countries towards increasing affluence and the movement of the underdeveloped countries towards deepening indigence are not unconnected. Together, indeed, they constitute a morbid organic nexus in which the former movement stands as ground and the latter as consequence.

And just appreciation equally has only one method. This consists both in the meticulous observation of the phenomena of African social processes, and also (and more especially) in construing the phenomena observed in terms of the underlying fields of force whose structure they express but cannot exhaust. Such fields, if we can adequately define them, will enable us to treat social phenomena in the same kind of way as the wave theory of light enables us to order the colours of the spectrum each to its proper wave-length.

We can be sure of one thing about the social fields of force we are hoping to identify. They are evolutionary in character. They presuppose a context of cosmic space-time, which we must take account of as best we may, because they are really intelligible only within that total context. In short, no social process can be understood until we have information not only about its current phase but also about its origins, its mode of development, and (in some ways most important of all) what it is by way of turning into. The student has a duty to make the best projections he can of its future states. Without these, information about its past and present can be very misleading. Organic growth cannot be justly interpreted except in terms which include its florescence. In the case of Africa's growth, florescence belongs to the future, perhaps to the far future. Certainly the real fruits of even such limited independence as the continent can be said to be enjoying in the 1960s have not yet begun to ripen on the tree. The inevitable confusions, errors, extravagances, misplaced hesitations, Yes, these are very visible. The results of the good work which the few public-spirited Africans have put in during the opening years of their lives as self-governing citizens, No, these are still quietly maturing below the surface. From 1980 onwards, the picture will start to look very different.

The better the student comes to identify the underlying dynamics of Africa's past and present, the more sanguine the form in which his forward extrapolations emerge. He finds he cannot stump this ambivalent continent without acquiring, besides a wholesome fear of the dreadful social storms by which it is tossed, a surprising confidence, a kind of tranquil trust, in the latent genius of the African peoples who are so unfairly condemned to ride them out.

The best human beings whom Africa produces today are no whit inferior in quality to the best who can be found anywhere else in the world. In all countries the best are few. But they are being added to more quickly perhaps in Africa than in most other places. It is on this moral and intellectual aristocracy and on the African peasantry that my tranquil trust most firmly fastens. When these two social elements learn to work together in close alliance for the balanced development of human and natural resources, Africa will have found its feet indeed. In their merger, in the expanding insight and wisdom of the one combined with the untapped reserves of all human gifts in the other, nestle the planted seeds of the African Renaissance.

CHAPTER 2

WHO ARE THESE AFRICANS?

IF YOU WALK about the streets near the centre of Benin City in Nigeria, perception soon becomes bemused from over-stimulation of eyes, ears, and nose. Disabling smells arise from ever-accumulating slops and refuse of every kind, which recall one's fancies of back-alleys in 18th century London. One does not indeed have to watch out overhead, but soakaways all seem to be choked, and a blue-black efflux with green edges seeps into the road.

Small piles of congealed tarmac, left over from past road repair work, obstruct the side-walk. Plenty of naked children run around, their umbilical hernias blinking broadly in the sun. The local tap or pump is besieged by women with buckets, and the surrounding area is red liquid mud. Large bright butterflies and dragonflies dance in the air, and a little higher up swallows and swifts hawk diligently.

Ears are assailed by pop-music blaring from transistor sets or record-players in the Honour God Football Pools booth or the God First Wee Wee Bar. Eyes note the painful disrepair of dwellings, shops, and offices. Even the thick mud-walls of the city, which at intervals carry plaques advertising their historic interest, are crumbling and covered with weeds. The moat is dry and half-full of rubbish. Abandoned cars have been tipped into it, and left to rust to pieces.

The people have a cheerful look and they acknowledge a greeting in a civil fashion. There are always some who like to get into talk with strangers. One such explained to me that, while he welcomed African independence, he wished that the white men would tell Africans how they ought to use it. Another, who described himself as priest and leader of the Cherubim and Seraphim, made a note of my name and address, and promised to write to me in England. (His letter has not yet arrived.) He saw no reason to fuss about the future of Nigeria, for he had information that God would provide.

A little later, when I was caught by a heavy thunderstorm, a glossy, enormously prosperous-looking Nigerian picked me up in his car, and most kindly drove me back to my hotel, as though assuming me to be entitled to such treatment.

Benin is no shanty-town, mushrooming up in hasty squalor between dusk and dawn. It is an ancient capital city of Africa, a centre of a once-brilliant artistic culture, where the tradition of the great bronze-workers has persisted for centuries, and still persists. The reaction to it of today's European passer-by is quite simply, "Where, oh where, do you make a start if you want to clean up this gangrenous dump?" To the average African, on the other hand, it is a national shrine which he is glad to hallow, but has no impulse to improve, or even to maintain in decent order. This characteristic mixture of unaggressive pride of race with slothful indifference puts a strain on a European's powers of imaginative sympathy.

It is a mixture which one constantly encounters all over Africa in variant forms and differing contexts. Thousands of miles from Benin, in the remote Lebombo hills whose scarp overhangs like a wave turned to stone in the act of breaking, where the clean air is full of the fragrance of acacia blossom, I stood by a drinking-trough under a grilling sun, watching a team of plough-oxen being watered after their morning's work. I was chatting idly to Mbangane, the driver of the ox-team, when he happened to make some deferential mention of Chaka, the Black Napoleon who was murdered by his brother Dingana in 1826.

"You speak as if you were sorry that the days of Chaka and his rule are past, Mbangane," I said.

He laughed and answered, "Oh, *Kosana*, Chaka was a great King and the Zulu were men in his time. But streams that flow strongly in summer dry up when winter comes."

"Chaka's stream ran red with the blood of his subjects whom he slaughtered. Is it a bad thing that it should have ceased to flow? Would you choose his summer rather than the white man's winter?"

"*Kosana*, the white people think that Chaka was only a cruel and destructive tyrant. The *bantu* remember that he was also a wise judge and governor, a thinker of deep thoughts, a skilled maker of music and of verses."

"Are then those tales untrue that tell how he struck down like flies, not only his enemies and the cowards in his armies but even those who served him best, even Mnyamana and Nongogo? Did he not delight to spill the blood of his young women chosen for their light skins and beautiful bodies?"

"For much of his life, *Kosana*, Chaka was better loved than any chief has ever been loved of his people. If in his last years a blackness came over his heart and he took to killing for killing's sake, that was because of the craft of evil spirits. The seed of evil sprouted and flourished in him because of the sin of his father."

"Say more, Mbangane. I do not understand."

"The union of Senzangakona and Mnandi was not sanctioned by the tribe or by their ancestors."

"But does that wash off from Chaka the stain of his tortures and massacres?"

"The *bantu* do not put that question, *Kosana*. They only know that Chaka was heir of the evil his father did in begetting him. Yet neither do they forget that it was he who first made a proud nation of the Zulu people, and one of whose story all the black races are proud, or will be in time to come."

In reflecting later on these exchanges, two things occurred to me. One was that here again appears the Benin complex of dignified gratitude to ancestors for a memorable example, combined with lack of any feeling of obligation to render analogous service to posterity by exertions of one's own. Of the Homeric spirit there is no trace—"Our real praise is to make ourselves better men than our fathers."

My second conclusion was this. To be forcibly subjected to foreign domination, however unbrutal that might be, is more subtly injurious to the African nature than any incidental cruelties of a system organic to itself.

The unhomeric outlook is surprising, in view of the tragic significance of childlessness for Africans. To be unrepresented in the generations to come by the fruit of one's own loins is seen as a threat of extinction for current life-breathers and departed ancestors alike. So strong is this feeling that the birth of a child rather than the act of intercourse is commonly regarded as the consummation of a marriage. Yet the emphasis is still on quantity rather than quality.

The type-African desires to have sons, but does not ask that they should be improvements on himself. The big man, the man of power, is he who begets many children; the question of their cultural potential is not examined. Still less is there awareness that the offspring of a man's mind, his deeper insights into the nature of the habitat or the working of human affairs, may be more precious than the children of his body. Africa needs a strong dose of Homer to give her strength to tackle her vast problems of self-modernisation. Meanwhile, the prospect of spiritual childlessness is not, it seems, felt by Africans as painful.

On the ill-effects of foreign domination, and even of well-intentioned foreign meddling in political and economic matters, the historic record is conclusive. There is a curious and generally unnoticed relationship between the fact that the A.A.L.A. gap first began to open up in the 1860s and the fact that the last shipment of African slaves left for a transatlantic harbour in 1865.

For the previous three and a half centuries that destructive traffic had continuously disrupted the traditional forms of African social order. By the 1860s most indigenous institutions had substantially rotted in the face of it. The ending of slavery and the slave-trade might have been expected to bring in a new era of social harmony and peaceful development throughout the continent. This was certainly the powerful hope of the emancipators of the day. To be sure, few would argue today that Africa would now be in better shape if the slave-trade had continued. On the other hand, it is incontestable that Africa is in many important ways further behind the advanced nations than it was a hundred years ago, and that the old emancipators would be broken-hearted if they could see what the intervening century has brought forth to present so much comfort and joy to white supremacists.

As long ago as 1841 the English emancipators, with strong support from the British Government, organised the so-called Niger expedition. It was intended to introduce into Africa the "positive" policy, as obverse and complement of the universal abolition of slavery and, it was hoped, of the slave trade. The principle of that policy was "the deliverance of Africa by the calling out of her own resources"—a phrase which might almost serve as the slogan of the Organisation for African Unity today.

The Niger expedition was wrecked by malaria and other obstacles to tropical settlement. The opening-up of Africa was in the event conducted not on the lines of the Positive Policy, but in accordance with the demands of the market-mind whose sole principle is to buy cheap and sell dear. The continent fell among emancipators of another kind, who deemed duty to be done if the trade in slaves was replaced by the trade in gin and firearms. This trade flourished concurrently with a protracted series of wars of annexation, crowned at last by the Congo Basin treaty. By the time the colonial regimes finally attained stability at the turn of the century, their minds were on law and order, and on the trade that follows the flag. The calling out of Africa's resources and the expansion of European commercial interests in Africa had somehow come to be treated as one and the same thing.

It was not until after World War II that African development once again began to be approached in the spirit of the emancipators of a century before. But by now the ending of the British Raj in India had opened the flood-gates of colonial independence everywhere. In consequence independent African governments and African development planning entered the scene hand in hand, and in circumstances which strongly suggested that the second was the offspring of the first.

In some ways this impression, though not substantially misleading, may do less than justice to some of the colonising powers who withdrew politically from Africa in and around

1960. It is true, indeed, that their primary concern between 1900 and 1960 did not waver from specialising the African economy as supplier of raw materials to industrial countries and as consumer of manufactures from them, and that the development of African human and natural resources was treated as secondary to this. Such is the spirit of Lugard's Dual Mandate, and such its discrepancy with the Positive Policy.

Yet it is also true that in those same sixty years there were colonising powers who put in much solid work in building the infrastructure which is now at independent Africa's disposal as a springboard for African development properly so called. Work of this kind was seen at its best in central and local government, health services, and educational and community services, though it brought benefits in other spheres also.

None the less, throughout nine-tenths of the sixty-year period the aims of colonial governments were not those which Africans would have chosen for themselves, and their policies were not such as would have been recommended by planners of African development.

The A.A.L.A. gap is the upshot. It is estimated that in 1860 the average income per head in the group of countries now described as industrialised (the affluent group) was about $170 at 1960 prices. In the group of countries now described as non-industrialised (the indigent group, which of course includes Africa) it was about $100, approximately what it remains today. Thus the inter-group difference was about 70 per cent. By 1960 it had increased to 900 per cent, by 1965 to 1000 per cent, and it is still fast increasing.

To put the point in another way, the affluent group in 1860 comprised one-fourth of world population, and produced one-third of world output. By 1960 it comprised 30 per cent of world population, and its share of world income was about 80 per cent. Conversely, 70 per cent of world population (the indigent group) is currently living on rather less than 20 per cent of world income. It is a remarkable triumph for the principle of cheap buying and dear selling; and if the principle continues to be followed on a global scale, its results will soon be much more remarkable still. Not confined to economic relations either.

It is possible to identify some of the social side-effects on Africans of the century-long economic process which has discriminated against them so disastrously. It has, for example, undoubtedly weakened the power of initiative in them. Many educated, or half-educated, Africans grasp a situation well enough and see clearly what needs to be done about it. But some inward flaw makes them turn aside from responsibility. They become professional magnifiers and multipliers of difficulties. They tend to decline any activity which they are not specifically appointed and paid to undertake. Or, more feebly still, like our Benin Cherub, they think it suffices to recall that the Lord will provide.

Such attitudes are direct legacies from colonial days, when Africans were other people's subalterns, and when it would have profited them nothing, and might have cost them dear, to think and act for themselves. Today to do that is precisely how they may deserve best of their country. But, the tiny group of first-class men apart, they cannot make up their minds to it. Nor in point of character do they measure up to demands of self-sacrifice. The incidence of voluntary belt-tightening *pro bono publico* is not high among them. Indeed, Africans in general strain downwards or sideways congenially enough; upwards they puff and blow and work against the grain.

One day in January 1966 I found myself sharing with an African a luncheon table in the University of Ghana. He was a lawyer engaged on post-graduate studies, and therefore a man of unusually high educational attainments. Over the chicken and rice he surprised me by commenting with violent contempt on the hypocrisy of monks and nuns. I asked him what particularly he had in mind. "I cannot stand," he replied, "their pretence of setting aside their genital drives and disinteresting themselves in sexual activities."

I pointed out that some such people, in addition to vows of chastity, take vows of poverty, and even of obedience into the bargain. And I ventured to add that Ghana might be greatly helped if a good supply of this type of hormone were active in the bloodstream of the local population. At this his snorts turned from steam into fire and smoke. Patiently I sought to explain that it was not always unreasonable, still less dishonest, to exchange immediate satisfactions for long-term ones. I expounded the psychological principle of sublimation, and added some carefully chosen words about the conservation and management of psychic energy.

To no avail. The Ghandian notion that civilisation might consist not in the multiplication, but in the deliberate and voluntary limitation of wants, and that such limitation alone can promote real contentment and enhance the capacity for service—all this lay well outside the range of this rather capable man. Of course, he was young, and no doubt his blood was full of a blinding hey-day. I should like to resume our conversation in fifty years' time.

Every human need sets a problem which can be solved only by experimenting and reflecting. Since Africans, like everyone else, are surrounded by the myriad things, they have to know both the nature of their needs and the nature of things, if they are to decide which thing can satisfy, or be manipulated to satisfy, which need. But Africans' knowledge both of the nature of things and of the implications of their own motives has remained rudimentary and stagnant to a high degree for a long time.

They therefore remain weak at identifying and interpreting their own needs (except on an uncritical level of immediate personal gain or enjoyment), and at discovering how to satisfy them. They are only now showing the first stirrings out of this condition. They still move by incoherent fits and starts, with no control but what a very subjective logic can offer.

No wonder that African society, from top to bottom virtually helpless in face of the challenge to modernise, yet constantly prodded by it, constantly aware also of large unassuaged, indeed unfocused, desires, should feel oppressed by frustration.

The chief prodders, the chief exposers of African inadequacy in matters of modernisation, are the purveyors of foreign aid. So no wonder again, to one who watches the bustling duplicity of foreign aid milling around all over the continent, that a conspiracy hypothesis should have formed in the African mind, according to which a world-wide neo-colonialist plot seeks to deprive Africa of economic freedom and progress, after a disingenuous acquiescence in political independence.

The hypothesis has a convincing ring for Africans, partly because some activities of some foreign aid agencies can really be accounted for along such lines, and partly because it provides them with a way of accounting for their own frustration without self-blame. Thus Africans, like early Protestants, remain at liberty to embrace the comforting view that, if only they can leave Rome behind them, it will be impossible to miss the way to heaven. Neo-colonialism is to them what the Counter-Reformation was to Calvinists; and foreign aid is a replica of the Society of Jesus.

The tasks of African self-modernisation, as the next chapter will show, are gigantic. The last five hundred years of African experience, dominated as they have been first by the slave trade (championed throughout as foreign aid) and latterly by the colonial system (championed throughout as political enlightenment), prove to have done little to prepare African countries for modernising reform. Viewing themselves as the end-result of this dual process, African countries find that they are frustrated yet further by the demographic condition and the organisational structure of their populations.

These populations are very young. More than half their members are under twenty years of age. In some places (Kenya is one example) half are under sixteen. They are therefore heavily weighted on the side of inexperience.

Next, few of them will ever be old. Death claims a quarter of the new generation before it can mature. In tropical African countries the expectation of life at birth is said to be thirty years at the bottom end of the range and forty-six years at the top. The whole population is weakened, some more, some less, by the morbidity which the high death-rate reflects. It is not very wide of the mark to say, as I have heard it said, that an 18-year-old African has a mental age of 10, and by the time he reaches a mental age of 18 he is usually dead.

Last, four-fifths of them are functionless, so far as the building of a modernised social structure is concerned. They live their lives at a tangent to the framework of constructive and productive industry, contriving an unimproved subsistence in a harsh rural habitat. These are people who for centuries have been emptied from vessel to vessel.

The type-African today is an aged child, in whom bitter constraint and huge perplexity turn the hair grey before he can grow up. To him a premature senility must come before a punctual maturity can. In a society so composed, youths of quick conscience and bright wits, who should be the shaping spirits of their era, get frosted in the bud. And this same type-African constitutes the raw material out of which the social Reformation and the cultural Renaissance are to be made *now*. By whom?

He watches his old world collapsing. He knows that it has lost for him the protective power it once had for his fathers. He is without fidelity to proved institutions, because he has no proved institutions to be faithful to. The only institutions he has experience of have been disproved.

This throws an ever-increasing strain on his interior resources as an individual. But he has no developed interior life; the span between the cradle and the grave is too short for that. He may have had a brief taste of schooling; he may have made some contact with Islam or Christendom. In spite of all the efforts of all these agencies, he cannot be said to be trained in any validated knowledge or disciplined in any creed that wins his comprehending assent. The witch-doctor is always round the corner in his mind, if not at the front of it. In such circumstances the collapse of his institutions often leads to a complementary crumbling of such inner powers of adaptation as he might have gained by way of enduring institutional support.

He thus remains equally remote from the self-sufficiency of the Stoic and the self-dedication of the Puritan. Disinterested kindness seldom coming his way, he has little sense of social indebtedness, or of duty to make his contribution to a diffused common good. The precept of *noblesse oblige* touches him no more than the virtually non-existent examples of nobleness[1] in the bearing of others towards himself.

Planning is the cry that goes up all around. The type-African cannot help hearing it. But he does not believe that life is a thing to be shaped by man's endeavour, least of all by his own. He does not even know that the earth is his home, to be cherished and ordered as such. He is apt to talk hotly about the dignity of man, without any inkling that this consists not in power, prestige, publicity, and pelf, but in the capacity and enterprise he devotes to serving his fellows.

It is fatally easy to make of the neo-colonial Rome a hissing and a reproach; it is fatally difficult to reach a common mind on what form its replacement should take.

Hence in many quarters one finds, very understandably, a hectic worldliness of youth rejoicing to run its course without thought. In others, every time the social outlook appears more charged with doubt and menace, the more frantic become the slogans that are hurled in the air, the fiercer the dogmas for which colliding groups contend. And the closer Africans cling to the theory of organised foreign meddling against them, the more they come to mistrust their own compatriots as being in league with this or that external enemy.

---

[1] But not altogether non-existent. In Nigeria on 29 July 1966 mutinous troops assassinated Major-General Aguiyi-Ironsi, then Supreme Commander of the Nigerian armed forces. General Ironsi was at the time staying in the house of the Military Governor of the Western Region, Lieutenant-Colonel Fajuyi. When the mutineers entered to take the General away to the place of execution, Col. Fajuyi confronted them and told them that it was incumbent upon him as host to see that no harm befell his guest under his own roof; before they laid hands on the General, they would therefore have to reckon with himself. Col. Fajuyi was not on the proscribed list, and the mutineers had no orders to molest him. After his intervention, however, he was led away with the General and killed alongside him.

CHAPTER 3

THE WORK THERE IS TO DO

AFRICA IS THE continent of the future. There can be no doubt of that. And in order to affirm it with assurance, one does not need to foresee in detail what shape Africa's future will assume, or how "future" it will be. Within the first decade of independence, however, we have already been sharply taught that we must think in terms of generations. The *mise-en-valeur* of a continent much of which has been badly neglected, much wickedly manhandled, is no short-term exercise. Moreover, if it is not to be subject to needless disappointments and frustrations, all major steps have to conform to a maturely considered grand strategy, which itself must be firmly based on the principles of ecology and conservation. Short-cuts and crash programmes invariably waste more time than they save.

Africa is the largest continent. It has about three times the area of the U.S.A. or six times that of Europe (excluding U.S.S.R.). Its population approximates to 300 millions, average density being of the order of 10 persons per square kilometre (as against 20 in U.S.A. and 90 in Europe, excluding U.S.S.R.). The area of land under cultivation per person is 0·8 hectares, or about twice that in Europe.

The climate is of the Mediterranean type north of the Sahara and south of the Limpopo, tropical or sub-tropical in between. Almost every known crop can therefore be grown somewhere. Mineral resources are rich, especially in gold, diamonds, copper, bauxite, iron ore, manganese, and uranium. Geological surveys are still far from complete, and new discoveries (e.g. of iron ore and oil) are constantly being made.

Hydro-electric potential is high in the Niger, Congo, Nile, and Zambesi basins, but it is concentrated in relatively few areas and for proper exploitation requires better economic and political co-operation than exists at present. The conservation and distribution of water supplies is the chief limiting factor on development, and there are huge regions where dry-land farming is precarious or impossible, owing to erratic and insufficient rainfall.

Output per head in U.S. dollars for all Africa (excluding the South African Republic) was in 1960 $92, of which $40 was ascribed to agriculture, $4 to mining, $11 to manufacturing, and $37 to other sectors. The level of productivity is thus among the lowest in the world.

This is speaking in continental averages. There are, however, very important variations between the individual African terrtories. Income per head in 1960 ranged from about $40 in Upper Volta and Malawi to $60–70 in Tanzania, Uganda Kenya, Nigeria, Chad, Mali, Niger, Dahomey, and Togo, then again to $100–250 in Rhodesia, Zambia, Mauritania, Cameroon, Ivory Coast, Senegal, and Ghana, and finally to over $290 in Gabon. Income per head at the top of the range is some seven times as high as at the bottom. This differential is about the same as the differential between Africa as a whole and western Europe as a whole.

This is speaking in terms of territorial averages. If one turns from average income per head to actual personal incomes, the spread is much wider in Africa than in Europe. The disposable personal incomings of a Tshombe, a Nkrumah, or a Houphouët-Boigny are almost certainly greater than those of anybody in Europe and the spending money of a nomad in Upper Volta is almost certainly smaller than that of any European unemployed or retired person, not excepting the people of Sicily.

When independence came and the new African political leaders began seriously to ask themselves what use to put it to, they naturally fell to thinking in terms of reducing some of these terrible disparities. And since it is so much easier to be impressed by the mote in another's eye than by the beam in one's own, naturally also they tended to place their prime emphasis on the gap between the overdeveloped and the underdeveloped countries of the world. They cannot be charged with turning a blind eye to the gap between the richer and the poorer countries within Africa itself, or to the gap between richer and poorer groups within individual African countries. But they certainly gave a much lower priority to these issues, and in approaching them they showed themselves much readier to will the end than the means.

It is already clear that this was a grievous error which violated the principle of first things first. In Africa today the first thing of all is that African countries should group themselves together, politically and economically, in such a way that each is enabled to put its own house in order. Efforts to emulate the over-developed countries have no relevance to this first thing.

It is a misfortune indeed that the new Africa started out on this false trail. To continue on it would soon prove a disaster. Luckily there is still time to retrace the faulty steps and plot a new course on a bearing which Africa will in any case have to follow in the end if it wishes to attain its rightful place in the world.

The trouble arose because the African leadership, drawn from the middle-class agitators who had led the independence move-ment, could command neither the leisure nor the intellectual equipment to think out the problems of African modernisation from first principles. There was nothing in the rather casual African Revolution to correspond with the systematic brain-work which Lenin and his colleagues had put into the planning of the Russian revolution in the years before 1917. Nor was there anything in the rather casual counsel that African leaders got from their non-African advisers to repair this defect.

In consequence, the basic assumptions of the strategy, generally followed from 1960 in the new Africa, and now shown to be mistaken, were these. The cardinal problem is not internal to Africa, but consists in correcting the uneven distribution of world income as between affluent and indigent countries throughout the globe. If the indigent now put their best foot forward and follow at a brisker pace the path followed by the affluent over the last century, a tolerably final solution of the world's economic problem can be reached in something like fifty years. Suitable financial and developmental aid from the affluent countries, combined with plenty of coaching in techniques, can bring such a programme within the scope of practical politics.

The privileged living standards currently enjoyed by the affluent countries only really began about a hundred years ago. They are results of an unfinished industrial revolution which, from the nature of the case, could not have taken place simultaneously in all parts of the world. The indigent countries are those which for one reason or another did not go over with the first wave of the revolution. What is required is that they should go over in a second wave now. If they do that, they will begin to advance in echelon with the first wave, and will even begin to catch up with it, if they can maintain the higher economic growth-rate of the two.

The present contrast between the increasing affluence of the affluent and the stagnating indigence of the indigent is accounted for by a modest differential in annual economic growth-rates of $1 \cdot 8$ per cent a year since 1860. It should not be impossibly difficult for a hardworking and intelligent indigent country to achieve a growth rate quicker than that of affluent countries by more than that differential. The main problem is to work out the concrete technical details for achieving a differential of such an order of magnitude.

A blueprint for Africa as a whole was presented by Surendra J. Patel in the *Journal of Modern African Studies* 2.3.1964. An annual growth rate of about 7 per cent for total output could, he suggests, be attained by the following means:

Over the period to the year 2000 a seven-fold rise in the output of agriculture, forty-fold of industry, sixteen-fold in the total of goods and services, and about twenty-five-fold in university enrolment. A rise in real income per head from $100 in 1960 to $260 by 1980, and to $700 by 2000. Capital formation of some $215 billion between 1960 and 1980, and $900 billion between 1980 and 2000. External aid of about $40–50 billion between 1960 and 1980.

Not only in Africa but throughout the underdeveloped world, the indigent peoples made a gallant shot at this kind of leap forward. In 1964 their advance over the previous year was 7 per cent in mining, 6 per cent in manufacturing, and 3 per cent in agriculture—an overall expansion of 5 per cent. Total export earnings were nearly 8 per cent higher. This was self-help on a creditable scale, resulting in a growth-rate a good deal higher than the U.K., for example, has been able to touch in any recent year.

Yet such efforts, though far from unsuccessful, are even farther from matching the need. From the standpoint of catching up with the affluent countries, a painfully significant fact is that in the year when the export earnings of the indigent countries went up by 8 per cent, world exports rose in value by 11 per cent. Often the indigent countries were diddled by the terms of trade, as the case of cocoa illustrates. In 1965, for instance, owing to the drop in cocoa prices, the rise in the value of cocoa exports from Commonwealth countries was only 9·4 per cent, whereas the rise in the quantity was 38 per cent.

Since 1960 the average yearly economic growth rate for the underdeveloped world as a whole, according to United Nations reports, has been about 4 per cent, little more than enough to keep pace with population increases. Food output per head has fallen consistently. In some countries it is now less than it was thirty years ago. The forecast is that economic disaster will engulf first Asia, then Africa and Latin America, if the current projections of population and production are maintained for long.

In recognition of Africa's surge towards political independence, the United Nations in 1960 launched what it called a Development Decade. The plan was to "put in the aid, mobilise local resources, and within ten years the young economies will be well on their way to self-sustaining growth".

These are the hopes which have irretrievably crashed. The practical progress made has been "totally and pathetically inadequate", as Lord Caradon pointed out to the U.N. Economic and Social Council in Geneva on 5 July 1965. The U.N.

Secretary-General, U Thant, added that among the indigent nations, which comprise two-thirds of world-population, the problems of health, housing, and hunger added up to a progressive misery which threatened to grow worse in the second half of the decade. A crisis has arisen which clamours for radical re-analysis of their situation by the indigent countries and their friends.

The strenuous endeavours of indigent countries to help themselves are being cancelled, to their own peril and to the peril of affluent countries alike, by three factors:

1. dependence on highly unstable foreign markets, which entail for the indigent falling export prices and rising import prices;

2. the requirements of debt repayment on account of international aid, which by 1965 was absorbing 15 per cent of all export earnings and is steadily mounting;

3. uncontrolled population growth.

All Africa, as part of the teeming company of the distressed peoples of the earth, is astray in a dark wood, harsh, dismal, and wild. It has to find another road.

CHAPTER 4

THE DARK WOOD

IN SEEKING THAT alternative road, the first fallacy Africa is bound to discard is the notion that its salvation lies, or can possibly lie, in following the development trail blazed by the industrial countries since the mid-19th century.

This becomes clear as soon as certain key questions are asked. Why did the affluent-indigent gap start rapidly opening on a world-wide scale just over a century ago, and not at some other time? Why did industrialisation spread from its original centre in Britain to a small number of countries in Europe and North America, and no further (Japan excepted)?

The answers are to be found in the facts of political and diplomatic history as well as in the concepts of economics.

The mid-19th century, besides being the period in which the affluent-indigent gap began to widen sharply, is also the period in which a number of the great nation-states of the modern world took shape. Britain and France, indeed, could already claim the status which Germany, Italy and the U.S.A. now assumed. These five countries all managed to construct a home base extensive enough to exploit the advantages of large-scale production which the new industrial power-machine, combined with the factory system, offered.

No sooner had this hard core of industrial nations coagulated than they were all seized with an intense desire to swell into empires. They quickly found that an economic home base which was broad enough to make output easy was also narrow enough to make sales difficult. Home production of industrial goods could not, it seemed, be prevented from outrunning the possibilities of home consumption. The machines, moreover, were ravenous for raw materials. Their appetite soon outran home supplies, and the consequent need for assured external sources began to cause anxiety.

Hence from 1870 onwards the race for fresh export markets and fresh external sources of raw materials controls with increasing insistence all other forms of policy in all the larger powers; and the pace becomes hotter as the level of industrialisation rises.

Britain, as the pioneer of the industrial system, had made the earliest start, and in two brief wars in 1842 and 1857 had secured an entry into the markets of China. India was brought into full conformity with the economic policies of Britain after the protest which was crushed in 1857. In 1859 the U.S.A. broke into the Japanese market in a thrust modelled on the British thrust against China.

At about the same time, corresponding advances were made by Russia in Siberia and Central Asia, and by the U.S.A. in Central and South America. The scramble for Africa began in earnest in the 1880s, and the partition of that continent among the great powers was completed by 1900. The lion's share inevitably went to Britain and France, but good hunting was also had by Italy and Germany.

In the exploitation of the external markets and sources of raw materials thus acquired, the export of capital from the industrial countries soon assumed pronounced importance. The device was found useful as helping the new dependencies both to finance the importation of industrial goods from their overlords, and also to step up production of their local raw materials for export to their overlords. More particularly, it was useful in establishing a permanent creditor-debtor relationship between overlords and dependants.

Finally, as keystone to the whole arch of the new colonial structure, a system of world-wide shipping services was developed under the control of the industrial nations.

Evidently it is no coincidence that the economic cleavage of the world into an affluent one-third and an indigent two-thirds has developed step by step with the division of global territory into colonies, protectorates, and spheres of influence of the industrial nations. The two movements are indeed no more than distinguishable features within a single process. The special growth of income per head in industrial nations could not have taken place as it did, if the rest of the earth had not been carved up into preferential markets for their exports and semi-exclusive sources of raw materials for their industries.

In short, the A.A.L.A. gap is just a new name for the industrial, commercial, and financial supremacy which the affluent have been at enormous pains to achieve in the world, which as a very bellicose group over several generations they have succeeded in achieving, and which in muted and now somewhat precarious forms they still maintain.

The U.N. Development Decade programme and the general economic strategy of most of the new African states have broken down because they did not grasp, or would not acknowledge, this simple equation—that the affluence of the overdeveloped nations is, through the mechanism of the market, related to the indigence of the underdeveloped as cause and effect.

Once the world situation, dominated as it fundamentally is by the A.A.L.A. gap, is construed in this more realistic way several striking inferences impose themselves, so far as the new Africa is concerned.

In the first place it follows that it is idle either to hope or to fear that Africa may repeat, at a time-interval of a century or so, the developmental experiences of the affluent nations by which they attained their status of economic overlordship in the world. No country can exercise the patronage and draw the benefits of overlordship, unless it has a group of dependable clients to work on and draw from. Equally no client country can cross the line which divides it from its patron simply because it feels the enhanced status would be agreeable. Crossing the line would upset the symbiotic balance of patron and client, just as an army would disintegrate if privates could all become generals merely by coveting that rank.

A patron who depends on his dependants cannot allow his dependants not to depend on him. To suppose that the strictly circumscribed success of the African liberation movement over the last ten years has had, or can ever have, that result is to be tricked by a misuse of words.

Nor is it any more feasible for African countries to set up a similar symbiotic system of their own, in which they would be the overlords and other people the clients. In the present state of the world, there are just no unattached clients available; and Africa is in no case to try detaching from their current overlords clients who already form working parts of the N.A.T.O. symbiotic system.

As we have seen, the success of the N.A.T.O. powers in operating a system of this kind is due to four main preconditions, none of which exists in the case of any part of Africa. Africa is not yet grouped into nation-states on the model of Lincoln's American Union, of Bismarck's amalgamated Germany, or Cavour's redeemed Italy. (It is permissible to hope it never will be.) Africa comprises no economic unit (not even Nigeria—yet) sufficiently large and compact to form a viable industrial base, as that term is understood in the affluent countries. Africa is not in a position to open up by aggressive violence new markets and sources of raw materials outside her borders. Africa cannot use the large-scale export of capital as a means to her own economic expansion. Africa enjoys no monopoly of world transportation.

A good deal of current discussion appears to be based on the view that obstacles of this sort can be surmounted by "international development aid". Enough has perhaps already been said to show that it is precisely because the N.A.T.O. countries and the A.A.L.A. countries are joined in a bond of market forces by which income per head in the one gets constantly larger, and in the other perennially stagnates, that most of the present modes of development aid work disastrously for the borrowers.

Tied loans, suppliers' credits, foreign-controlled enterprises installed on African soil do not in practice lead even to the modest objective of increasing Gross National Product in Africa quicker than the growth of population there—much less to a quicker increase of average real income in borrowing than in lending countries.

Sixty years ago these devices used to be known as economic imperialism. After World War I, dual mandate was deemed a more soothing title. In the 1930s the word popularised by the Japanese was co-prosperity. Today in Africa they are called neo-colonialism. In N.A.T.O. circles the term used is International Development Aid, and the lending countries are given the honorific of "donors".

The name varies, but not the methods or the effects. As in the beginning the methods were important factors in opening up the A.A.L.A. gap, so today they ensure its continuous widening.

As to the effects, so far from facilitating the proper development of natural and human resources in Africa, they constitute the main obstacle that stands in the way of it. I offer an illustration from the experience of Ghana; parallel cases can be found in abundance in every African country.

By October 1964 it had become clear to all competent observers (including presumably the British High Commission in Accra) that Ghana was on, if not over, the brink of bankruptcy. In that month the U.K. Government directly guaranteed a contract for a frigate to be built in Glasgow for the Ghana Navy at a cost of over £4m., repayable over seven years at 6 per cent. At about the same time, another contract, also endorsed by the U.K. Exports Credits Guarantee Department, was signed for six fishing trawlers at a cost of over £3½m., repayable at 5½ per cent over five years, although it was well known that Ghana already had 34 trawlers on order which she could neither operate nor pay for.

Such transactions are indiscriminately classified as aid to underdeveloped countries. But it can fairly be deduced that uppermost in the U.K. Government's mind was its own drive for exports, and not the defence or the development or the modernisation or the solvency of Ghana.

If Ghana's frigate and trawlers are characteristic of the material workings of "aid", what of the psychological workings? These are no happier. In the borrowing countries they take the form of a settled attitude of mendicancy, a tendency to blame on the stinginess of "donors" troubles that spring from their own inadequate management, and a distaste for strenuous efforts to solve their own problems for themselves. "Donors", on their side, are tempted to suppose that people as wanting in self-sufficiency as the borrowing countries are meet to be twisted round anybody's little finger.

The upshot is that most important economic decisions in Africa are taken neither on the economic merits of the case nor in the light of the need to harmonise the various development plans. What count are cold war considerations (in spite of professed non-alignment), the hunt for the least stinted "alms", and the promise of the fattest graft.

By 1965, just half-way through the Development Decade, "aid" had already developed to a point where the borrowing countries were transferring to "donors" more for the service of existing loans than they received by way of new loans. Within five years of independence the net outward drain from Africa had begun. This might be thought to be the object of the exercise from the "donors'" standpoint. But they do little to ease the process of their debtors. If African countries increase their exports of primary produce, prices fall on the world market. If they turn to industrialisation, "donor" countries place restrictions on the importation of African-made goods.

The African jest "These lenders don't even want their loans repaid" has some point. And for a small country like Mali, for example, which against a recurrent yearly revenue of £5m. has piled up, or had thrust upon it, an external debt of £100m., the fantasy of new loans to meet the cost of old loans begins to look quite realistic. If this is aid, Africans begin to say, let us see what a bit of honest damage can do for us. As Nicholas Kaldor puts it, "There is a glaring inconsistency between the professed aim of the developed countries to assist in the development of the poor nations through large-scale economic aid, and their commercial policies, which prevent such aid from bearing fruit."

Of course, the story is an old one that ante-dates independence by many decades. Surendra J. Patel estimates that since 1900 European interests have received from Africa $100–$150 billion at 1960 prices. International "aid" is, and has been for generations, very much a two-way traffic, with the balance of advantage tilted away from Africa.

Though African countries may cry a plague on "aid", their need of true help from more developed parts of the world remains desperate. The proper criterion of true help is, as the sequel will make plain, the extent to which it promotes the economic viability of the continent and rural reconstruction within it. The criteria of the disutility of "aid" are (a) the extent to which debt repayment comes to monopolise foreign exchange earnings, (b) the extent to which upkeep and renewal costs of "aid"-financed installations come to monopolise local revenues, (c) the ratio borne by eventual transfers from borrowers to initial transfers from lenders.

A high proportion of foreign finance goes into urban industry and commerce and their accessories, and into the extraction of minerals; virtually none, apart from some road construction and some hydro-electric schemes, into rural development. Reflecting this imbalance in development programmes, a localised domestic version of the A.A.L.A. gap opens up within the mini-economy of every nationette in Africa. This domestic gap is here called the Onitiri gap.

Dr. H. M. A. Onitiri, Director of the Nigerian Institute of Social and Economic Research at Ibadan, made the following remarks in his Presidential Address to the Fifth Annual Conference of the Nigerian Economic Society in January 1966.

"The relationship," he said, "between rural areas and growing urban areas is very much like the relationship between the underdeveloped and the developed nations of the world.

"The underdeveloped nations have frequently argued that if the economic relations between them and the developed countries are left to be determined solely by market forces, their competitive position will be so weak as to cause their development to lag substantially behind that of the developed nations.

They have therefore pleaded for special action to be taken, sometimes in direct opposition to the dictates of market forces, in order to ensure that they are not left behind by the rising tide of development.

"The same argument can certainly be put forward in connection with the economic relations between rural and urban areas of an underdeveloped country. For a number of reasons, such as growing attractiveness of life in urban areas, more effective trade union activities, unfavourable terms of exchange for the products of the rural areas, and so on, the rural areas are likely to be greatly disadvantaged in a growing economy, unless special effort is made to create conditions for a more balanced development."

In these perceptive observations Dr. Onitiri is really raising the whole huge problem of what principles should determine the interdependence of the rural and urban sectors in Africa. He is, in a word, challenging his audience to define the Positive Policy. As that issue lies at the heart of the African renaissance (and indeed of the global renaissance too, if there is one) we shall be constantly recurring to it.

Meanwhile, we should note this. Since in all the new African nationettes the economy is based on agriculture, on which an average of some 85 per cent of the population is dependent, the main mass is, in the conditions described, stood off from the work of national development. If income per head increases among those urban élites who were initially the most prosperous, it dwindles among the poor, especially the rural poor.

The Onitiri gap thus threatens the internal political unity of African mini-states as gravely as the A.A.L.A. gap threatens the peace of the world. It is one of the main factors to which the continuing leadership crisis throughout black Africa can be directly traced.

From the theorem that domestic political unity is unattainable save by way of the closing of the Onitiri gap, two corollaries are derived. One, that without political unity inside African states there can be no united Africa; the other, that without united Africa, there can be no balanced drawing out of the natural and human resources of the black world—in short, no Positive Policy, and hence no African renaissance.

Both A.A.L.A. gap and Onitiri gap pose crucial problems for Africa, in the sense that both call for immediate action if any general cultural headway is to be made. Both arise from inappropriate forms of economic organisation. But the methods of handling the one will differ radically from the methods of handling the other.

The A.A.L.A. gap is a feature of the relations between the N.A.T.O. countries and the rest of the non-communist world. For Africa it is tangential, a circumstance from which it is in principle possible for Africans to cut themselves off, if they care to show the necessary resolution. It may be likened to a barbed wire entanglement in which the African peoples are at the moment caught, but which they can struggle out of if they act strongly together and ignore scratches and torn clothes.

A successful effort of this kind would bring important net advantages to Africa, because the type of civilisation which the N.A.T.O. countries embody does not furnish a suitable exemplar for the social and economic development of peasant populations in a tropical and sub-tropical habitat—perhaps not in any habitat.

The principle of matched dependence on N.A.T.O. models is pointless and necessarily self-defeating in African conditions. The continent's problem cannot be significantly formulated in terms of catching up economically with the N.A.T.O. Joneses. Indeed, many pressing difficulties arise because the mistaken view prevails that social health and international standing are measurable only by comparative income per head, and that African salvation lies only in adoption as a N.A.T.O. fosterling.

Africa does not have to solve the problem of the A.A.L.A. gap; that is a N.A.T.O. job. All that Africa has to do is to get shut of it—to learn to turn its back on the world-cleavage that the gap so deplorably connotes, to reject decisively the helot status that the N.A.T.O. involvement commits it to, to attend to its own affairs in a genuinely and thoroughly African fashion,

2*

in a word, to lay hands on the second and final instalment of its own independence.

The Onitiri gap is a very different kettle of fish. Its problems are not tangential, they are radial. They are rooted deep in the social physiology of the African continent. They express disorders which threaten every development plan from every side. Their solution is Africa's responsibility and Africa's alone, since none but the sons of her own soil can say what constitutes a solution. Here is the task that must engage the continent's concentrated endeavour. All else is but distraction.

CHAPTER 5

ESCAPE

AFRICAN EXPERIENCE SINCE the coming of political independence has shown that it is madness for any part of the continent to found a modernisation policy on the production of foodstuffs and raw materials, in the hope of disposing of these profitably in international markets. All indigent countries have learnt to their cost that all the benefits of international aid schemes and of all their own efforts to increase export earnings over many years can be neutralised in five minutes by a fall in export prices.

In the long term Africa has no option but disengagement from the world market—disengagement whose rapidity will be governed, step for step, by the finding of outlets for African products within the African continent. This is the first point in a general economic strategy for the new Africa.

It does not mean, of course, that the work of the United Nations Conference on Trade and Development (U.N.C.T.A.D.) is necessarily useless. U.N.C.T.A.D. was set up in June 1964 to promote the integration of international trade and financing, so as to raise living standards in non-industrial countries whose economies depend largely on the export of primary products. Clearly the U.N.C.T.A.D. approach of seeking by rational argument to extract trade concessions from N.A.T.O. countries, and by the same token to counter the preposterous irregularities of the international market, ought to be pressed for all it is worth.

However, the years since 1964 have conclusively proved that N.A.T.O. countries have no warm welcome either for U.N.C.T.A.D. as an organisation or for the principle of re-shaping world trade in the interests of economic growth in indigent countries. There is little sign of willingness within

N.A.T.O. to surrender any substantial part of those vested privileges in world markets which they still enjoy as an inheritance from the thrusting imperialism of the last century.

U.N.C.T.A.D. has never ceased to urge that the problem of the widening A.A.L.A. gap can no longer be considered merely in economic terms, any more than the problem of maintaining world peace can be considered merely in political terms. Neither will be solved until both are treated as one. Such suggestions leave N.A.T.O. unmoved—no doubt because they strike at the heart of the N.A.T.O. countries' hopes of increasing growth rates in their own economies.

Having fought a number of wars to preserve their 19th century legacy intact, it is inherently unlikely that the need to avoid further wars would appeal to the N.A.T.O. countries as a cogent ground for sharing out the legacy now. They have not yet implemented any of the recommendations accepted at the U.N.C.T.A.D. meeting of 1964. The most important of these was that by the end of 1965 the industrial nations should have abolished all tariffs and charges on primary products. The U.N.C.T.A.D. meeting in Delhi in early 1968 confirms that there is no prospect of this ever actually happening.

From the African standpoint the reorganisation of the world market is the most forlorn of all forlorn hopes. Not for many years will Africa be equipped to beat the N.A.T.O. countries at their own game. In 1964 the cocoa-producing countries tried to hold up sagging cocoa prices by forming a ring of their own. They had no grain of success. It is simple prudence to acknowledge that the spread of well-being in Africa will have to serve other aims than export trade.

Disengagement from the world market does not imply complete severance at any stage, any more than it calls for abandoning the U.N.C.T.A.D. effort. African countries will certainly make use of the world market in a marginal and selective way, whenever for the time being it offers some tangible advantage. But African dealings with the world market will become increasingly subordinate to the building up of regional and continental markets within Africa.

There are particular products, such as copper, tin, gold, diamonds, and petroleum, which may prove semi-permanent exceptions to the rule, though the day will come when these too will be disposed of to the greater general benefit inside Africa itself. As regards food products, the lines of advance are two. One is to process them fully before exportation, the other to limit total output, by agreement between African producing countries, to the volume indicated by foreseeable sales.

There will always be scope also, perhaps great scope, for bilateral trading arrangements with non-African countries. In this context, indeed, Africa badly needs the services of a few experts who could provide in a good cause and in advisory form the kind of financial wizardry that the late Hjalmar Schacht provided for the Third Reich in executive form in a bad cause.

In all this range of policy, then, the one fundamental requirement is that no African country should ever again be placed in a position of basic reliance on world markets for its standard of living and its growth.

So long as we envisage the A.A.L.A. gap simply as a range of differences in income per head, there is little reason to think that it can ever be closed. Certainly it will never be closed by operations in world markets, by the export of loan capital from industrial nations to Africa, or by most of those forms of outside interference which are currently misdescribed as aid. Historically such institutions and devices have come into being to serve the interests of N.A.T.O. countries, and are indeed one expression of their economic overlordship. They are intrinsically one-sided in their working. They have no knobs to switch them over to performing a like office for the indigent.

This is not an augury of gloom. On the contrary, it is a message of hope, of prospective escape. It proclaims that, in respect of the paths of economic development they have followed, the N.A.T.O. countries are rather warnings to be heeded than models to be copied. A high level of income per head is neither necessarily desirable in itself nor in point as a measure of social progress.

What sensible African would wish to estimate success in the modernising of his country by the level of public expenditure on armed forces—especially if he is aware that world spending on armaments equals the whole income of the 2,000 million members of the A.A.L.A. group? Or by the level of private expenditure on drinking, smoking, gambling, habit-forming drugs, psychiatric services, the decimation of his fellows in traffic accidents, and organised crime—especially if he is aware that crime in the U.S.A., for example, is increasing four times faster than population?

What African patriot would hope to see his country's economy geared to permanent war, and his government's policies swayed by half-submerged military-cum-industrial lobbies, representing the tortuous complex of interests which benefit when "defence" spending is increased? N.A.T.O. countries are admired for their technology, their elegant comforts, and their gracious living. Yet those other features also are numbered among the consequences of their high income per head.

Living standards which the African disposition will delight in as satisfying and worthy, are not assessable in income per head at all. They will be discovered as Africans build for themselves a new kind of—African—civilisation. They will be attained when the African population places itself in dynamic balance with the African habitat at an adequate technological level.

Their attainment is a task for Africans who have learnt to work eagerly and constructively together. It cannot be made lighter by shuffling off its trickier parts on to other people. If it is discharged at all, it will be discharged by men and women, deeply rooted in the soil of Africa, who have confidence, initiative, and above all a clear sense of direction. These things are not dropped by "donors" into the rice-bowl of "aid".

Half-way up Zomba mountain, several thousands of feet above Malawi's little administrative capital, is a plateau on which has been built a low rambling structure known as the Ku Chawe Inn. There are vast views of matchless beauty all around, and a few miles southward a lake looking like the sea, quite endless, with the great hump of a bare sugar-loaf on guard beside it.

The mountain rises to two splendid peaks with a saddleback between them. Below the peaks the slopes are cut up into deep coombs and gorges, thick-wooded with eucalyptus trees, conifers, and all sorts of indigenous timber, for this is a well-managed afforestation area.

The coombs, which remind me of the deep Exmoor coombs under five-fold magnification, have friendly streams and waterfalls, not too big and not at all harsh in the way that Africa can be harsh. I delight to walk along the broad rides between the trees, glowing in the intenser day that I share with bright-coloured birds, with butterflies both small and huge, blue, yellow, orange, white, and black, and with flying grasshoppers whose top wings are green, underwings red. The occasional clearings are thick as thick with wild ageratum spread in pools of powder-blue that ripple in the strong sun.

One day, as I turned my head towards luncheon at the Inn, I saw standing in the ride thirty paces ahead of me a pair of *duiker* in prime condition, whose glistening coats were sleeker than one would have dared to imagine. In friendly wonder their great film-star eyes gazed at me. Nobody moved for a long minute. Then the little creatures loped off into the underbrush in that lovely diving-bounding flight of theirs.

Half a mile further along the road, I came on a large log-cabin with a level field in front of it. The village primary school, as I knew at once by the goal-posts at either end of the field. It was the time of the morning break, for as I walked by fifty or sixty small African children came surging out of their classroom shade into the sunshine, hopping and dancing, singing and shouting. With absolute unanimity they expressed absolute joy in being alive. The small girls wore blue cotton·frocks, the small boys khaki shorts and shirts. African totos, before they begin to blacken under the pressures of the adult ambience, rank high among the most entrancing objects in the world. They can even stand alongside my *duiker* without loss of face.

A few minutes later the Inn came into view, and I had a third encounter. A shabby-looking African, weighed down by a torn Army great-coat three sizes too big for him, was slouching along in a dead-beat kind of way. I raised my stick in salute, as I normally do, gave him good-morning, and asked "How are you?" He stopped, with slow dignity pulling himself up to his full height. "Very drunk, Sir, thank you," was his reply. After the briefest pause he added "And thank God".

Amused, but obscurely saddened too, I went in to luncheon.

As it chanced, I took my meal alone, and was able to reflect on these incidents of my morning walk. They seemed to me to symbolise in miniature the great African predicament. Over the coffee I opened a book I had found on the po-stand in my bedroom. It was a copy of the Bible, put there at the instance of solicitous American Rotarians who very decently wished me to get right with God. My eye lit at random on the magnificent, dark, Delphic, Pauline phrase "But we glory in tribulations also: knowing that tribulation worketh patience; and patience, experience; and experience, hope: and hope maketh not ashamed."

I applied my rule of trying to interpret every episode, every observed event, not so much as the end-result of assignable causal antecedents, but rather as a changing phase in a growth-decay process of indefinite duration.

In what such process were the *duiker* involved, and where was it taking them? Alas, the answer here admitted of little doubt. They were involved in the general disappearance of Africa's fauna. There was high probability that in thirty years time their species would be extinct. My schoolchildren would have become in their degree responsible for the extermination.

And the schoolchildren themselves? In thirty years time would they be counterparts of the pathetic layabout who thanked God he was drunk? What sort of hope would experience work in them? And would that hope, once wrought, make

them ashamed, or not? Certainly they had a fine prospect of
meeting with tribulations of many kinds. It was not easy to
believe that they would glory in them. Where could they gain
the basic faith which alone turns tribulation into a source of
glory?

As for the layabout, he would obviously be dead long before
thirty years had gone by. But the evil, or the good, he might
have done in life would by no means be interred with his bones.
For he was an African, praying after his fashion that his people
might be free and mature. His prayer would go on rising from
more and more African throats. Nor was he merely an African;
he was also a type-member of the A.A.L.A. group. So were his
sons and daughters, his nephews and nieces, among the schoolchildren.

Where would the A.A.L.A. group be standing in thirty years
time? Here was the key-question. In the answer, perhaps, lies
the justification of the layabout's life.

The A.A.L.A. peoples are overwhelmingly rural by residence
and peasant by occupation. They all have coloured skins. They
are increasing in numbers at a speed which by all criteria is
excessive, and which in any case is much higher than that of the
N.A.T.O. countries. Though in Latin America there are many
Christians as well as non-Christians, the A.A.L.A. group is
predominantly non-Christian; it includes the worlds of Islam,
Hinduism, Buddhism, Taoism, and Confucianism.

Their habitat is the tropics and the sub-tropics. The northern
parts of China and the southern parts of South America
excepted, they all live in a zone that circles the earth between 30° North and 30° South of the equator. This zone is
ecologically their preserve. No industrial nation is found within
it.

The industrial nations are all located between 30° and 60° of
north latitude. They do not, however, occupy the whole of this
northern zone. About one-third of it, the area between 20° East
and 140° East, is territory of the U.S.S.R., North China, and
Japan. Nor is there any industrial nation anywhere in the

southern hemisphere, unless one counts the outlying satellites of Australia, New Zealand, and the South African Republic as industrial nations.

For the century between 1860 and 1960, while the A.A.L.A. gap was opening, the non-industrial countries made spasmodic local protests, but were obliged one by one to submit to a fate that seemed inexorable and the same for them all. No concerted general resistance was put up, or even appeared feasible. With the spread, however, of political independence in the Far East from 1947 and in Africa from the late 1950s, their self-organisation as a group, conscious of their situation and their potential, began.

Today their accidental features of homogeneity—their semi-starvation, their pigmentation, their tropical and rural habitat, their peasant ways of life, their non-Christian beliefs and desires, their stupendous rates of population growth, their recollections of oppression by white men—these are being converted into factors of calculated and purposeful solidarity. These two-thirds and more of the people of the world are organising for a dual overriding aim—to shake off the contemptuous domineering of the N.A.T.O. countries, and to make of themselves upstanding and modernised societies.

Leadership in the grand mobilisation of the *plebs pauperum* throughout the world is being applied for by the Chinese People's Republic. The Chinese possess all the formal qualifications required for the appointment. They are non-white and non-Christian. As sufferers from colonialism they are pre-eminent. In their own person they embody about one-third of all the have-nots of the earth.

At the same time, they are clearly moving at speed out of their have-not status without moving into that of an industrial nation on either the N.A.T.O. or the Russian model. They are establishing a quite novel regime based on the peasantry, with rural development and the subordination of the cities to the country-side as its social strategy. In combination these qualities generate a broad gravitational field surrounding the population and territory of China, powerful in the long term to draw into orbit about them all the peasant peoples of the tropical and sub-tropical zones.

To be sure, the tense quarrellings between C.P.R. and U.S.S.R., together with the "cultural revolution" in the former, together too with the low level of Sino-Indian and Sino-Indonesian relations, suffice at the moment (1968) to neutralise this gravitational pull. These are phenomena of the short term, sharp turbulent oscillations, local and transient, within the general curve of long-term change. The enduring bond between China and the A.A.L.A. countries at large lies not in the realm of sentiment, but in the fact that their basic social problem being similar, its solution must follow corresponding lines.

In N.A.T.O. countries the meaning of the current divergence of the Russian and Chinese paths has been ill understood. Too much has been made of the emotional heat and ideological argumentation which have accompanied it. At a certain level the breach is, of course, real and dangerous enough. Yet, if two communist regimes at different stages, and following different directions, of development should adopt different foreign policies, and get cross with one another for doing so, what is there in this to rejoice their enemies, frighten their friends, or surprise anybody? It happened before in the Jugoslavian case, and will doubtless happen in other cases after the Sino-Russian row has died down.

Meanwhile, the genuine debate which underlies the row is of high and serious sociological interest. It may well strengthen the communist cause in the long run, by introducing new breadth and variety into communist modes of social organisation. The more this happens, the more attractive, in one guise or another, will communism become to A.A.L.A. countries.

In any case, the Chinese, by virtue of their standing within the A.A.L.A. group, hold three strong cards. First, their fellow-members, not blinded by the hysteria of western reporting of the "cultural revolution", see that in China today society and mind show more of rational order and co-operative cohesion than in any other human grouping of comparable size. Going forward among the Chinese people, in the heart of the world's most venerable and in some ways most successful civilisation, is an intense and profound renaissance which never fails to impress even the least sympathetic observer. These things embody the very talisman of which all Africa is in search.

Second, the Chinese rulers persuasively suggest that by proper application of the Maoist theory of the Chinese revolution, the fundamental issues of rural reconstruction can be solved in Africa as well as in Asia. The development in due sequence of farm work-teams, then higher-stage co-operatives, and finally communes provides a model which will be closely studied throughout Africa and, with local modifications, substantially adopted. The commune, which after all its ups and down persists in China as the basic structure through which agrarian policy works, and as the definitive solution to the problem of uncontrolled urbanism, will, it is thought, be quite quickly adapted for a similar role in Africa.[1]

Third, in spite of some appearances, there is nothing opportunist about China's bid for leadership of the have-nots. On the contrary, it proceeds in accordance with a maturely deliberated world strategy. The current "cultural revolution" is but one of the preparatory exercises designed to fit the Chinese people for that role.

China is quite as much struck as anyone else by its total success in the twenty years struggle against the armies of Chiang Kai-shek. That success was gained by a type of guerilla warfare that denied to the city-based enemy the countryside in which the cities were embedded. Enemy strength was thus effectively sealed off in urban complexes that could be supplied either not at all, or only from the air. By this plan, executed with practised skill and unflagging determination, Mao's troops won the civil war against American-backed forces three times their number and well equipped, as they themselves were not, with modern arms.

Essentially it is the same plan that the Chinese now propose to

[1] See Appendix D.

apply on a global scale in order to overcome the superior material strength of the over-industrialised and over-urbanised N.A.T.O. powers.

In terms of geography these powers are already encircled by the people of the tropical and sub-tropical belt, who present an unbroken railing, as it were, between them and the southern hemisphere. The Chinese conception involves transforming this purely positional encirclement into a real denial of access to and communication with all these huge underdeveloped regions, except on terms which the latter themselves will stipulate.

The wide manœuvre can be regarded as an offer by non-white people everywhere to relieve the white man of his burden. Or as the final peasant revolt against the towns, which has been intermittently raging since Roman times. Or as a class war of dispossessed proletarians against the avarice of owner-masters. Or as a religious war of all other faiths against a Christianity identified with the oppressions of the white race. It is each and all of these things. There is nothing new about it, except that it unites under one banner the underdogs of race, colour, class, creed, occupation, and technology, and re-edits their struggle in a supra-national and world-wide context. It pin-points, too, their single and common enemy.

Such a programme must take time, though quite possibly less than the forty years that were needed for China's own domestic revolution. It is being speeded up by the devoted industry with which the white race is currently digging its own grave, under American leadership in Indo-China and under Afrikaner leadership in southern Africa.

There is little enough of unity yet among the Afro-Asian countries, and Chinese leadership, though active in the necessary preliminaries, has hardly begun to make itself felt. Latin America, whose basic interests are identified with Afro-Asian interests and whose full commitment to A.A.L.A. group policies can therefore only be a matter of time, still occupies a relatively detached position, although some change has set in since the Havana Conference of 1966. The proximity and pressure of U.S.A. are still enough to prevent the sub-continent declaring for non-alignment, let alone showing overt leanings in the Afro-Asian direction. A great deal of work remains for China's gravitational field to do.

The United Nations, notwithstanding that China is excluded from it, will probably for a number of years furnish the main arena for the international activities of the A.A.L.A. group. The Afro-Asians by themselves had (in 1967) 58 member states out of the 117 to which the total rose with the admission of Gambia, Singapore and the Maldives in 1965. Another 10 countries form the Soviet group, so that whenever the two groups make common cause, they can outvote in General Assembly the N.A.T.O. powers and their satellites, with or without the Latin Americans.

The position in the Security Council, though on paper less favourable, is not dissimilar. Of its 15 members, 5 are chosen from Africa and one from East Europe, making (when U.S.S.R. is added) 7 in all. All this gives both scope and incentive for learning the arts of diplomatic collaboration. The U.N. can serve as the group's technical college for international politics.

Such a disposition of forces does not promise long life and fruitful accomplishment for the U.N. in anything like its present form. The N.A.T.O. powers will have but a dwindling motive for backing a world organisation which can no longer be reliably swung in support of their several national policies or even of their joint interests. In proportion as N.A.T.O. esteem for the U.N. wanes, the weakened organisation will become a less valuable forum to the A.A.L.A. countries. In short, neither the U.N. nor any other would-be universal association of nations is adapted to resolving fundamental global conflicts of interest such as that expressed by the widening A.A.L.A. gap.

Furthermore, one third of the have-nots (by population) are not merely outside the U.N., but in active opposition to it. At the time when Indonesia withdrew, nearly half were outside. True, Indonesia has now applied to come back in, but its return would hardly bring much accession of strength. It is unlikely that China would now accept membership, even if it were offered—which is perhaps equally unlikely. It seems wise to regard the whole A.A.L.A. group as, in potential, a rival club where have-nots only would be eligible.

If the long-term prospects of the U.N. appear less than bright, those of the N.A.T.O. powers appear more than sombre. Permanently kraaled in the top left-hand corner of the map, like the *Par Avion* sign on an envelope—a corner bounded on the west by California and Alaska, on the east by the Adriatic and the Baltic—they will constitute a splinter group destined for progressive isolation from the rest of the globe, almost all of whose peoples they have furnished with the best of grounds for antipathy. They, the cast-offs of the world, are riven by internal feuds more intractable than those which plague the A.A.L.A. countries, and they are deeply infiltrated with large numbers of persons whose pigmentation or ideological affinities or both are much akin to those of the have-nots.

More threatening than this, the N.A.T.O. group are under the truly frightful handicap of having put all their eggs of faith and aspiration into one basket—the basket of power. Of power they have vast accumulated stocks which they have no idea what to do with. They have nothing but power. The A.A.L.A. countries have little power, but they have almost everything else. The N.A.T.O. group makes itself so muscle-bound with power (which in the age of mind is empty of relevance) that it loses capacity for adaptive action in its environment, thereby tending, at the heels of many an earlier species in like evolutionary case, towards extinction.

The N.A.T.O. countries are no longer able to give. They cannot give at all, in the sense of behaving with a measure of yielding deference to those whose value-systems differ from their own. Nor can they give at all, in the sense of showing generosity untied to calculations of their own advantage. Beyond a punch in the face from their power, they have nothing, therefore, to offer to anybody. Even among themselves their grip loosens on natural human happiness, and they are driven to make do with the equivocal substitute, the sorry curiosity, of organised gambling and entertainment.

Their only notion of social order is power at the top, fun at the bottom. So jejune a formula will not do for the age of mind. It is the musty formula, now many centuries out of date, used by the grandeur that once was Rome. Rome, which fell at last because the lesser breeds would not stop nibbling at its frontiers.

CHAPTER 6

THE POSITIVE POLICY:
GENERAL IDEA

L'Afrique a les pieds dans le néolithique et la tête dans le thermo-nucléaire. Où est le corps? Il se débrouille comme il peut.

Débrouillage may perhaps be freely translated as "artful dodging". It is not pretty to watch. Even those who use it most cleverly and whose lives depend on it most completely call it *cette forme athée du salut*. It corresponds in social, political, and economic life to dirty play on the football field. To say that it consists in seeking mean gains for yourself by doing other people down is to say all that there is to be said about it.

During the first stage of a political independence which is also non-independence, *débrouillage* is inevitable in African conditions. There is therefore no sense in pointing accusing fingers at it. It is more even than a set of disreputable devices for steering clear of worse disasters than the one you are in at the moment; it is *par excellence* the African way of life in the current crisis, the only adjustment open to people compelled by circumstances to meet hideously difficult challenges with hideously inadequate social equipment.

To the observer who uses his eyes, *débrouillage* appears to be universal in Africa. So in one sense it is. All social strata have recourse to it at one time or another, and some at all times. But the observer who uses more than his eyes becomes aware that, however universal it may be, it is also superficial, transitory, and local. It is an immediate surface reaction to passing exigences, and can and does co-exist with reactions of very different quality at deeper psychological levels. The shrugged shoulders and the muttered *il faut vivre* do not exclude a determination to impose on life, as time goes on, some satisfying meaning.

Sociologically speaking, *débrouillage* is localised. It is a condition of Africa's body, not of its head or its feet. Africa's feet are firmly planted in an ancient and vital culture, of which Africans of every grade and type are proudly conscious. Africa's head is busily working out principles, strategies, and organisations for modernising the continent, such as will progressively become both cause and effect of diminishing *débrouillage*. Africa's head is, in a word, planning the drawing out of the continent's resources in the spirit of the Positive Policy, with a view to closing the Onitiri gap.

It would be idle to pretend that there is yet much agreement in different parts of Africa and at different social levels as to the precise shape the Positive Policy should take. But objective analysis of the current frustrations of African countries suggests that the overriding aims of that Policy call for effectual social planning in five main areas. In briefest outline they are these. They are here arranged in logical order of importance, but conceived as all operating concurrently in practice.

First, the adjustment of the quantity and quality of population to functions which productivity policy strictly requires and can worthily reward.

Second, the progressive re-structuring of rural areas into a series of small, compact, carefully designed community habitats, which offer to their members a fuller and more congenial way of life than the towns, and which conserve and improve the resource-base for community needs.

Third, the enforcement of limits to urban growth.

Fourth, the transformation of the domestic market into a system of distribution endowed with both wit and will to seek a balance of all human interests by correlating costs with capacity to bear them, utilities with some fit measure of need.

Fifth, the planned development of the services-amenities sector at the quickest pace which material output makes possible.

Once a social order architectured on such lines begins to take confident shape, it will become manifest that what is in fact emerging is a new pattern of civilisation, rural in its general character.

Alternative to, and incommensurable with, the urban industrialism to which the N.A.T.O. countries are committed, taking as its governing concern the conservation and improvement of the land, it will attach the highest priority to all that belongs to the countryside as the prime resource-base and the fountain-head of human satisfactions.

It will give second priority, from the standpoint of economic development, to light industry as an essential complement of rural production. The light industry plant will in the main be installed within the rural communes themselves.

Heavy industry suffers relegation to a third grade, admitted only in so far as needed to supplement light industry.

It is well indeed for Africa that it still has time to choose the rural alternative, in preference to the galloping urbanism which has already brought so much of human culture to the verge of collapse. It is well indeed for the world that the whole African continent may pioneer, in ever-closer alliance with co-workers in Asia and Latin America, in fact as the bridge between these, the coming advance beyond the tainted achievements of the N.A.T.O. enclave.

Such are the chief prerequisites, and such the chief consequences, of closing the Onitiri gap in the only way it can be closed (namely by a grand strategy of African rural reconstruction), and thereby of opening up the continent to political and economic unity.

Two further prerequisites, however, which in the present state of African affairs are bound to prove formidable stumbling-blocks, call for emphatic mention.

No serious rural development is possible until the intertwined problems of the fragmentation of land-holdings, the short-dated tenure of land, and the insecure title to land are solved. These issues lead to strife between communities, much wasteful litigation, and shocking obstruction of development openings. But they are rooted deep in the kinship structure and in the religious outlook of African peasant society, and hence deep also in the traditional pattern of village rights. They cannot be swept aside. Yet so long as statesmanship still fails to find some way of loosening the log-jam, the channels of rural growth must remain choked, and the Onitiri gap must remorselessly widen.

A second type of fragmentation is no whit less obstructive of any effort to modernise and develop, namely the political fragmentation of the whole of tropical Africa into mini-states monstrously overloaded with superfluous politicians and civil servants, much too weak economically to provide a springboard for growth, and much too crooked to serve any straightforward public interest.

Of 27 such states in tropical Africa, all purporting to be independent under African rulers, 9 have a population of two million or less (Mauritania, Liberia, Sierra Leone, Dahomey, Togo, Congo, Brazzaville, Gabon, Gambia, Central African Republic); 11 have a population of 3–5 million (Upper Volta, Chad, Niger, Malawi, Zambia, Ivory Coast, Mali, Guinea, Senegal, Rwanda, Burundi); 4 have a population of 5–10 million (Kenya, Uganda, Ghana, Cameroon); only one, Tanzania, with a population of some 12 million, passes the 10 million mark.

Nigeria and Congo-Kinshasa, though numbered among the 27, stand outside this classification. For, while as geographical areas they are more populous (45–50 million and 15 million respectively), they are without any effective political unity at all.

In political isolation from their neighbours, or, in the case of Nigeria and Congo-Kinshasa, as in-patients crippled by domestic animosities, not one of the 27, not even Tanzania, can have any substantial prospect of modernisation, balanced development, internal political unity, or stable government. Among them no régime that maintains such isolation has an expectation of life of more than a few years.

Yet all régimes cling to it as if it were their passport to immortality. It is not hard to fathom the contradiction, when one realises that (in Dahomey, for instance) two-thirds of public revenue are spent on public salaries, and that the military coups of December 1965 in Dahomey and of January 1966 in Upper Volta arose directly out of movements to reduce civil service wages and to control prices.

For any African ruler in his right mind it is an infuriating impasse. But the real point is that, so long as the practice of the leaders upholds the balkanisation of states, leaders have no standing for urging peasants to give up fragmenting their farmlands. In the absence of a solution of these twin fragmentation issues, agricultural and political, Africa literally has no future. The Renaissance cannot even begin. If the current crop of leaders do not produce such a solution, they will be replaced and replaced until leaders emerge who can.

Finding a solution would in any case be a searching test of African wisdom and goodwill, even if these were free to work without external nagging and meddling. At present it is made virtually impossible by the four-sided cold war in progress all over the region between the Brooding Presences of France-Europe, Americanism, Communism, and Islam.

In a social soil such as has been analysed above, responsible statecraft, equal to the mounting challenge of modernisation, cannot quickly germinate. Inevitably it is the fate of pioneering political leadership to be constantly rejected. The new Africa is indeed ripe for the violent change which it is now continuously undergoing. All its friends have to realise, however ruefully, that more intense and more subversive forms of conspiratorial politics are in prospect, and many heads of discredited politicians have still to roll before a stable and constructive system emerges. But, as I shall explain in later chapters, the faint outline of such a system is already faintly discernible.

The sequence of upheavals, based on no ideology or principle of political philosophy, will no doubt be punctuated in future as it has been in the recent past, by army mutinies and take-overs. These occur sometimes in revulsion against the current crop of politicians (as in Nigeria and Ghana), sometimes by behind-the-scenes arrangement with them (as in Dahomey and Upper Volta). In either case, though they are essentially directionless, they are not pointless. Their point, which is universally understood, is to put paid to the unimaginable abuse of public resources that is universal throughout Africa and much sickens all moderate men.

From the political angle, therefore, the Positive Policy is obliged to mark time, because social soil of the present type in Africa appears to suit the growth of only one kind of political leadership. It is a kind which can be turned for a while to the uses of an "independence" movement, but has no point of contact with a strategy of development and modernisation.

It sprouts in the shape of small oligarchies, many of whose members have, or soon acquire, a vested interest in resisting agrarian change, fairer taxes, reduced public salaries, better education, cheap housing schemes, and other ingredients of social democratic reform. Income per head, in consequence, increases quickly in the higher income groups and stands still as death in the mass of the nation. Then the tendency is for two embittered, mutually hating Africas to confront each other. We are up against the Onitiri gap once more—this time in its political manifestation.

Once more also we are up against a problem which is not soluble within the structure that creates and sustains it. Not even "international development aid" can help, so long as that structure remains intact. What is needed is a new sociological basis for African political life. I refer again to an alliance between peasantry and intelligentsia whose objective is rural reconstruction.

Assuredly it should not be forgotten that these African phenomena are merely local specialisations of a predicament common to much of the world. On the other hand, it should not escape notice either how broken-backed is the notion that political power, in the form described, can work as a creative force of civilisation. Yet it is clear that precisely this notion is tenaciously held by the majority of African leaders today. This tenacity is another reason why they do not last long.

What a strange kind of neo-colonialism it is. Here are representative Africans, themselves heroes of the liberation, embracing the characteristic fallacy of the old imperial interests against which they and all Africa besides are in revolt. Having freed themselves from a foreign colonial system, they hasten to set up a facsimile of it within the bosom of their manumitted society.

The self-deceiving rationalisation which used to go by the name of the White Man's Burden was that by the proper exercise of political power a wise minority could raise all mankind to a higher plane. The old expansionist nations each bore witness to their private dream of a great world empire, in which beneficent law, and sound custom backed by law, would bring happiness to everybody. When at length they woke up, they all found themselves, at home as well as in their colonies, in a position of over-centralised isolation, with the shallow foundations and the ebbing support which render even the most gilded of imperial systems as top-heavy as a leaning tower.

African Governments, whether civil or military, are headed in a similar direction. They too suppose it safe, and even laudable, to concentrate the business of governing their wildly disorganised societies in the hands of a small clique around the Head of State. They too confuse over-centralised isolation with the reality of power, when in fact the arrangement does little more than offer themselves as a sitting target for the next military coup.

It is hard for the new governments of Africa to acknowledge that this *is* confusion, because political power of a sort, brief and precarious, is all they possess. The fact remains that creative force and plastic stress do not reside in any dominance, external or internal, political or economic. They reside in the pattern of organic relations which constitute a well designed social scheme and promote high-fidelity communication between persons and between groups. It is such an organic pattern that the Positive Policy strives to establish.

Endeavour of this kind on an all-Africa scale exhibits the

tragic continent at a historic turning-point of high significance and creative potentiality, to be linked with which any of the heroic figures in European history over the last two and a half thousand years would have been proud. Alas, the modern Europeans, eyes skinned for the right band-wagon and nothing but the right band-wagon, find little in the new Africa to interest them. Their disenchantment grows more marked as African independence becomes more real. Their racial susceptibilities are affronted by African abuse of their "kith and kin" in Rhodesia. Except when a chance offers of a pretty profit on a business deal, they write off the continent of the future with an ill-humoured grunt "Let it stew in its own juice." They never ask what trials and tribulations is Africa facing, and why.

Africans, on their side, since beginning to manage their own affairs, have rumbled the European too. They see that something in his constitution stops him from identifying himself simply and generously with their cause. They read him as a character who has to be holding something back; who, should he seem to give, gives out of his superfluity only, and only for a stiff price.

When of the introverted type, he dresses up a taciturn indifference as laconic wisdom; if an extrovert, he hides his real self-seeking under an easy laugh and friendly banter. Africans understand well that his strength lies in his ingenuous mistaking of his own cultural peculiarities for forms of universal excellence which in his view happen, *de facto*, to be exclusive to himself. They perceive that his motives are typically no more than a reflection in the sphere of action of his immunity from self-criticism.

He strikes them as alike empty of contrition for their past and of sanguine expectation for their future. They know it is beyond him to say even to himself "We have done enough harm to Africa; it is time we went." In the aggregate these seem damning disabilities. In face of them the African of true public spirit, who labours to lay in his own life-work and by his own serious and strenuous deeds the foundations of a worthy African order, is apt to dismiss the outlook and practice of visiting Europeans as an intrusion and a contamination. They get no real welcome, but they are tolerated on the basis that not to have them would for the time being be worse.

II

THE POSITIVE POLICY:
SPECIAL IDEAS

CHAPTER 7

REDUNDANT MEN

CECIL RHODES HAD a word for Africans—LOAFERS. In this usage he exposed the unteachable racism of his outlook. He believed that Anglo-Teutons were the cream of humanity, Africans its dregs; the former being entitled therefore to rule the globe, the latter sentenced to chopping its firewood.

About Africans he was astonishingly wide of the mark. African women must be among the most industrious human beings who have ever lived; and even African men, who admittedly cannot hold a candle to their sisters and their wives, work as well as any, and better than many, in work-conditions they understand and regard as congenial.

But, although Rhodes was grossly mistaken, he had, let us grant, a muddled point. African men, at any rate, do appear to have a marked flair for identifying conditions unfavourable for work. Often, very often, when they engage in activity which a European would class as work, they exhibit no joy in making, no sense of the dignity and responsibility of labour, and they pack up when the job is by any standard no more than half-finished.

Observing this, my friend Dr. L. N. Jackson, who accompanied me as an expert in family planning on one of my missions to Africa, commented "The trouble with these chaps is they've no feck and no gruntle"—his way of saying that they tackle their work in a feckless and disorderly manner, and their emotional state while engaged on it is marked by a kind of disgruntled tenseness, or perhaps mere boredom.

Most Europeans who import into Africa their own ideas about efficiency, must at one time or another have muttered to themselves, after watching an African waste a whole morning in botching a simple job, "If he weren't doing that, I wonder what more useless or more harmful thing he would be doing."

No doubt the typical African demeanour in the presence of "things that need doing", as a European would put it, is largely due to an upbringing which includes little training in handling tools and materials, and in which no sharp distinction between work and leisure and play is drawn. But it is intimately connected also with the first great tragedy of African social life, namely that while there are millions and millions of jobs everywhere that cry out to be done, and millions and millions of jobless Africans everywhere who are bored to death by inaction, no power on earth seems capable of bringing the two sides together.

Hence, to take one small example, street-refuse collection in most parts of most towns is either not effectively carried out at all or is very sketchily done by classes of schoolchildren under a sort of corvée system, because the local authority cannot afford a squad of dustmen.

The fact is that African numbers are too many for the employments the economy can furnish, and for the attention which parents and social services can give to their health, education, and training. It is this quite specific form of redundancy, this bursting at the seams of the garment of social provision, that is proving fatal in every issue of social and economic development.

When a planning team was first got together in Upper Volta in the second half of 1961 to evolve a method of comprehensive economic planning, one of its first steps was to estimate the number of man-workdays per year needed to achieve the targets set for agricultural production.

A calculation was made of the actual number of production units in the rural areas, counting an adult male as one unit, an adult female as ·7 unit, a child as ·3, and an old man as ·2. Next, the number of workdays available from these units was reckoned up, regard being had to the local farming calendar, the prospects of labour-saving technical progress, and the population projections. Finally, output targets for the main crops intended for industrial use or for export were related to the estimated number of workdays left over after the necessary food-crops had been allowed for.

The amount of human investment actually required to fulfil the commercial crop programmes were negligible in comparison with the amounts calculated to be available.

In other words, Upper Volta, even if its population were not increasing at all, has at its disposal reserves of human capacity which it would take many years to train and deploy for productive purposes. In this particular respect, Upper Volta is typical of all Africa.

Human capacity that runs to waste in this fashion is, in fact, of such dimensions in every African country that it is unrealistic to suppose that gainful employment can ever be found for any important part of it either in the public sector, or in urban industry, or in mining, or in trade, or in crafts, or in farming, or in all these together. The inference is either that the waste capacity can be absorbed nowhere, or that it will have to be absorbed in rural development and in the services-amenities sector. The latter is the alternative presented here. But subject to one condition—that the surplus capacity is itself concurrently reduced.

Some insight into this undodgeable necessity for reduction can be gained by a brief glance at the public sector, and at urban industry and mining.

The public sector is already heavily overstaffed throughout Africa. In a large number of mini-states the burden of costs it imposes on the economy puts any kind of economic or social development out of court from the start. The only possible long-term policy, consistent with meaningful modernisation, is to cut down its ratio to the total employed labour force and to limit its total size by reference to the functions it actually performs.

In regard to urban industry and mining, it is enough to recall one finding from the U.N. document *Industrial Growth in Africa* (New York 1963). "In Africa (excluding South Africa) over the last two decades industrial employment has increased by about 1 million. During the period nearly 25 million persons of working age were added to the labour force. Thus although the pace of industrial expansion in Africa has been rapid, it has so far had only limited influence on raising the level of income per head, transforming the economic structure, or providing new employment." There is no evidence to suggest the reversibility of this trend.

In a situation like this prudence and logic vociferously urge that the first point of policy can only be to train and deploy your living reserves of manpower first. Merely on the principle of first come first served, these live reserves have a claim on society's concern prior to any that can be advanced on behalf of the unborn. Moreover, to raise productivity per existing production unit makes more economic sense than to call up (at above replacement rate) new reserves whose marginal productivity must be zero for many years, and might well never rise above zero.

This is how the business world works. Employers are perfectly clear that, in order to manage their firms with success, they must have a trained and stable labour force, a force where quantity is rigidly forbidden to wage war on quality. For this reason they limit their establishment to conform to a strict interpretation of their efficiency needs. What is true of the needs of the individual firm is also true of the needs of the social order in general.

The principle, indeed, is fully acknowledged where foreign immigration is concerned. All political societies in Africa as elsewhere, think it reckless to collect resident personnel to whom they cannot offer a satisfying life, and whose entry into the social order must make it harder for the citizen body itself to encompass such a life. African governments are much slower to perceive that the same principle equally needs applying to their home-born population. An immigration law for the human foetus.

Throughout Africa the erosion of the soil caused by primitive methods of cultivation is matched by an erosion of human resources caused by primitive methods of reproduction. The precipitation of babies is so heavy that the channels of home, environmental hygiene, school, and employment cannot control the run-off. The folk cry out to be conserved by measures comparable to the conservation of the land. As the development of the physical environment depends on the one, so the development of the social environment depends on the other. The chances of gaining social stability and the political motivation necessary for co-operative construction would be much improved if the population were less torrential.

Let me illustrate from the case of Tanzania. In that country, which has by no means one of the highest population growth rates, the population rises every 18 months or so by a number equal to all Africans employed in the labour market.

What becomes of all these new arrivals? Assuming that the present ratio of wage-earners to subsistence farmers does not alter, roughly 10,000 a year would be born into urban homes, and 190,000 into rural.

Using figures given in the 5-year Plan, one may calculate that some 66,000 (about one-third) will die before they are old enough to begin repaying the costs of their upbringing. Those who survive continue always under the threat, and often under the impact, of epidemic disease, chronic infection, parasitic disease, and malnutrition.

At present half the school age population is in Standards I to IV of the primary school. If this proportion is to be maintained, 100,000 new places each year, or 20 per cent of the current enrolment, will have to be provided in these four Standards.

Only 1·7 per cent of the school age population is found in the first four forms of the secondary school, so that the yearly human increment will have less than one chance in fifty of attaining to post-primary schooling.

The 5-year Plan intends that the number of school leavers at the various levels of academic and technical education should tally with the manpower demands of the economy, without giving rise to a surplus of educated and semi-educated persons to aggravate the problem of unemployment. One sees the point,

3*

without feeling much conviction that uneducated unemployed can be relied on to cause less difficulty in the end than educated unemployed.

Children born into urban homes will be brought up in dwellings half of which are overcrowded and in need of major repairs, and two-thirds of which have neither direct water nor organised sanitation. Each year about 7,000 of them will begin to seek work at the age of 15 or 16 and will add themselves to the 77,000 one-time wage-earners whose jobs have evaporated since 1960. The total of 84,000 persons who may then be classified as out of work or seeking work will represent about 25 per cent of the whole labour force.

The 190,000 children born into rural homes will have an even simpler history. They just get swept under the carpet of subsistence agriculture (whose condition we shall be taking a look at in a moment). Here it is enough to note that death rates and disease rates are as high in rural areas as in the towns, and sometimes higher. Education is considerably harder to come by.

The new African countries strove for their independence because they were resolved to establish their human dignity and self-respect, and to shape their future for themselves. How will the new generation feel about dignity and self-respect when they discover that one-third of them are called on to die before or during adolescence? How will they feel about freedom to create their own future, if in preparing themselves for this exacting task half of them cannot even spend four years at the bottom of an ill-founded primary school? Would it not be kinder, indeed more truly hospitable, to ask them to postpone their visit to this world for a time, while the current generation bends itself to settle part at least of its account with poverty and disease, and builds a school system that is at least approximately complete?

When the unhappy experience of the Development Decade is studied jointly from the angles of economics and of demography, one conclusion hits one incontrovertibly in the face. The fundamental factor that queers the whole pitch is the unmanageable growth rate of the African population. In a word, if all other development problems are solved, and the demographic problem is not solved, there will still be no African development.

The greatest menace to real economic growth in Africa since the Development Decade began is embodied in those economic strategists who argue that even a 3 per cent annual growth of population will automatically take care of itself, provided it happens in the context of a 5 per cent growth of the economy. This misapplied Micawberism, of course, has a wide appeal. In Africa, as in all other parts of the world, there is no dearth of sophisticated self-dupes who paddle with alacrity in the comfort of this facile and vulgar evasion.

Such an outlook will always be pointless and unnecessary. What would greatly help in Africa now are people who fully grasp how crucial and how central to every issue of social development are the particular modes and rates by which one generation replaces another on the earth's surface. Only such people can seize the importance of quality in a population, or the interrelation of quality and quantity, or how little chance there is of raising quality, so long as quantity is determined by the random forces of thoughtless fecundity operating at or near the physiological maximum.

Insight into these issues brings with it appreciation of the pressing need for a general productivity policy. Such a policy would enable planners (and planning has come to stay in Africa) to *begin* by asking what is the work which the social order requires to be done, and *then* go on to produce and train the personnel for doing it. "Given our present social structure and stage of growth," the planners would say, "how many people, busy on what precise functions, do we need in order to provide a satisfying life for all?"

This sequence of events will in the end eliminate, and from the start moderate, the distressing waste entailed by the present method, by which planners are compelled to accept the haphazard delivery of personnel in quantities quite unrelated to any social need, and then to run around in hysterical circles trying to invent work for it, no matter whether the work they may succeed in inventing is socially useful or not.

Evidently such a productivity policy implies the ability to regulate the growth rate of a population. Once regulation is established, the age-sex structure can be modified and total numbers can be allowed to rise, whenever there is good reason to believe that an increment would conduce to improvement in the quality of the common life. Alternatively total numbers can be reduced, if on the same criterion, that trend seems preferable. Flexibility of this kind will soon come to be regarded as one of the normal skills of living together that responsible citizens learn as a matter of course.

Such flexibility will not only greatly facilitate the raising of the cultural level of African populations. What is equally important in the long run, it will for the first time in history make possible a practical approach to the problem of raising the genetic level as well. Genetic improvement and cultural improvement are intimately interlocked in such a way that the one will always enlarge the scope of the other.

Africans, like all humans, are not a stationary end-product of an evolutionary process which was once active but has at length come to a halt. Evolution, now as always, is constantly in progress in all races. Its product and its vehicle, the unit in and through and towards which it works, however, is the breeding population itself, not the component individuals.

Misunderstanding on this matter leads to much darkening of counsel. The point that statesmanship is urgently challenged to grasp is that what develops in evolution, and is actively promoted by selective forces, is an increasingly complex pattern of genetic differentiation embodied in the human population as a whole.

That proposition is immediately complemented by a second, of equal force and cogency. Human populations, in Africa as everywhere else, are now obliged, by reason of the evolutionary level they have reached, to assume responsibility for their own changing genetic structure. It is surprising that African leadership is so slow to see in that responsibility a form of African independence more fundamental, and less exposed to erosion by any neo-colonialism, than the political and economic forms.

The question is not of drawing up a specification for a new African genotype, and of launching a novel kind of human organism built to that specification. It is simply of the business-like management of the gene-fund of the race. It is the devising, in deeper understanding of the genetic variants which present themselves for selection or lie in wait for their evolutionary opportunity, of a population that exemplifies new patterns of genetic richness, better adapted to the life and function of humanity in the age of mind.

The social argument in favour of a systematic productivity policy may be summed up, then, by saying that a population growth rate of the dimensions now current throughout Africa (this is a Pan-African issue, if ever there was one) threatens the bankruptcy of the social services. It perpetuates the Onitiri gap because it makes impossible the radical reconstruction of the countryside on which the growth of the African economy depends, on which depends, indeed, Africa's new civilisation.

There are linked economic and cultural arguments also which powerfully reinforce the social one.

To glance at the economic argument first. Development plans all seek to increase the country's wealth as a means of raising its manpower levels, and vice versa. To this simple and admirable aim there is one stupendous obstacle, subsistence farming. Its practitioners comprise some 85 per cent of the African population. They live in family groups engaged in growing food crops for their own consumption, with only an infinitesimal surplus for disposal in the market and therefore with only infinitesimal money incomes.

It is a mode of life adapted to sustaining itself with a minimum development of natural resources, and as an inevitable consequence it issues in a minimum development of human resources. Philosophers might urge that this represents the ultimate in mortal wisdom. But from the standpoint of the planner subsistence farming is one vast vicious circle.

It is almost entirely divorced from the commercial and investment life of the country that harbours it, though the practice of growing a cash crop alongside the self-feed crop is indeed spreading—at a snail's pace. Of the foodstuffs eaten in the whole region of East and Central Africa 80 per cent pass through no trade channels at all. Of the agricultural exports of Tanzania, for example, 40 per cent come from the 1 per cent of the country's land which is owned by non-Africans.

No economy can flourish and no plans for upgrading man-power can succeed, if total life-earnings per head are less than the costs of rearing and schooling per head. Child welfare and health services are very sketchy in the subsistence areas, and no more than half the children born there get as much as four years in a primary school. Even so, the cash cost of this treat-ment probably exceeds the cash incomes subsequently earned by themselves and by their contemporaries who receive no schooling at all.

Again, the greater the number of persons that the economy is unable to absorb into productive work, and the greater the numbers it can use only at low manpower levels, the lower will average life-earnings be. Few people in the subsistence areas work more than a 150-day year. The effect of subsistence farming routines is to keep manpower levels as low as is humanly possible.

And when, owing to the high growth rate, half the population is under 16 years of age; when also, owing to the high death rate, the average expectation of life is about 40 years; then the productive effort, such as it is, is made by a negligible propor-tion of the total production units available. In such circum-stances, the injection of a human increment of 3 per cent a year makes the weight of inertia impossible to lift.

On the other hand, were the new generation fed into the social system at a rate which the framework of health, education, and employment provision could adequately accommodate, not only would the ratio of earners to non-earners rise, but so also would the ratio of income-earning life to total life. In such conditions, development plans would have a chance, and there would be a chance of enlarging the absorptive capacity of the social frame itself.

The population's numerical outgrowing of the social frame available for sustaining it is reflected in the emergence of a widespread class of Africans without land, without skills, without means of self-employment, without hope of employment by anyone else. It is idle to think of the victims of this trend as well-grown, able-bodied citizens for whom somebody sometime is bound to find a job. The whole point is that most of them could not do a job if they had one. A maladaptive economy, therefore, simply vomits them forth as wholly indigestible. The fact seems to be that unemployment of this kind is increasing in all parts of the continent.

The cultural argument is this. Among the expanding class of African unemployables are many who literally should never have been born. They represent redundancy in its most unqualified form. Their mere presence on earth is a blight on a social order that can offer them no life worthy to be called human. Only badly underdeveloped countries could be so lavish in producing them; their continued production is a guarantee that their countries will remain underdeveloped. They are a pitiable squandering of the most precious wealth— the potential of man. It would be hard to characterise aptly the cruelty of an order that condones their birth and then finds itself powerless to cherish them.

The paradox is that this cruelty is itself the offspring of mercy. It is the product of medical science going about its life-saving duties, but going about them in an unbalanced frame of mind, waging a trance-like war on death, heedless of the consequences for the quality of life. This is not the spirit in which a competent estate-manager works.

Already in some parts of the world all the power and the glory and the single-minded devotion of medical science have been compressed into a single bitter fruit—the keeping of more people alive longer in increasing misery. In those places mercy has truly murdered the very possibility of the good life. This is what is visibly beginning to happen in Africa also. Today the gravest of the many grave obstacles to the development of human resources there is precisely this corruption in the work of the health services.

The health services have created this problem. It is just that they should be called upon to solve it. To go on reducing the death-rate regardless of the effects on the growth-rate of populations is medical delinquency as reckless as the reproductive delinquency of parents who follow a maximum progeny rule.

Nobody, of course, wants to see a rising or even a static death-rate. Everyone without exception wants to see a death-rate as low as medical science can bring it. But on one indispensable condition; that every reduction is balanced by a countervailing reduction in the birth-rate, to the level required for the solvency of the system of social provision. In present African conditions it is in an absolute sense vital to reduce the overall growth-rate until it stands at about half its current figure.

Medical science may not plead that it did not understand what kind of social catastrophe its maladjusted acts were preparing. The concept of a proper health service has to be revised and amplified to cover not merely the saving of disease-threatened lives, but also the protection of a birth-threatened social framework.

It is not yet well understood in Africa that parenthood can be undertaken at two widely separated levels of culture, or (to repeat the term so often used already) of manpower. At the one, family size is determined by desired sexual behaviour.[1] At the other, sexual behaviour is determined by desired family size—desired, be it known, by both parents. The form of human development of which Africa stands in most urgent need is that which would raise her parents from the first level to the second.

[1] When discussing this point with Major-General G. R. Smallwood in his house at Karen outside Nairobi, I happened to say that a high birth-rate was in one sense natural in a country where it was dark from 6 p.m. to 6 a.m., and few people had artificial lighting in their homes. Drily he commented, "You'd be surprised what goes on in the afternoons."

Countries which do not make a general transition of this kind
will find the road to true decolonisation beyond measure hard.
To those which do make it the future of the world belongs. It is
within this context that lies hid the most damaging of all points
of racial discrimination against Africans. No external agency
can impose it. How tragic if it should be self-imposed.

Perhaps it won't be. The idea of planning a family, still more
a population, is very foreign to Africans, both emotionally and
intellectually. It is much to their credit, therefore, that they
have not rejected it out of hand, as so many others less forth-
right and more religious have. Imagine my surprise and
pleasure, when, as I watched the television screen on the
evening of 15 March 1966 in the University of Ibadan,
Nigeria, a programme came up which dealt with this theme.
It was beautifully put over by a panel of four Africans, two
of either sex, plus a comic stooge. The four sang the praises of
family planning clinics, and exhorted African women to attend
them. The stooge was an elderly Moslem sceptic, who quoted
the Koran against the whole idea and got floored by the four
every time. He seemed to enjoy the experience, and staggered
to his feet smiling after every count. The programme was
sponsored by the Western Nigerian government.

Governments of many countries in the underdeveloped
world are now operating, in one shape or another, population
policies based on the planning of small families by married
couples. Among these are Turkey, Pakistan, India, China,
Chile. In Africa national family planning programmes are
being introduced in Tunisia and Morocco, and considered in
the United Arab Republic.

So far as tropical Africa is concerned, the pioneer is Kenya,
whose government in April 1965 published a White Paper
entitled *African Socialism and its Application to Planning in Kenya*.
"The Government's capacity to achieve its objectives," the
Paper states, "is restricted by our limited resources, which
restrain our ability to expand, and by our high rate of population growth, which rapidly increases the size of the task. . . . A

high rate of population growth means a large dependent population, lowers the rate of growth (sc. of the economy), and makes exceedingly difficult the task of increasing social services. . . . Immediate steps will be taken towards family planning education."

Much experience has now been gathered together from many parts of the world about methods of implementing family planning programmes on a nation-wide scale. It can be found instructively set out in published form (see, for example, *National Family Programmes : a Guide*. U.S. Population Council, Dec. 1964). No government, no voluntary body, can complain any longer that it does not know how to set about the job.

Moreover, the United Nations has now reached a point where, at the request of member governments, it will provide advisory services and training in action programmes. The U.S. Government goes further, and will "consider requests for technical assistance in family planning, including assistance in professional training, the financing of vehicles and education equipment, and the local currency financing of programmes for family planning."

The current position in black Africa may be summed up by saying that nowhere have family planning methods yet been used extensively enough to cause any appreciable change in the birth-rate or in the volume of natural increase.

In the francophone countries this is likely to remain true for rather a long time. Their outlook is still far removed from the spirit of the Kenya White Paper. Most of them retain French laws prohibiting or greatly restricting the import, manufacture, and sale of contraceptives, and the performance by doctors of operations to induce abortion or sterilisation.

There is in these countries, therefore, little use of modern devices by the African population, and little talk of establishing family planning services. In many francophone areas influential circles are very conscious of what they regard as underpopulation (interpreted as a large number of square miles of territory and a small number of people per square mile). However, most African leaders do regard the legal restrictions on contraception as a legacy from the old colonial power, which might some day be re-examined to see if they are in the best interests of African independence.

In the anglophone countries contraceptives are legally sold, and presumably could be legally manufactured. In Kenya and to a lesser extent Uganda, in Nigeria, and in Ghana some organisational foundation already exists for an extension of services which might produce important effects. The voluntary agencies which could become the vehicles of change are handicapped by lack of finance, shortage of trained personnel, inadequate publicity, and doubts about official approval.

Whether external aid in spreading family planning services (this, as was said, is now available) would be resented in these countries may depend on its source and manner of presentation. There is increasing apprehension about certain aspects of a high rate of natural increase, especially the implications for investment, and the economically inefficient age-structure of rapidly growing populations.

As all cynics will have guessed, a "thief-of-time" school of thought exists (it is strong among economists), which holds that since population policy cannot produce quick results, it makes little odds where you start on it this year, or next, or the one after that . . . or (by autosuggestion) ever. This plea's very repugnance to logic heightens its attractions for the lower reaches of human nature, especially in harassed politicians on the look-out for chances of ducking the really awkward questions.

And of course it is perfectly true that population policy is a long-term affair, whose speed of action is limited by the nature of the medium it works in. The demographer, however, infers from this that to waste another moment before starting is merely to add avoidable troubles to unavoidable.

Let us suppose that African countries should find it possible, say between 1970 and 1990, to bring about a fall in the birthrate of the same order as that which has already been attained in Japan. This would mean reducing the current African average of somewhere about 45 live births per year per 1000 population to 25 per 1000 in 1990. The growth rate would then fall from 2·5 per cent in 1970 to 1 per cent in 1990, the average rate being 1·7 per cent over the period. At compound interest, therefore, the total population would have increased by 40 per cent in the 20 years.

On the other hand, without a population policy and with a 3 per cent annual growth rate, as in Kenya and a number of other countries, the population would approximately double in the same period.

There is no shadow of doubt that, if the Japanese demographic experience were to be repeated in Africa between 1970 and 1990, the continent would enter the twenty-first century with every favourable prospect miraculously enhanced and most of the unfavourable ones providentially removed.

Some economic strategists feel safe in dogmatising about the impossibility of dropping the African growth rate to 1 per cent. From this premise they conclude that, since for the demographic strategist the area of manœuvre is small, he would be wise to refrain from using what he has. For their part they envisage growth of Gross National Product over the next 20 years of 124 per cent, or 220 per cent, or 366 per cent, under "low", "medium", or "high" assumptions. There is no need, they assure us, to worry about population, provided the growth of G.N.P. is quicker by an appropriate margin.

This attitude is countered by a sharp appeal to facts. If the Japanese did it, why shouldn't Africans? At least encourage them to try. Economists may indeed *envisage* growth rates for the economy of 10–15 per cent a year. But these are far removed from the rates which African economies actually *achieve*. If the record to date of the Development Decade is anything to go by, they never will achieve them, so long as the demographic issue is just shrugged off.

CHAPTER 8

OPERATION HABITAT

MY CARDINAL ASSUMPTION throughout is that the promise of an African renaissance can fulfil itself only in step and in line with the closing of the Onitiri gap; and that the Onitiri gap can be closed only by appropriate measures of rural reconstruction, as distinct from urban industrialisation. It is time now to outline as clearly as I can the meaning attached to the term rural reconstruction.

At present there is in use in Africa a broad spectrum of meaning which ranges from the mere improvement of farming methods and the expansion of cash crops for export at one extreme, to the invention of a new non-urban type of civilisation at the other. Understandably enough, African thinking for the time being tends to huddle round the former. It is with the latter, however, that the continent's long-term interests are bound up, and it is the latter that I shall be mainly discussing.

The experience of relative stagnation in the rural sector is common to all the new Africa, although in particular countries particular crops may for a while make a fairly lively showing. Such stagnation is typified by the case of East Cameroon, where, during the period of the first Plan (1960–65), value added annually in the agricultural sector averaged 2·2 per cent, compared with 7·2 per cent in G.N.P. as a whole.

The figures no doubt reflect some real difference in productivity. But they do not take into account either changes in price levels or the growth of population. In the case of Ghana, however, we are supplied with figures which show the overall growth of G.N.P. in real terms.

Year	Per cent increase
1960	7·5
1961	3·2
1962	5·3
1963	2·7
1964	4·5
1965	1·2

Thus economic growth, allowance being made for price changes, averaged 4 per cent over the six year period. Over the first three years the average was 5·3 per cent, and over the second three 2·8 per cent.

Viewed in the light of the concurrent population increase of about 3 per cent a year, real income per head rose, on average over the whole period, by some 1 per cent a year, but stagnated from 1963–65. It would follow that in the rural sector it actually declined, at any rate in the more recent years. There is no reason to think that Ghana experience in this respect differs much from the generality of African countries.

It will not do to jump to the conclusion that manpower levels in rural areas are necessarily stagnant in the same way and the same degree as material output. Some African countries are creeping towards 100 per cent enrolment in the primary school; Ghana indeed claims to have reached it. It may well be that in a few years time the process will begin to show a dividend, not yet fully earned. If so, we may expect some corresponding rise in rural productivity a little later still.

The expectation at least would accord with the biological principle that organism and environment are different facets of a dual-aspect unity, and that development of either takes place only by way of the interaction of both. Natural resources, that is to say, are developed only by human resources directed to their manipulation, and human resources are developed only through efforts made to manipulate natural resources. The refashioning of the rural habitat must, on this view, carry with it the refurbishing of the physical condition, the mental cultivation, and the system of motives of the rural population. The converse, of course, also holds.

The problems of rural reconstruction fall into three main groups. They are complex and refractory to an extreme degree. In Nigeria, for instance, government-sponsored land settlement schemes have been attempted for 50 years. They have consumed a lot of money, and the failure rate among them has been high. Since independence much hard work and much intelligence has gone into pilot schemes and experimentation in many parts of the continent. Undoubted progress has been made; some insistent questions have been answered. But it still cannot be said that assured results are such as can be assembled into a working model for the strategist of reconstruction.

The three groups of problems are, first, land allocation and land use in a peasant community; second, to invent technically efficient systems of full-time profitable farming with a minimum of initial capital investment; third, how to phase the planning and execution of reconstruction schemes.

To give the non-African reader some impression of the real nature of the first group, how complicated and at the same time how primitive they are, I offer a brief sketch of the Akoliufu Farm Project.

This project started on 1 June 1964 in a village-commune of 4,144 inhabitants, situated 18 miles from Umuahia, Eastern Nigeria, to which it is connected by a tarred road. The participants had only their matchets and hoes to work with, and no funds for other equipment. Apart from the project, they continued their normal food crop farming with the rest of the village. No hired labour was employed.

In the initial stage, 119 acres of communal land were cleared for tree crops (oil palms). This acreage comprised 966 different parcels of land owned by a large number of different persons (some, however, owned more than one parcel).

The 966 parcels, which had previously been poorly cultivated for food crops by their numerous owners, were consolidated into a single holding, and leased for 99 years for cash crop cultivation under modern agricultural methods. The signing of this lease is regarded as a major breakthrough in the reorganisation of the productive assets of the village.

The 99-year lease was acquired without payment of compensation or fees, because it was agreed (a) that the lessors should retain the right to re-enter the land, should the project be wound up at any time before the lease expired, (b) that the lessors as a body should receive by way of rent three and one-third per cent of the project's net earnings, (c) that only persons born in the village should participate in the project.

As the lessors were many and so were the participants, it soon became convenient for each side to be represented by a single legal entity.

The lessors therefore appointed the village union as their trustee, and executed a power of attorney to that end. The participants formed themselves into a multi-purpose co-operative society which held the land on their behalf.

The immediate aim of the project was to earn for each participant the same income as he could have expected to earn in paid employment, viz. £132 p.a.

The target was to be reached (a) by establishing an oil palm plantation to give a steady income when, in 5–6 years from planting, it came into bearing, (b) by planting annual cash crops in rotation as inter-crops between the oil-palms, first maize, then cassava, then groundnuts (the first season's maize crop amounted to 21 tons, or about 6 cwt per participant), (c) by establishing nurseries of oil palm seedlings for sale (in the first season 13,000 seedlings were sold), (d) by establishing market gardens of tomatoes and pineapples, (e) by keeping poultry and goats, (f) by introducing some processing and craft industries, the four planned being weaving, brewing, palm oil extraction, and garri processing.

The total income earned in the first season, when only three out of the range of planned enterprises were working, was £1,050—about three times the government subsidy to the project.

In selecting the participants the village preferred that each extended family should make nominations. This procedure was found to work remarkably well, and to add greatly to the goodwill generated by the project in the village. A total of 113 persons were nominated.

About one-third of the original nominees dropped out, most of them during the bush-clearing stage when the work was heavy.

The total of participants at October 1965 was steady at 73. Of these 27 had attended primary school, and 46 had not.

The agreement as to the work-quota that participants should devote to the project was 2–3 days a week. Of the 113 persons first nominated as participants, those seeking full-time work were in a minority. Most were looking to supplement their other earnings in the village. And the supplementation looked for was to the livelihood of families rather than of individuals.

The breakdown of the 113 was into 43 unemployed, 49 farming, 6 teachers, 15 practising other trades, including tailoring and masonry.

One cannot claim, obviously, that Akoliufu solves the problems of land allocation and use even in Eastern Nigeria, and still less in any more general sense. But it does show that a number of interesting relevant and promising discoveries are being made. It gives some indication of the lines on which solutions may eventually be reached. And it paints a picture of the massive commonsense which the African peasant, under conditions of independence, can bring to bear on difficult issues which baffled colonial governments for decades.

Akoliufu has the further advantages (a) that its low cost would allow it to be universalised, other things being equal, (b) that the new enterprise is developed from within an existing community of settled farmers, so that no migration of population is involved, (c) that, within a given radius of the parent village, a project can grow indefinitely, so long as there is land to be had and a supply of volunteers to work it.

The second group of problems, concerned with technically efficient ways of full-time profit-making farming for whose sake the peasant will cheerfully move forward from his part-time subsistence methods—these cannot be said to have found a large-scale practical solution anywhere either. But here again the manifold efforts that are being made in a number of countries are bearing some first-fruits. If one were to try to generalise about the stage reached in the more favoured farming areas in the new Africa at large, one might fairly venture at least the following conclusions:

To consolidate fragmented holdings by consent into viable economic units is very time-consuming, but not impossible.

Human investment in farming land can yield a satisfactory return.

Consequently the old resistance to farm work among primary school "graduates" can be broken down. In the south of Nigeria, for instance, even the Farm Project income-prospect of about £150 p.a. attracts quite a flood of educated youth.

Rural development can go forward, and rural employment openings can be created, with only moderate calls on investment from outside.

Substantial local capital can, with suitable organisation, be raised in rural areas, and the credit needs of farmers and village industries can be met from it. (A thrift scheme has been launched by the Co-operative Bank of Eastern Nigeria. There are a million individual farmers in Eastern Region. If each of them deposited £2 a year for five years, the Bank would have at its disposal for credit purposes a capital of £10m.)

As an example of the results that are being gained, the supply of eggs from the new farm settlements has driven imported eggs out of local markets in Western Nigeria. As the various rural development programmes get under way, this effect is likely to repeat itself in other places and in respect of other commodities.

Finally, in the years since 1960 a cadre of indigenous experts has been built up who can handle rural development ventures with considerable efficiency and confidence. The relative ease with which new schemes and projects are now set up anywhere in southern Nigeria, for instance, bears speaking witness to this construction.

The principle, in short, has been established that "The land can do it". What remains is to devise an organisation of human resources to do justice to the agrarian potential.

The biggest single programme of agrarian reform so far undertaken in Africa, and certainly one of the most instructive, is the so-called Million-acre Scheme in Kenya. Primarily this aimed at the resettlement with African smallholders of mixed farming areas in the "white highlands" previously owned by European settlers.

In 1960 European estates in the white highlands comprised 3,600 holdings, the average size of which was about 2,100 acres. The total acreage therefore was about 7·5 million. There was, however, wide variation from the average size. One-third of all these holdings were under 500 acres, and another third between 500 and 2,000 acres. About half a million acres went to the big plantations, and the balance to the ranches.

The mixed farming lands, which were chosen for obvious reasons by the Kenya Government as the immediate target for African settlement, amounted in aggregate to about 3 million acres, owned by something under 3,000 individual Europeans. The Government's task was to make a quick start on the orderly transfer of lands and assets from these Europeans to selected Africans. After experience had been gained in two probing enterprises involving about 180,000 acres each, the first phase of the main campaign—the Million-acre Scheme—was decisively launched in 1962, eighteen months before Kenya's full independence.

By mid-1964, 750,000 acres had been bought in by the government, rather more than 750 white settlers had sold out, and 17,500 African families had replaced them. By 1966 the opening phase was complete; the first million acres had been acquired, and 30,000 African settlers installed. The Government was proceeding on two assumptions: first, that each new settler would on average employ one other African; second, that the average size of African families would be six. If in practice the assumptions prove correct, then 1,000 white settlers and their families (say 4,000 souls) will have been replaced on the same land by 30,000 African settlers and their families, and 30,000 African hired hands with their families (say 360,000 souls in all).

No doubt the change represents an important enhancement of status and opportunity for 180,000 Africans (the settlers and their families). Whether those Africans employed by them who previously worked for white settlers will be aware of a corresponding improvement in their lot is perhaps less certain.

In assessing net advantage to the African community, one has to remember that the net increase in employment places for African farm hands is not spectacular. It is represented by the difference between 30,000 and the number previously employed by 1,000 white settlers, a figure which does not appear to be precisely known, but which, when added to the aggregate of the white settlers' domestic servants, must amount to a good many thousands.

Moreover, in the strict economic sense the Million-acre Scheme would not achieve success, unless land development and farm output of the 30,000 African smallholders both showed increases over those of the 1,000 displaced white settlers. This, in turn, requires that the human investment of Africans should by itself involve higher productivity than the human investment plus the cash investment plus the volume of African farm-employment provided by white settlers.

But of course the importance of the Scheme, though it includes economic factors, is not primarily economic at all. It is political, administrative, technical, tribal, and racial. It is the one direct, full-scale attempt at present in progress to restructure African society on a non-pyramidal pattern, and to bring about the true Africanisation of Africa in the sense intended by the Positive Policy. It symbolises the eviction of the European trespasser, and the continent's inoculation against the European virus.

At the same time, it is a form of insurance against racial conflict. It was feared in many quarters (including the colonial Government before independence) that independence might be followed by a land-grabbing stampede, in which self-selected

Africans would move into European farms *en masse*, and drive the owners out. Organised African settlement was devised to meet this risk half-way, on the principle that if one is to have an agrarian revolution, it is good sense to keep it as unbloody as one can. In the same spirit it was decided to select African settlers, not for special knowledge of farming nor for disposable investment capital, but on the simple qualification of being landless and jobless.

This way of absorbing into productive commercial agriculture relatively large numbers of distressed Africans is a godsend to a new régime hard-pressed by stubborn problems of unemployment. It has also served remarkably well so far as a prophylactic against racial violence. How remarkably strikes one the more forcibly, the better one grasps the full dependence of the Scheme on careful advance planning, and on the punctual availability of a large number of distinct but interlocking factors at interlocking times.

The Scheme's basic social significance lies in the hope it offers of raising the purchasing power, and therefore the social and political standing, of the African mass at the base of Kenya's racial pyramid. Urban industrialism cannot yet do this, and probably never will. It has openings for but a tiny fraction of the mass, and in present conditions the level of wages and the volume of employment cannot rise together. A rise in one, indeed, must entail a fall in the other.

In the Scheme each holding has attached to it a target net income which, having regard to its size and to the soil and rainfall conditions, it has been constructed to produce. If on the average these target incomes are achieved, the role of Africans in the economy will be much enhanced, and a long step forward will have been taken towards higher production, more employment, and a fairer distribution of national income. The Onitiri gap, in short, will begin to close. Production targets are in general, acre for acre, some 50 per cent above production levels under European ownership—a by-product of the much denser settlement of the land.

All holdings are designed to yield roughly the same target net income. Hence holdings differ greatly in size and shape, according to the peculiarities of soil and climate. On land of the highest grade the income target may be furnished by as little as 7 acres, while on less favoured land other holdings may rise to 40 acres for the same income. Farm budgets showing how the income is to be reached are worked out for each class of holding. Conservatively framed, the budgets have a number of safety devices built in. The planners believe that any man of average skill and commonsense is capable of keeping to them successfully, and that a good farmer can do much better.

The Kenya Development Plan 1964–1970 propounds the principle that "the combination of co-operative farming with individual holdings gives the best promise of maximum productivity". Accordingly, the new African smallholders of the Million-acre Scheme are turning progressively towards co-operative organisation for marketing their produce, for performing mechanical work beyond their individual resources, for pooling labour supplies, and for operating water supplies, processing plants, and dairies.

The Million-acre Scheme is all very well for Africans. It is both an earnest of many of their good hopes for the future, and a token of the righting of grave wrongs in the past. Looking to these gains, many observers might think it a matter of natural expectation rather than surprise that cases of personal violence by Africans against Europeans in the white highlands have been very few since the Scheme's inception.

What of the reaction of the white settlers on their side? Those who have not actually been displaced are threatened with displacement. The Million-acre Scheme is known to be but the first instalment of a work which will be pressed forward until the whole 3-million acres of mixed farming lands have been transferred. Meanwhile it is difficult for any white settler who has not yet been bought out to continue running his relatively enormous mixed farm in the middle, or even on the fringe, of an African resettlement area. Those who try find themselves constantly harassed by thefts of stock and fencing, illegal timber-felling, and the incursions of illegal squatters. Police protection is neither readily available when sought nor of lasting effect when found. The Kenya Plantation and Agricultural Workers' Union, guided by slogans that farming must be made impossible for white people, calls for their mass evacuation and deportation, to accompanying threats of non-cooperation, go-slow, and spasmodic strikes.

Such is the context in which the remaining white settlers watch, not merely the crumbling of the European highland-stronghold, but also the whole enterprise of African resettlement balancing on a razor's edge, and swaying above deep gulfs of possible disaster either side.

For the sake of the advancement of African interests, they are losing their land and some part of their investment. They have lost their status as a social elite. They are losing an occupation and a career. They face a future full of doubt. Unlike displaced members of the colonial service, they are appeased with no golden handshake. Their only crime is to have been overtaken by events for which their personal responsibility could not on any reckoning be thought significant. They are, indeed, the sole losers in the entire transaction.

To be sure, many of them feel, or have felt, bitter. Which of us in their shoes would not have? The bitterest, rightly, were the earliest to leave the country. Citizenship in the new Kenya can hardly be for the likes of them. But as a rule settlers are, it seems, too logical or too magnanimous to project their bitterness upon Africans, whom they regard indeed less as authors of their troubles than as fellow-victims of an ill-conceived settlement policy that failed in the end to work. They recognise the counter-policy of African resettlement as historically inevitable and poetically just.

When they leave their farms, they are often at pains to see that the African farm-hands who worked for them are well looked after in the new conditions. If race-hatred should raise its head again between black and white in Kenya, it will not be at the prompting of these men. They have turned their faces towards the wind of change and accepted its consequences in the best way of Kenyan patriotism, with an equal mind, a decent resignation, and a proper goodwill for the new order.

The focus of such hard feelings as they may have is no African, but Whitehall and the Central Land Board in Nairobi.

In July 1964 I was taken by Colonel John Kent, of the Department of Settlement in Nairobi, to Kinangop in the highlands, to visit the farm there which he and his wife had worked for many years. Some months previously he had been bought out by the Central Land Board, and the farm was now being carved up into smallholdings for Africans. Before we left Nairobi, Kent showed me an oil painting of the farmhouse and garden as they had been while the Kents were living there—house long and low, built of reddish stone that might have come from Devon or Cheshire, garden trim and green, splashed with colour from dahlias, cannas, poinsettias.

Emerging from the Rift Valley and arriving on the spot, one's overwhelming immediate impression was of neglect, of running to seed, of being out of men's minds. "Once," I thought, "this haunt was resonant. Now even the birds have flown. No one comes here any more. With root and knot and shuttling yarn, grasses and weeds overweave and ravel up the paths. The toothless gate sags, bent and idle. The place has died, though it still aches for full decay in the full dusk. Poor earth-bound spirit, grown numb in loneliness, whose inaccessible reserves banish the very fellowship they plead for. The ways of Africans can be warm and human, but they are not the warm human ways this place knew before."

Inside, the house was bare and empty everywhere, except in the back kitchen, where three silent African mothers sat on the floor, suckling their young.

John Kent, incredibly unsentimental, seemingly quite untroubled by any football in his throat, observed in a dead-pan voice, "You know, if I were an African, I believe I should think all this the dawn of a new day. Proof, you might say, of African strength."

I turn now to the third group of issues confronting the

strategist of rural reconstruction, those concerned with the planning and execution of development programmes.

It is evident from what has already been said that no scheme of resettlement or rural redevelopment can be just a matter of choosing particular persons and setting them down on particular parcels of land. Such schemes are much more like a combined military attack by land, sea, and air; and for the men directing them they pose rather similar problems. In Kenya, for instance, the Department of Settlement soon found that, in order to handle the elaborate tasks which the Million-acre Scheme involved, it was necessary to set up an operations room, somewhat on the model of a war-time headquarters.

Furthermore, a Department Planning Committee met fortnightly to gear together in a unified network at various levels the Surveys Department (which produced the aerial contour maps), the planners of the Agriculture Department (who used the maps as the basis of their plans), the Central Land Board (which bought the farms from their European owners), the Settlement Department's own field staff (who sited the new holdings), and finally the Administration (who produced the African settlers).

Thus from the experience during the last five years of what has come to be known as "integrated rural development" certain practical principles common to all Africa have been evolved—principles which show clearly in how wide a context one has to view a scheme, in order to direct its working with an adequate grasp of the implications of one's acts. They are these:

(1) The declaration of a development area and the drawing of its boundaries, taking into account the present and prospective needs of neighbouring areas which have been developed earlier or are to be developed later.

(2) Proper area planning, covering soil conservation, woodlands, wild life, roads, water supplies, power supplies, village sites, land for schools and other public purposes or communal amenities must be carried out at the start.

(3) Land use as laid down in the area plan must be strictly adhered to at all times.

4

(4) Only after these requirements have been met can sound economic planning, which is the basis for deciding production targets, target net incomes, and size and location of holdings, be undertaken.

In the area plan, so conceived, the claims of flora, fauna, and humans are met and reconciled in terms of the long-range possibilities of the area as a whole. The area plan constitutes at once the ecological basis of rural reconstruction and the development framework within which settlement programmes are called upon to operate. It is the blue-print for altering the character of the rural habitat so as to afford a fuller and more satisfying existence than the overcrowding and overstimulation of the towns, and to furnish townward-tempted men and women with reason and occasion to remain in the country with their families, caring for them and for the setting of their lives.

The footings of rural development can be provided only by modernised farming. But a vital complement is a versatile equipment of light industries, spanning the rural areas and involving many enterprises beyond the mere processing of farm produce.

It is being found necessary, in fact, to re-think the whole relationship between the countryside and the towns. It is already clear that when a pair of towns, such as Nairobi-Mombasa, Salisbury-Bulawayo, Kampala-Jinja, Yaounde-Douala, come to corner three parts of the wealth of their entire countries, national development is seriously distorted. It is of importance that the forces of inertia by which economic growth goes on gravitating towards such overblown centres should be resisted, and that other parts of a country should be given their chance in accordance with a considered scheme of equalisation. This entails, among other things, setting up administrative machinery to control the location of industry.

The current situation is a good example of what happens when economic considerations are thoughtlessly accorded primacy over ecological ones. The blinkered pursuit of imagined economic convenience leads straight to real economic inconvenience of a kind that painfully divides the nation.

It would be a disastrous error to think of Operation Habitat as an agricultural revolution of the 19th century type, which hounds men out of the countryside as fodder for an urban factory system. With the labour-capital ratio in industry increasingly and permanently tilted away from labour, the modern factory's appetite for human fodder is soon sated. Urban industry will do well if it manages to absorb even the natural growth of the urban population. Indeed, in proportion as rural reconstruction succeeds, and the increase of population comes under regulation, it is to be hoped that a certain exodus from the towns may set in.

On the other hand, a natural consequence of modernising farming methods must be to raise output per unit of labour and of land. To do just this is in fact an important part of the aim. All the same, when a given yield from a given area is maintained by fewer hands, what becomes of the hands displaced, particularly when the Operation's directives forbid them to invade the towns? To be sure, hands redundant in respect of a given yield may still be wanted for increasing yields. The Operation will certainly find that many an adequately trained peasant can be profitably absorbed in this way.

Scope for a rising farm output, however, though very wide in Africa today, is not unlimited. As we saw, export markets are beneath contempt so far as reliability goes, and domestic purchasing power is low. If the 85 per cent of the population who depend on farming were all doing a good day's work on efficiently run farms, home and export markets alike would be submerged beneath a flood of unsaleable produce.

It would be senseless to try to side-step this difficulty by keeping farming inefficient. The rational answer is to run the farms with the economic optimum of manpower, and to take up the surplus into secondary and tertiary production on the spot.

The introduction of the industrial factor into rural development is the chief innovation in the new approach, and its main justification for calling itself "integrated". Its potential contribution to the cause is threefold.

Being directly linked in the first instance to local farming, it can strengthen the economy of the village-commune by better methods of processing, packaging, and distributing farm products. Using local timber in woodwork and furniture-making, local hides and skins in leather work, local cotton in weaving, further illustrates how industrial activities can form a valuable complement to agricultural production.

Again, new small-scale industries such as ceramics, metalwork, the assembly of electrical appliances, and plastics may diversify local output and offer employment opportunities for men, while for women a like office can be performed by jewellery, confectionery, dressmaking, embroidery, beadwork, and home upholstery.

Finally, both local farming and local industry can be helped in the sphere of management (at present weak) by measures to modernise business methods, and to provide facilities for design and product development, adequate cost analysis, and better marketing. It is to pursue these objectives that, for example, the Industrial Development Centre in Owerri, Eastern Nigeria, has been set up; and similar institutions are, as might be expected, appearing in other places also.

Even this kind of rudimentary industrialisation within the village-commune needs, as has been said, a base of modernising farming to found itself on. But, that initial requirement being granted, the objectives are probably easier to attain than those of the farming process itself:

(a) Since it is not entangled, as that process is, with the fundamental rights and religious preconceptions of the villagers, emphasis can be laid frankly and without danger on pursuing the new rather than on reupholstering the old.

(b) Though it misses the economies of scale, it offsets this defect by its use of local materials for local needs, thus securing the economies of optimum location—"optimum" meaning where the cost of transporting materials and energy to the site plus the cost of transporting products to the market is lowest.

(c) Because of the labour-intensive character of the development, a job can be provided for an investment of less than £500 (often as low as £100), while the larger-scale urban industrial development requires an average of £3,000 or more per job created.

(d) It fits in well with the Farm Project type of development, because it too avoids population-shifting: it brings the work to the people, and not vice versa.

Operation Habitat, in a word, comprises an agricultural revolution and an industrial revolution carried forward simultaneously though in correct echelon, as wings of a single engagement. In correct echelon, again, with this interlocking advance, and supporting it in the rear, follow the strategic reserves.

These will consist neither of farming nor of industry, but of services-amenities. Until a couple of centuries ago the wealth of nations was measured in terms of the yield of the land, then a century later in terms of output of manufactures, later still in terms of the size and complexity of financial operations. Henceforward, the measure is in terms of non-material production, that is to say, in the spread and variety of the personal and group services which people render to one another, whether in sport, entertainment, information, travel, holiday-making, sight-seeing, or as ancillary to the arts, the sciences, and the technologies, or in new combinations of any or all of these. It is very fitting that the age of mind should hold in highest regard the diffusion and enjoyment of cultural resources.

The planners of integrated rural development are beginning to pay attention to the need for ordering the lives of rural communities to a civic design in keeping with their surroundings. There is growing realisation that the quality of community life turns in an important degree on the physical lay-out and the social architecture of the setting in which it is lived. This is an area of applied sociology in which architects and town-planners in many parts of the world have recently accumulated much useful knowledge—a good deal of it of vital relevance to rural reconstruction in Africa.

Human relations within a neighbourhood, for example, have repeatedly been proved to depend on the arrangement, design,

and density of dwellings, on the avoidance of ribbon development, on the zoning of different types of land-use, on open
spaces sited with taste, on convenient shopping centres and
other places of public resort, on buildings that embody the sense
of civic pride, and above all on trees, on trees in plenty,
strategically and artistically grouped.

The primary community in which Africans live face to face
with one another is sometimes a close-knit village, but often an
expanded and straggling agglomeration, with neighbours too
far apart, no communal focus, and no service centre. In planning a more convenient type of social architecture than the
latter, the first point is to bring people together into a compact
unit of appropriate size. The second is to find some device for
the physical separation of cash crop lands from food crop lands.

The spread of resettlement schemes is carrying the matter a
stage further. Not only is the lay-out of farm lands taken better
care of than a few years ago; efforts are also now being made to
develop village sites into better villages. In Tanzania model
village lay-outs have been drawn up in connection with the
resettlement programmes. In Kenya the Department of Settlement has its Town Planning Section, which sets criteria for the
spacing, siting, and size of townships, roads, schools, etc.

In West Africa settlers' farm houses and gardens have been
re-designed. Experience has shown that indigenous builders can
put up better planned, more durable, and less expensive
houses than those which were being built by foreign contractors
in 1960. Moreover, the Farm Settlement authorities are beginning to beautify village sites by planting ornamental trees and
shrubs and fruit trees early in the life of the villages.

The people responsible for rural development could save all
concerned endless pain and trouble if, from the very first, they
would treat each commune as an estate to be developed (or
gradually redeveloped) to a plan that follows the principles of
design now so well understood and so readily adaptable to the
African circumstance. This need cost no more and in the long
run might well prove cheaper than a more haphazard and less
considered method.

Apart from furnishing a pattern of living out of which agreeable community activities naturally arise and apart from keeping subsistence production off the cash crop lands, this kind of planned concentration tends to free women from carrying water long distances, to check the bilharzia menace, to provide a sufficiency of protein and protective foods in the diet, and to improve hygiene and sanitation. A communal water supply, especially, can grow into a strong unifying factor, painless in its operation.

Well-designed villages, each set at the mid-point of a farm unit of 3,000 acres or thereabouts, and forming a joint home for, say, 150 farmers and their families, are the social bricks out of which the reshaped countryside is built. They are arranged in constellations in which the component villages are 3–5 miles distant from one another. The constellations draw the circumference of a rough circle with a radius of 15 miles or so, and with a well-watered site for the centre. At this centre there will arise in due time a market town of some pretensions, destined to provide for a population of something like 5,000.

Such a town could well become an active and perceptive microcosm of African civilisation. It would be the commercial and financial focus of the area; the seat of local government, of courts of law, of secondary technical, and adult education; the intersection point of a system of road transport services; the location of several carefully selected manufacturing industries; the regional headquarters of some central government departments; the place of business of professional men and women, such as doctors, dentists, veterinary surgeons, lawyers, engineers, research staff, and teachers of all grades; the site of a wide range of cultural amenities from a public library, a museum, a theatre and concert hall, to a sports ground, a swimming pool, and a municipal park and zoological gardens.

Regarded as a whole, the market town and its grouped, farm-linked village-satellites would constitute an interwoven social complex large enough and varied enough to offer all essential means to a full and rewarding life. It would offer a series of career structures rising high enough to match the aspirations of the most capable members of the farming community, should they wish to relinquish their agricultural interest either wholly or in part. It would arrest the present frustrated drift from a scrub-countryside to the no less frustrating shanty-towns of the big urban areas.

Plainly it is of crucial importance to keep the size of such market towns within appropriate limits. How can these limits be indicated and why have I suggested a maximum of about 5,000?

In the first place, the market town is designed to inject into the countryside some basic virtues of urbanity without loss to the wholesome rurality of the habitat. The essence of such a scheme is that the market town should be and remain symbiotic with its village-satellites and should not be allowed to develop in ways not organic to the life of the villages.

N. O. Addo, in a valuable paper *Demographic Aspects of Urban Development in Ghana in the 20th century*, shows that, in that part of Africa at any rate, the functional frontier between the urban sector and the rural sector coincides with the population-contour of 10,000 for human settlements. By this he means that no "agricultural town" can exceed a total population of 10,000 without letting slip the distinctive quality of the countryside and changing its essence to urban.

This thesis offers a valuable warning to the planners of rural reconstruction that it would be wise to accept 5,000 or thereabouts as the upper limit for a market town, and to work out corresponding limits for both the size and the number of its village-satellites by reference to principles such as Addo indicates. Settlements between 5,000 and 10,000 in size should be avoided, and this numerical zone should be preserved as an unoccupied no-man's-land between rural and urban sectors. Thus planners will take out a measure of re-insurance against the submergence of rural speciality. And they will escape the charge of merely creating new cities in the country.

In the second place, whenever a market town runs into danger of passing the 5,000 mark, planning policy should be prepared to stop its growth, and to use the overspill to found elsewhere a new commune, if one may use that term to denote the complex of farm-based villages plus market town. Much planning work will consist in the careful pre-selection of sites for new communes against the time when the need for them should arise, and well in advance of it. A general determination on the part of planners that, while the number of communes may increase as needed, each commune must adhere closely to a predetermined optimum size, is vital.

Operation Habitat is a 30-year programme to which will be harnessed the main endeavours of two generations. Governments and their advisers will feel increasingly bound to achieve a span of apprehension limited only by a time-horizon at least thus distant. Long-range perspective plans taking the whole period, the whole population, and the whole area within their purview, will furnish the framework for consolidated short-term targets which specify the details of accomplishment.

In these schemes the development of the communes goes forward in a single movement with its necessary complement, the development of the reorganised primary school—to which our discussion will soon be turning.

CHAPTER 9

THE MENACE OF THE TOWNS

ANOTHER KIND OF danger that horribly besets the new Africa
is the rampant growth of towns. Like the population issue itself,
of which indeed it is in part one further painful expression,
urbanism is not yet acknowledged by African leaders as a top-
priority problem that has to be dealt with now if the next
generation and their successors are not to be overwhelmed by it.[1]

Actually, however, African countries (in common, as it happens with A.A.L.A. countries generally) are faced with a
dilemma which may be briefly, if crudely, put in this way.

If they *do not* raise their urbanisation rates (i.e. reduce the
ratio of country-dwellers), the rural settlements will collapse
under the pile-up of unproductive numbers. If they *do*, urbanism will assume the dimensions of a disaster.

Kingsley Davis in *The Scientific American* (September 1965,
231, 3) offers the following formulation. "It is becoming virtually impossible to create city services fast enough to take care
of the huge, never-ending cohorts of babies and peasants swel-
ling the urban masses. It is even harder to expand agricultural
land and capital fast enough to accommodate the enormous
natural increase on farms."

In the mid-nineteenth century, when the A.L.A.A. gap began
to open, no society in the world was predominantly urbanised.
Even by 1900 only one, Britain, could be so described. Davis has
calculated that in the Europe of 1600 the combined population

[1] The term urbanism is here used to denote the size of urban populations
as such. Urbanisation, on the other hand, signifies the proportion of the total
population which lives in urban settlements. Thus urbanism can rise without
any rise in urbanisation, provided the rural population increases not less
fast than the urban. In the U.K., for instance, urbanisation was 78·8 per
cent in 1926, but had declined to 78·3 per cent by 1961. In the interval,
urbanism (the number of town-dwellers) had nevertheless greatly expanded.

of towns with 100,000 inhabitants or more was 1·6 per cent of the whole European population, in 1700 it was 1·9 per cent, in 1800 it was 2·2 per cent. Urbanisation was minimal. But with the great increase in economic productivity which in the middle of the 19th century began to spring from the development of power-machinery and the factory system, a rapid speed-up of urbanisation began.

Today all highly industrailised countries are also highly urbanised, though never more highly than 75–80 per cent, which appears, at least at the present stage, to constitute a kind of natural ceiling of urbanisation. If the urbanisation rate characteristic of the decade 1950–60 continues unchanged, more than half the population of the world will be town-dwellers by 1990. By 1960 one-third already were.

In N.A.T.O. countries urbanism is still growing, but urbanisation, after having risen steadily for a century, is now beginning to tail off, whether permanently or temporarily nobody knows. This means that the A.A.L.A. countries are now mainly responsible for the continuing rapid urbanisation of the world as a whole. From 1950–60 their urbanisation was twice as fast as N.A.T.O.'s. In urbanism also they are far outstripping the city boom of the 19th century industrial revolution. By Davis's reckoning their town-dwellers will double in number every fifteen years, if present rates of urban growth persist.

In Africa, the experience of Ghana, which is the best documented, typifies the newly independent countries, albeit in a somewhat magnified way. In Ghana urbanisation increased from 9 per cent in 1931 to 13 per cent in 1948, and to 23 per cent in 1960. The rate of increase was more than twice as high in 1948–60 as in 1931–48. As for urbanism, the rate of growth over the three decades 1931–60 far exceeded a whole century's record in U.S.A., Sweden, and U.K. From 1948–60 it was 9·3 per cent *a year*, more than three times the growth rate of the total population.

We are not to suppose, however, that the new African countries are simply following, at a quicker pace, in the footsteps of the N.A.T.O. countries. The current African experience is radically different in quality. During the 19th century and later, urbanisation and urbanism in the N.A.T.O. world both arose from and contributed to economic growth. Urbanisation, grave as were the social distresses which accompanied it in countryside and towns alike, did at least go some measurable way towards solving the problems of the rural sector. It had the effect of consolidating and rationalising agricultural holdings, it encouraged their higher capitalisation, and it greatly increased the efficiency of the farming process. In U.S.A. today, for instance, the manpower needed to manage this far more productive farm system is less than two-fifths of what it was in 1910.

In Africa, on the other hand, neither the large rural-urban migration nor the unprecedented urban growth now under way stands to economic growth as ground or consequence or necessary condition. It stands rather as a stumbling-block. The growing towns are not reducing manpower in the rural sector and by the shift supplying their own employment needs. They are not putting the incoming migrants to work in producing goods and services that from their side help to modernise agriculture.

On the contrary, a permanent urban unemployment problem is being created without alleviation of the rural predicament. The growth of towns is in the main out of gear with balanced growth in the economy at large, urban development is increasingly unhinged from rural development. An altogether excessive share of development resources goes into the towns without bringing in its train any marked improvement in living conditions for the masses there.

In short, urbanism in Africa is more a demographic than an economic phenomenon. It is becoming more and more a mere function of total population growth, less and less connected with urbanisation, hardly at all with development or modernisation. If Africans wish to apprehend the shape of things to come in their countries, it is prefigured for them (allowance being made for differences of scale) in what is now going on for all to see in India. Kingsley Davis (op. cit.) observes "I have calculated that if India's population should grow as the U.N. projections indicate it will, the largest city in India in the year 2,000 will have between 36 and 66 million inhabitants."

The figures of urbanisation and urbanism in Ghana are much higher, as was suggested above, than those of the region as a whole. Davis, indeed, concludes that between the Sahara and the Zambesi average urbanisation at the moment stands at no more than 5–12 per cent, depending on how an urban population is defined. Yet it remains true that all that huge region begins to feel, in greater or less degree, the disruptive pressures that are undoing Ghana. All countries wish they could free themselves from the menacing constraint. None can.

It is Africa's good fortune that, unlike India, it still has a bit of time to play with. But the crucial question it has to face is not how much inconvenience this or that country may have to undergo in submitting to such pressures. It is (a) whether urban development, whose consequences are almost wholly negative from the standpoint of modernising a country as a whole, is at all a rational way of using economic resources; and (b) whether capital for investment in rural reconstruction can be liberated by any means which do not include the restriction of urban growth.

Lip-service is invariably paid throughout Africa to the principle that preference must be accorded to rural development. All the same, the keenest vigilance of governments and planners is beyond question still directed towards urban construction and industrialisation. This is part and parcel of their preoccupation with the hope of a rise in income per head, and the towns, they feel, offer the best prospects of quick increases in productivity. Ironically, the semi-instinctive concentration on supposed urban needs, which in a sense runs counter to their rational convictions, sometimes leads to the missing or muddling of opportunities for that rural development which is avowedly their prime concern.

A classic instance of this process is afforded by the Volta River Resettlement Scheme in Ghana. As a result of building the Volta Dam and flooding great stretches of the countryside above it, it became necessary to find new homes for 80,000 people whose old ones, comprising 700 villages, were to be submerged during 1965.

For this operation the original programme, which had many admirable features, contemplated the creation of 52 new villages or communes with populations ranging from 500 to 4,000. Each family was to be provided with a "core" house, to which more rooms could be added as needed. Both the villages and the houses were expertly designed. Cleared farm lands were to be available in varying amounts to different categories of farmers.

Here was a well-thought-out project which was intended to serve, and might well have served, to raise a large body of subsistence-type peasants to a new technical level of farming, expressed in relatively large-scale operations, a co-operative method, partial mechanisation, a scientific cropping schedule, and a cash crop output—precisely the kind of agricultural revolution that all tropical Africa is crying out for, and that the Akoliufu Farm Project and the Kenya Million-acre Scheme are, each in its own way, trying to achieve.

Alas, the Volta River scheme was doomed to failure from the moment the Ghana Government began falling behind the planned land-clearance time-table. The promised 12 acres per arable farmer proved far beyond the resources which the Government were able to command for mechanical clearing. The programme was cut from 12 acres to 6, at which rate the total area to be cleared came to 54,000 acres. By the end of 1965, when the Volta Dam hydro-electric system was already supplying power to Accra, and when therefore the flooding above the dam was practically complete, only 15,000 acres had actually been cleared.

In consequence, there was not enough agricultural development to support the new villages in food and income. Without these the good housing, the sanitation, the water-supplies, the social amenities, the conscientious social welfare and community development staffs quickly lost their point. A great trek of the resettled peasants ensued to areas where food was available, until many villages stood empty or decimated. People who stayed on did so only to meet grave difficulty in getting their crops away to market, and long delays in receiving payment for them.

A powerful prejudice had been created in the minds of all, whether they stayed or whether they left, against the whole conception of co-operative and modernised farming, which the Ghana Seven-Year Plan had declared its determination to encourage.

There seem to have been two main reasons for the failure of this promising enterprise. The first is that the Volta River Authority, with which the resettlement responsibility lay, was engrossed in the technical and ecological problems of the hydro-electric construction, and in the need to deliver power to urban industry by a fixed date. Thus it simply lost sight of the unique agricultural opportunity which the resettlement aspect of its programme offered.

The second reason is that the simultaneous pursuit of urban development and rural development, which planning schedules required, involved a weight of responsibility beyond shouldering by the numerically weak administrative and technical cadres at Ghana's disposal. When load-shedding has to take place, it is the agrarian interest which in practice goes by the board, despite formal protestations of rural priority.

Evidence could be adduced from many other countries besides Ghana to show how serious are the obstacles, political as well as administrative and economic, to making a reality of that preferential concern with the agrarian issue which is on all hands acknowledged to be imperative. If one kind of urban pull sucks in migrants from the countryside, there is another which surreptitiously influences the thought-processes of development planners. Yet a third actually imparts a parasitic character to the towns themselves. As N. O. Addo observes (op. cit.), "in Ghana rural cocoa production is the pivot of the country's economic progress; and in the sense that taxation from cocoa is the main form of government income from which expenditure on urban services is made, rural agriculture could be said to be the dynamic force working to maintain and advance the urban process."

Plainly there are deeply ingrained tendencies for development impulses to flock together, by unthinking routine, into the towns. The rule seems to be that such concentration will take place under a momentum of its own, unless resolute measures to prevent it are pressed home. The condition is one which nothing but effectual planning can deal with, because it arises from the unregulated working of market forces.

Those forces have no eyes to see the non-economic advantages of the rural habitat. Although they will sometimes speciously argue that increase of rural output and productivity is a prerequisite for assured growth in all other sectors, they feel no motive for developing the rural habitat in its own right according to its proper potentialities. They degrade the countryside to a mere utensil of rampant towns.

We are driven back to the fundamental issue raised by the Onitiri gap. What has to be done to secure a balanced development of economic relations between rural and urban sectors? It is an issue in which all A.A.L.A. countries, not African only, are equally involved. It needs to be grasped in its global import.

It can be analysed into six component questions. Is it to be an objective of development planning

(a) first to limit, then to reduce, the urban population?
(b) to ensure that urban industrial productivity shall increase faster than the urban industrial labour force?
(c) to regulate the settlement within the urban sector of people who do not constitute part of the urban industrial labour force?
(d) to ensure that the labour force engaged in non-material production shall increase only as material productive capabilities increase?
(e) to ensure that labour needed by the urban sector shall be found primarily from that sector's own labour resources?

(f) to keep the size of the urban population in phase with the development of rural production and the productivity of the rural force?

Those who find themselves in charge of development planning in Africa during the remainder of this century will, by the kind of answers they give or fail to give to these six questions, largely determine the type and quality of the civilisation which the continent is now struggling to bring to birth.

Probably for the N.A.T.O. countries it is already too late to attain any rural-urban balance on the lines indicated. They appear doomed, as their lives are moving now, each to become one vast polynucleated city with ever-rising population density, obliterating as they go the very distinction between urban and rural, at the expense of the rural. Kingsley Davis puts the point thus. "The bigger the city, the higher the cost of space; yet the more the level of living rises, the more people are prepared to pay for low-density living. Nevertheless, as urban areas expand and collide, it seems that life in low-density surroundings will become too dear for the great majority."

Perhaps Africa alone of all the continents still has something like a clean slate in this matter, with an average urbanisation, as we saw, of no more than 10 per cent, and an immense rural hinterland available for development as genuine countryside, exhibiting the full range and richness of rural variety.

Yet the invariable overriding qualification must never be forgotten. Even in these special conditions that so supremely favour Africa, it will prove impossible to achieve a wholesome town-country equilibrium, until development planners learn to treat the human reproduction rate as itself a plannable factor, and to frame policies of some intelligence and power for the purpose.

If they are unduly slow over this lesson, they may expect to find the N.A.T.O. predicament catching up with them.

CHAPTER 10

TRAINED MINDS

NATURALLY THE POSITIVE POLICY has its educational aspects. Troops who are to carry Operation Habitat to success must be properly trained for the job. And they must be good enough soldiers to comprehend what precise contribution is expected of them, and why. Since the main body of the army has, from the nature of the case, to be recruited from the rural population, the educational task may be defined as transforming the subsistence peasant into a yeoman farmer.

Wherever in Africa the régime of subsistence agriculture holds sway, the countryside is three parts dead. The purpose of Operation Habitat is to give it a strong shot of life. A French commentator has well remarked *Pour animer ce milieu, il importe de le bien comprendre et d'épouser sa condition.*

In many ways this community principle, as I like to call it, is native and congenial to the African peasantry. The conception of fellowship in a group of kindred, almost one might say in a common bloodstream, which encompasses animals and plants as well as men, is of all the varied cultural heritage of Africa the element most worthy of, and best fitted for, development in a modernised educational system. The western nations to their deep loss, have been strangers to it for many centuries. Africa is, one dares hope, destined to restore it to them and to all the world.

But unhappily among the present-day African peasantry the community principle, so interpreted, has dwindled to a myth and a sentiment. It has no power upon their action. While they might find it picturesque to hear the rural habitat spoken of as their bride, they are too ignorant of the nature of things, and they perceive their own real motives and interests too dimly, to attach practical meaning to their responsibilities as bridegroom. So bitter for them has been their experience of the last hundred years that they are drained now of proper feeling for the countryside and its agonising troubles. One of the most frightening features of the whole African scene is the indifference, the hatred often, which countrymen and town-dwellers alike feel for rural life. To spend one's days on the land is to wave goodbye to all ambition, almost to abandon hope.

In Cotonou in the early months of 1966 I made the acquaintance of a Dahomean journalist, who had plied his trade with success in Ivory Coast and Senegal as well. Gradually I gathered from him quite a bit about his outlook on life in French West Africa. Dahomey, he explained, is a poor country, startingly denuded of everything—except the bare land itself. Sons of the soil who aspire to spend their lives in anything better than an unending corridor of grinding penury contemplate with an angry scorn this desert that they sprang from and must return to. Scratching the barest of bare livings from it is viewed as an affront to human dignity.

"The one road forward for fellows like me," he said, "was to become a *scolarisé*—in other words, to convert myself into a French bourgeois intellectual. I only half-succeeded, of course. Often poverty and hunger took my eye off the ball. I was always short of time and means really to get outside French education. I can't remember a time when I wasn't being forced to make do with swallowing mere morsels of knowledge, mere grains of thought."

"And what did the half-loaf do for you?" I asked.

"Well," he replied, "it gave me a chance to burst out of the suffocating net of kindred, of protégés. The tribal rules are strict. At home in Dahomey, I must cherish and support these people. If I don't, my life is in danger. The way out is to escape abroad into some kind of white collar job—in my case journalism."

"And if you can't get abroad, your life would be literally in danger? How do you mean?"

"Dahomey's a place where people feel insulted if they have to watch a kinsman or neighbour doing better than the average.

They take it out of him by making him pay blackmail to a large family group of spongers."

"And if he refuses?"

"This may sound strange to you, but then he really does lose his right to live. As a form of life-protection, he has no option but to take out a subscription with the witch-doctors. It's no fantasy that the old practices of sorcery threaten him. Make no mistake about that. The fetish-merchants can literally create a cloud of hatred and jealousy under which man and man, village and village, may tear one another to pieces."

"How much use to him is a life guaranteed by this sort of means?"

"Little enough," he said. "That's the trouble. He stays alive, of course—for a while anyway. But he can never become a proper member of the kindred again. What he does is to grow a shell of individualism, under which his new francophone interior life can shelter. He invokes 'modern values' as a defence against the importunities of his kin-group. When he fails to escape abroad into physical exile, he falls back on this spiritual exile that he struggles to impose on himself at home. It's the most painful of all kinds of division from his own people."

"On the other hand," I said, "I suppose it is psychologically impossible to renounce his bourgeois intellectualism. Once an intellectual, always an intellectual."

"You've got it," he said drily.

As I found later, this is not quite the end of the story. Dahomean "*scolarisés*" who score the initial triumph of escaping abroad do not really come off much better in the end. It is now often held against them that in pre-independence days they stood too close to the colonialists and all their works. They tend to be regarded as strangers in Africa, as bogus Africans inlaid with a white veneer, as collaborators in short. Other Africans easily give up thinking of Damohean semi-intellectuals as brothers, and, egged on by the shallow and imbecile little nationalisms of the day, look to the time when they can pack them off home again.

Independence, of the current balkanised type with its narrow codes of nationality, gives them their opportunity; which has been seized by Ivory Coast and Niger, Gabon and Congo-Brazzaville. From all these lands, to name no others, Dahomean expatriates have been deported, robbed and naked, to their country of origin, where they burden the budget and vegetate without work.

The tragic story well illustrates a pattern of education which might have been designed to make Operation Habitat impossible, because it works towards the erosion of rural elites instead of towards their construction. High-level manpower in Africa at large has been seduced into turning its back on the countryside and ignoring its crying needs. This fact presents the main educational problem of the next thirty years.

Almost everywhere in Africa the old elites were rural. No doubt, in face of the European occupation they proved ineffective. No doubt, the turn of the urban elites was a phase that had to be lived through. That phase is now starting to close. The new elites, if they are to exercise any control over the course of events, will have to become rural once again, identifying themselves directly with peasant needs, and committed to a a scheme of priorities in which industry and commerce serve the requirements of the countryside, not vice versa.

In principle, the job of the reformed pattern of education is, in one and the same movement, to provide the peasantry with the schooling it needs and to put it in organic touch with the body of high-level manpower. The leaders of rural reconstruction will not emerge in mere spontaneity. They have to be sought out, placed in the way of training, however simplified, and, by the self-identification of their own goal-interests, imbued with the will to achieve goals.

The leaven of the rural revolution consists in a blend of trained excellence of peasant character with trained excellence of intelligence at graduate level, such that the character conceives the end and the intelligence perceives the means. In the early stages of mobilisation for Operation Habitat, peasant education comes through activity, not ideology or planning; from reflection on the nature of some practical task; and from discussion with co-workers of the concrete problems it poses. This alone will permit a progressiveness and coherent raising of the level of awareness among the peasantry and prepare it for dedication to rational goals and the objective needs of modernisation. This is the first step in fitting peasants for that campaign in the course of which they will transform themselves by transforming the countryside that is to nourish them as they nourish it.

The ultimate victory aimed at is the domestication of a gigantic and often harsh habitat to a point where it takes on the sanctity of a human home. Then a social order emerges that adds a new dimension to the order of nature. And Africans begin to realise their characteristic dream of a humane communion in which mankind and nature's forces share an enlarging life that by degrees purges itself of destructive antagonisms.

If, on the one hand, the education system is to form the advance guard of the rural reconstruction army, the practical processes of rural reconstruction have in their turn to inspire radical changes in the pattern of schools, training institutions, and universities. Those who re-plan the structure of formal education will want a realistic picture in their minds of what those processes are, so that they may deduce from them the new kinds of teaching provision by whose aid they are to be carried out.

The decisive break-through, the casting off of the crippling fetters of tribal land-mismanagement, is likely to come, not everywhere but in a sufficient number of key places, in the next 15–20 years. Within that span, the boundaries of the money economy will have been extended to take in many African farming areas. Many semi-nomadic tribes will have been launched on grass-managed ranching. Consolidation and enclosure of old farm lands, together with African resettlement on good new lands, will have made headway.

Moreover, a growing weight of investment will be directed into roads and communications, into farm equipment and processing factories, and into farm training centres, the extension services, community development, and adult education. Regional networks of improved marketing arrangements will develop, structured in the main on co-operative principles. Again, there will be more investment in plantations, linked with outgrower schemes. More field research stations will be set up, with functions similar to those of the Henderson Research Station at Mazoe in Rhodesia and working in close contact, where possible, with a local university. Government irrigation and reclamation schemes will be enlarged. Plans for water conservation, afforestation, and the wide distribution of electric power will be pressed forward by urgent central authority.

Developments like these, if they are not to be constantly held up by heart-breaking frustrations, require in the first place a cultivated and responsive peasantry, with minds well enough trained to grasp the principles involved in the environmental challenge, and to make, under proper encouragement and support, the informed response that ecological science indicates. The second requirement is a corps of specialists of various kinds to furnish trained peasants with such support and encouragement. The nucleus of such a corps already exists in the field staffs of the extension and community development services.

It is beginning to be realised, further, that besides the expertise of planners and of professional and technical staffs in Departments of Agriculture, Departments of Settlement, Departments of Natural Resources, Survey Departments, and so on, rural reconstruction will call for many managerial skills at many levels, and of the highest order at the highest level.

In agriculture there will come into being operating units of new structural forms, such as group farms, farm machinery pools, or the organisation representing the clan-ownership of an 80,000 acre grass-managed cattle ranch. Large co-operative organs will arise with unified responsibility from production to marketing, including the distribution of farm credit. "Hot lines" of communication and participation will be built from centre to circumference, so that rational discussion can continuously proceed between the base and the summit of the nation. New communities springing up in resettlement areas, whether in "white" highlands or in Government reclamation and irrigation projects, will require co-ordinated direction from a business organisation and business managers on the lines of a Tennessee Valley Authority. For such tasks the quality of expert business sense, of public relations flair, and of disciplined sociological insight ought not to be less than the best.

These are some of the capabilities which an effective Corps of Commissioned officers, from general to subaltern, may be expected to exhibit, and which the education and training they are exposed to should aim at implanting. Evidently Operation Habitat offers plenty of scope for high-level manpower.

I turn to the prime consideration of all, the ground troops, the cultivated peasants who are to grow into yeoman farmers. How far can the educational influences that impinge upon them be shaped into coherence and convergence? Viewed in the perspective of Operation Habitat, possibly the influences of greatest importance, actual and potential, are family upbringing, rural health centres, and primary education.

In the lives of most African children in the rural areas, there is at present too much home and not enough of the health centre and school. Nothing but confusion in the child's mind will result, however, should he come to feel that the three, or any two of them, stand for conflicting value-systems. If the three, aided by nature's process of maturation, are to make it possible for the child to become a cultivated peasant, it is vital that they should all honestly work together on what one might call an agreed syllabus.

Few would deny that tribal upbringing has become mainly divisive in its social and political effects. The tribe and the clans and families composing it form too narrow a base for the kind of socialisation that African children now need, if they are to grow up into creative citizens of the new order. Moreover, the tribe is the channel along which the system of magical beliefs and witchcraft practices is transmitted—practices and beliefs which sever in a dreadful way all but the most superficial communication between rural Africa and those tutored Africans who have learnt their way to something of the scientific attitude. For these and many other reasons the political leadership never tire of girding at the evils of tribalism—which indeed politically, economically, and socially has become a devastating nuisance everywhere.

This, of course, is not to deny that some features of tribal culture possess survival value even in the context of independence, and have a claim to active participation in a modernised system of upbringing. But clearly the many evils of tribalism will persist without much change, so long as most of the population spends almost all its time immersed in the social pressures of the tribe. And as long as tribalism persists, so long also will subsistence farming. The pressures of the tribe will begin to weaken only when forms of social co-operation which cut across tribal boundaries are widely and officially demanded, and when the re-designed primary teaching itself is both made ubiquitous and also converted from a localised organ of clan or sect into a true institution of an ampler society—in short, a genuine instrument of group-communication consciously contributing to the cohesion and unity of all African social life.

Before 1960 one basis of the demand for independence was the need for that universal education which the colonial régimes could not, or would not, supply. Since 1960 it has been unquestioningly assumed that independence must remain unreal and modernisation unattainable without universal education—which means, first and foremost, 100 per cent enrolment in the primary school. Most African countries, therefore, have been and still are making sustained efforts to develop their educational systems towards that goal.

From the springboard of the three years 1962–3 to 1965–5 projections were made by U.N.E.S.C.O. which suggested that 100 per cent enrolment could be reached by 1970 in Ghana,

Guinea, and Senegal. By implication the other African countries would follow suit at shorter or longer intervals. Such projections, especially when mistaken for predictions or even for dated targets, proved to be much too optimistic. The primary school in the new Africa, so far from bowling along at a brisk pace towards universality, finds itself on the contrary in a state of crisis which calls for a thorough re-thinking of its workability, and indeed of its suitability too. Let us take a look at the educational position in Senegal, by way of illustration.

On ne peut être indépendant dans l'ignorance, observes President Senghor, as he decrees *la scolarisation totale du pays dans un délai de dix ans*. He might have added "There can be no social growth in a population, unless its average level of education is rising". Accordingly, the target of the first 4-year Plan (1961–65) was declared to be an enrolment percentage of 51. This was apparently thought of as bringing 100 per cent enrolment by 1970 well within reach, having regard to the West African average annual rate of increase of 12 per cent between 1950 and 1962.

The percentage in fact achieved by 1964–65 was not 51, but only 36 (representing 202,500 pupils). Inevitably the usual difficulties of buildings, equipment, and teaching staff were encountered. But the main reason for the underfulfilment seems to be that both the rate of population increase and the proportion of school-age children to total population were misestimated. The latter figure, for instance, turned out to be 17 per cent as against the Plan's assumption of 14·5 per cent.

The error is not repeated in the second 4-year Plan (1965–1969), as this table shows:

Year	Total Population	School-age Population	Pupils Enrolled	Percentage Enrolled
1964–65	3,309,000	562,500	202,500	36·00
1965–66	3,382,000	575,000	216,500	37·65
1966–67	3,457,000	587,500	230,900	39·30
1967–68	3,534,000	601,000	245,900(est)	40·91
1968–69	3,613,000	614,000	261,300(est)	42·55

Here the key-assumptions are a population growth rate of 2·25 per cent a year and a school-age population of just over 17 per cent of total population. On what assumption the increase of enrolment is based is not clear, but the increase as shown is about 1·64 per cent a year. What is clear, however, is that the prospect of 100 per cent enrolment has withdrawn into a remote future.

If one extracts from the above table the numbers of school-age children *not* enrolled, one finds that they were 360,000 in 1964–65 and are estimated at 352,700 in 1968–69—an average annual decrease over the four years, of 1,825. And if one goes on to calculate how long it would take to reduce the 352,700 to zero by annual subtractions of 1,825, the answer works out at slightly under 200 years.

Senegal is better placed than most African countries. At any rate some reduction of the unenrolled is going on there. Elsewhere it often seems to be assumed that, because the percentage of children in school is rising, therefore the numbers of children without a place in school are falling. The fact is that both magnitudes are generally increasing together. So long as this remains true, the goal of universal schooling must recede.

100 per cent enrolment having first been agreed upon as vital to independence, and now being found to be out of the question, one might have expected eager discussion to arise about the best alternative policy. This is not Africa's way. Instead one meets muffled complaints about the high cost of educational programmes, and muffled scepticism about their value. What, after all, does schooling do beyond making pupils unfit for life in the villages, and giving them ideas above their station?

In any case, more than 50 per cent of the school output are unable either to continue their education beyond the primary stage or to enter paid employment on leaving it. Efforts to expand primary schooling therefore simply exacerbate the problem of the unemployed school leaver. If one cannot avoid a high level of unemployment, all those jobless boys will surely give less trouble if they cannot read or write. It may even be wise to reduce the primary school population to the numbers needed to fill post-primary school places and vacancies in the juvenile labour market. The watchword for the coming years should be consolidation rather than expansion (a euphemism for leaving the fundamental problem of education to look after itself).

Viewed in the context of Africa's need for modernisation, attitudes of this kind are merely futile. It is not particularly alarming that universal attendance day after day for full-time education inside the four walls of the primary school should be found impracticable. After all, this is a purely European conception which may well prove superfluous in the development of African culture. Even in the most advanced countries of Europe it was treated as impracticable until a hundred years ago, and there are still parts of Europe where it remains unrealised. But what is truly menacing is that the whole principle of universality should be dropped in furtive silence without a struggle. There seems little appreciation in Africa of the risks of selective schooling at the primary level.

This blind spot is remarkably odd, since the whole educational experience of Africa throughout the colonial period demonstrates with great clarity that the crucial flaw in the cultural sphere has been the failure to draw the peasantry into the main stream of education, and to give them literacy and vocational training and technical leadership. It is this failure which still cancels out any and every programme of social growth. The result is a fatal division of the community into a *scolarisé* minority and a *non-scolarisé* majority, neither of which is capable of any productive communication with the other. Such a division is incompatible even with social order, let alone social growth.

The outcome of all educational provision is thenceforward a parasitic urban "elite", eaten up with snobbery and selfishness because, forsooth, they have tasted post-primary schooling, plus a rabble of maladjusted unemployable louts who call themselves "primary school graduates". The great bulk of the mental capacity with which the total community is endowed remains latent, untended, even unidentified in the unschooled peasant youth. No country can stand such waste without going down-hill.

It may be true, of course, that the illiterate rural adolescents are nicer people to meet than the primary school "graduates", or for that matter than the products of secondary and higher education. The myth of the noble savage retains a shamefaced charm even in Africa. But how is it possible to draw the inference that some children are improved by schooling while others are better off without it (which is the position increas-ingly taken up, it seems, by African Governments)?

The proper conclusion is very different; namely, that if you cannot afford to provide primary instruction which is at once scholastic and universal, what will have to go is the scholasti-cism, not the universality. In other words, if the system of full-time formal schooling at primary level, as at present organised in Africa, cannot offer a school place for every child of school age, it will have to be replaced by new kinds of institutionalised teaching from which there will be no exclu-sions.

Every human group has some systematic way of transmitting the knowledge of the elders to the new generation. The indi-genous African methods followed lines of social initiation and apprenticeship rather than of schooling in our formal sense. In practice, and from their own standpoint, they were unusually successful, largely because they were the same for all. They therefore simultaneously promoted social cohesion and equality of opportunity within the common life.

The current crisis in first-level education has grown out of the wooden and mechanical attempt to copy the European primary school as an institutional form. The first decade after independence has sufficed to show that such a model is unsuited to the present stage of African development, and that it acts as a brake on social growth rather than as a stimulus to it.

In a number of African countries the content of first-level

education is being more and more oriented towards rural science. Much of this new material is better imparted in the field than in the classroom; and better too by instructors with special knowledge of social welfare, health, nutrition, agriculture, community development, and the co-operative movement than by school teachers as such.

Most countries have some form of community development service, of agricultural extension service, programmes of rural development works, programmes of family nutrition and home development. Such services and programmes concern themselves with improving water-supplies and the physical conditions of home and their surroundings (diet, food-storage, kitchens, latrines, etc.), with village planning and hygiene, with building roads, bridges, and houses, above all with more efficient farming methods and the conservation of the habitat.

All these concerns provide ready-made instruments of education, and have the advantage of being presentable as part of active field projects whose working can be observed and assessed. They can easily be used as pegs on which to hang simple arithmetical calculations, and literary exercises such as the keeping of notebooks. If instruction is properly organised around them, they may be the means to better-rounded courses than can be provided by conventional classroom teaching within the four walls of conventional primary schools.

The field staff of the Departments of Agriculture, Health, Social Welfare, and Co-operation would be drawn into the day-to-day work of teaching the 6–12 age group, and trained school teachers would concentrate on organising the curriculum and co-ordinating the instruction. By the rearrangement of the fundamental stage of education on these lines, village by village or by groups of villages, the entire 6–12 age group would be given a general preparation for the kind of life it will have to live, for its station in that life, and for its duties and opportunities in that station.

Besides such general preparation there are two other irreducible essentials which the primary school in all countries is accustomed to provide, and which any effective alternative to the conventional primary school must also be able to provide. These are literacy and selection for post-primary schooling.

In the kind of alternative we are now discussing, literacy training itself would be organised in the context of the total programme of community development, and in conditions where the necessary reading matter is prepared by the villages themselves under the direction of the local representative of the Department of Education. It would have links with the literacy work going on in the field of adult education. All literate members of the village community would be expected to take part in it, since well-known techniques exist in accordance with which the actual teaching can be done by almost anyone who is literate himself and capable of carrying out a simple set of instructions.

For the last two years of this new 6-year course of fundamental education, pupils aged 11–12 would enter on a period of formal schooling on more conventional lines. The main objectives here would be (a) to consolidate and extend the skills acquired during the 4-year phase of what may be called field-initiation, with special emphasis on polishing up the 3 R's; (b) to select that minority of pupils who showed themselves best fitted to proceed to further schooling at the secondary level; (c) to award a certificate to all pupils who had satisfactorily completed the 6-year course.

Administratively the 6-year course in its entirety would, needless to say, be planned, directed, and integrated by the Department of Education as the sole competent authority. The *premier cycle*, however (i.e. the 4-year course of field-initiation undergone between the ages 6–10) would be the particular responsibility of a small Joint Action Committee at Ministry level, supported by a special unit within the Central Statistics Office. The Committee's chairman would be appointed by the Department of Education, and its other members would be drawn from the Departments of Agriculture, Health, Social Welfare, Community Development, Adult Literacy, and from the Co-operative movement.

The *deuxième cycle* (i.e. the 2-year course of formal schooling

undertaken by the 11–12 age group) would take place under
qualified teachers in the buildings and with the (supplemented)
equipment of existing primary schools. Buildings and equipment which are inadequate to accommodate the whole of the
6–12 age group would presumably be sufficient, or could soon
be made sufficient, to provide proper teaching space and
facilities for the whole of the 11–12 age group.

Obviously a general scheme of this kind calls for thorough
testing by means of pilot schemes in many varying conditions.
If it survives its feasibility tests, it will first of all do something
which has never yet been done in Africa, namely survey and
deploy the totality of a population's intellectual and artistic
endowments. Secondly, it will apply to all children without
exception the same treatment in respect of their fundamental
education. Thirdly, in the first four years of the course it will
bring schooling to life and life to schooling in real and practical
terms; and in the last two years it will offer a rigorous and
emulative intellectual discipline geared to defined rewards.
Fourthly, it would tend to equalise differences in achievement-
motivation between different ethnic groups within the same
political society—differences which have wrought such havoc
in Nigeria and elsewhere, but which none the less can be
changed by changes in the social environment that produces
them in children.

It is submitted that some such scheme offers the only way
out of the present critical impasse in the primary school system,
and could in its working be a great improvement on much of
what is spuriously dignified by the name of primary schooling
today. Above all, it would save the vital principle of universality
in the system of fundamental education.

Education is already one of the largest and most flourishing
of African industries. In Nigeria, we are told, it employs some
125,000 persons, which is more than the number employed in
the modern sectors of industry and commerce combined.
Between 1950 and 1959 the average annual rates of growth in
enrolments in a number of selected countries south of the

Sahara were 12–14 per cent at primary level and 21–24 per cent at secondary level. The rates have been quicker still since independence.

Teacher training programmes are stretched to the limit, and have difficulty in keeping pace with the increases in enrolment. Primary schools therefore suffer from dilution by what are little more than pupil-teachers, and secondary schools from a very costly dependence on expatriate teaching staff. Even in enrolment there is a long way still to go. In 1962–63 40 per cent of the school age population was attending primary schools in West Africa, 69 per cent in North Africa and 46 per cent in Africa as a whole. In secondary schools the percentage was 3·8 for West Africa, 12·2 for North Africa, and 6·9 for Africa as a whole.[1]

The general pace of educational advance in Africa is none the less much quicker than any other indicator of social progress. Educational development stands roughly where the N.A.T.O. countries stood seventy years ago. The educational distance between Africa and N.A.T.O. is significantly shorter than the economic distance.

Africans, of course, are in the education industry at all levels in massive ways, and the prospects for its thorough Africanisation, which shall be at the same time true modernisation, are better than they are in any other branch of industry or commerce. This is of cardinal importance, since industry and commerce at large can be Africanised only by way of the Africanisation of education. The educational system, designed as a balanced whole, is viewed as a key-factor in any strategy for modernising the economy and the social framework alike.

It is evident that a new phase of educational development is opening. In the decade immediately following independence the system finds itself heavily tilted towards the output of "high-level manpower". In view of the proper resolve to replace

[1] U.N.E.S.C.O. has set the following targets for Africa by 1980: 100 per cent enrolment in primary schools, 23 per cent in secondary schools, and 2 per cent in institutions of higher education. There is no chance of their being generally reached.

expatriates by Africans in the public service and elsewhere, it cannot be argued that this bias was mistaken. But it has inevitably led to some distortion of the system. The time is at hand when expansion of graduate output (especially of non-scientific graduates) will have to be given a lower priority than expansion of secondary schools, and expansion of secondary schools in turn will be shaped by the need to overhaul the concept and practice, the aims, methods, and organisation of primary schooling.

Emphasis is already being laid on these principles in some African countries, of which Uganda may stand as an example. "Somehow," the Ugandans say, "we have got to get away from mere rote-instruction in the 3 R's and enter the paths of true learning. The entire system from the first years of the primary school onwards must become child-centred. The development of the school child, not the advantage of government or parents or priests must determine policy. The syllabus must be Ugandised; text-books in history, nature study, geography, arithmetic must reflect the life and culture of the people of Uganda. Unless we lay this sure foundation, we cannot build securely for the ensuing years.

"Questions of organisation, responsibility, and control of the schools obviously have great importance in this context, and they have to be suitably settled before co-ordinated reform can be undertaken. But the ultimate key that regulates the extent and the quality of the school services as a whole is the training and supply of teachers.

"The key to improving the basic primary course, the key that opens the gate to true learning, the key indeed to all development of human resources on a nation-wide scale, lies in raising the entry standards and the passing-out standards in the teacher-training institutions, concurrently with a significant increase in their output."

If the education industry is to become the thriving concern that African modernisation requires, it will be essential to eliminate waste from its working. At present, unit costs are extremely high. At some universities, indeed, they are comparable with costs in the most expensive academies in the world—mainly because of their residential character and their founders' lavish ideas about lay-out, buildings, and equipment. Average costs are high in secondary schools also for similar reasons; they are normally boarding schools with a high proportion of expensive expatriate staff, and they are normally built of imported, not local, materials.

In primary schools the high cost of producing a pupil who has satisfactorily completed the course is largely due to the high proportion of drop-outs and repeaters. In ideal conditions it should take six years to work through the primary course; one U.N.E.S.C.O. study shows that in some African countries an average of four times this duration is in fact needed.

Viewing Africa as a whole, and education at all levels, it would probably not be wide of the mark to estimate that the school-university system at its current stage of development functions at about 30 per cent efficiency.

As one way of improving this figure, it would be a constructive move to explore the possibilities of inter-territorial co-ordination, especially at the level of universities and teacher-training institutions. It is clear that many of the existing nationettes can no more provide complete self-contained educational systems than they can create self-sufficient economies.

THE RACE ISSUE

THROUGHOUT EAST AND Central Africa the first task that independence laid on African political leadership was the removal of the colour bar in all its forms. In West Africa, since it was not an area of white settlement, this particular problem did not arise.

The colour bar in colonial days was in practice more extensive and elaborate in some countries than in others, or more firmly entrenched in the statute book, but in none of them was it unknown. Even in Tanganyika (now Tanzania), in which, as a Trust Territory, legal discriminations on grounds of race were not admitted, discriminatory customs none the less crept in from across the borders. Their modes were very various, affecting many matters, including land ownership and use, place of residence and of business, employment, access to public amenities and facilities, education, housing, health, and social services generally.

So objectionable were the disabilities thus imposed on non-Europeans, and so inappropriate the structure of race relations founded upon them, that the General Assembly of the United Nations on 15 December, 1960, adopted Resolution 1536 (xv) which recommended "the cancelling of all laws and regulations which tend to encourage or sanction, directly or indirectly, discriminatory policies and practices based on racial considerations", and urged the discouragement of such practices by all other means possible.

The Resolution reinforced a movement which had started two or three years before in a number of African territories, but was still at the stage of a protest campaign. In Northern Rhodesia (now Zambia), for example, the first real breakthrough on the social front had occurred just previously with the passage on 1 September, 1960, of a law that opened hotels, cafés, bars, cinemas, etc., to all races. Thenceforward, helped by United Nations support, the crumbling of the race-barriers went on at an accelerated pace, and even began to manifest itself here and there in Southern Rhodesia (now Rhodesia). In one aspect, the whole process was part of the break-up of the Central African Federation, the last fortress, north of the Limpopo, of the segregation principle.

The attainment of independence furnished the occasion for a final, all-out, frontal attack. In Kenya, whose method springs from motives and attitudes common to all the African nationalist movements in the region, the attack was incorporated in the text of the Independence Order-in-Council itself.

From its coming into force in December, 1963, the Order made all citizens of the country equal before the law and specifically protected all persons from discrimination on grounds of race. It required that "no law shall make any provision that is discriminatory either of itself or in its effect"; and that "no persons shall be treated in a discriminatory manner by any person acting by virtue of any written law or in the performance of the functions of any public office or any public authority".

Discrimination is defined as "affording different treatment to different persons attributable wholly or mainly to their respective descriptions by race, tribe, place of origin or residence or other local connection, political opinions, colour or creed whereby persons of one such description are subjected to disabilities or restrictions to which persons of another such description are not made subject or are accorded privileges or advantages which are not accorded to persons of another such description".

Once-familiar types of racial segregation were banned by the provision that "no person shall be treated in a discriminatory manner in respect of access to shops, hotels, lodging houses, public restaurants, eating houses, beer halls or places of public entertainment or in respect of access to places of public resort maintained wholly or partly out of public funds or dedicated to the use of the general public".

These measures constituted a revolution of the first importance. They were a necessary, though not a sufficient, condition for the establishment of that non-racial society which the terms of the Kenya Constitution presume throughout, and which the new African Governments throughout the region have made their objective.

In some vital matters they have, to be sure, become immediately effective. Whether a person can exercise the Parliamentary franchise, stand for election to Parliament, own land, hold office in the public service, and freely enjoy the public amenities available in his country, now depends not on his racial description, but on his status as a citizen.

This, however, is not to say that all causes of friction between the races, or all impulses of favouritism which each race entertains towards its own members, have been or can be abolished by a stroke of the law-maker's pen. Attitudes ingrained in all races through long years of colonial rule will need time and conscious tolerance and sincere mutual aid before they can be changed into spontaneous fellow-feeling.

The point can be illustrated from the Kenya Civil Service, substantive appointment to which, under the new Constitution, is open only to Kenya citizens. The new Constitution creates Kenya citizenship for the first time, and confers it on every person born in Kenya who was previously a British subject or a British protected person, provided also that one of his parents was Kenya-born.

A considerable proportion of Asians and Europeans did not fall within that category, while almost all Africans did. Such Asians and Europeans therefore became ineligible for substantive appointment to the civil service, unless they took out citizenship in some other way. The law provided that they might do this by applying for registration as a citizen within two years of independence (i.e. by December 12, 1965). The option was open to them if they were born in Kenya, or if, having been born elsewhere, they had resided in Kenya for five years out of an eight-year period.

The discrimination here is between citizens and non-citizens, not between members of different races; moreover, the restriction of civil service posts to citizens is by no means peculiar to Kenya; it is common form in many countries all over the world. But in a number of individual cases in Kenya the two lines of cleavage happen to coincide, and the restriction is felt, illogically if you like, as if it were imposed on racial grounds. This was a problem of the transition, which was bound to settle itself before the end of 1965. Any Asian or European affected could settle it for himself by opting for Kenya citizenship. Those who delayed no doubt considered that they had good reasons for caution, and ought not to suffer if they availed themselves of the full latitude the law allowed. The African view, on the other hand, tended to be that if opportunities slipped through the fingers of the hesitant, that was a price they must expect to pay for not making up their minds promptly.

Asians and Europeans looking to first appointment in the Government service were not the only ones to feel the effects of this situation. Others who were already members of the service before Kenya citizenship was created, might also be touched by it when promotion was in question. The Government might be reluctant to promote officers who, on their side, seemed reluctant to identify themselves with the new country and who, if in the event they failed to opt for citizenship by December, 1965, might be required to leave the service then. The upshot was that preference was sometimes given to Africans who would not on personal grounds have been regarded as the strongest candidates.

The fact, then, that the composition of Kenya's citizen body had not yet been definitively settled could and did work out to the benefit of Africans, where the public service is concerned; and this for reasons which it would not be just to call racially discriminatory. But in other sectors, such as commerce, industry, education and the hospital services, the bias was the other way. The non-racial policy and outlook of the new Kenya has had little power yet over long-standing African disabilities.

In the private sector of business, where political pressures are harder to drive home, it soon became clear that Africanisation was a trickier business than it was in the civil service. So far there has been little increase in the vertical mobility of Africans in the labour market at large. In the business world their career prospects remain very much what they have always been. They are still acutely aware that making headway is a question of crashing through race-barriers, that good performance on the job cuts little ice, and that political influence plus formal educational attainments are the only keys that can open the door to preferment.

African official circles are apt to become restive in consequence. Local and overseas firms are warmly urged to recruit and train Africans at higher technical and managerial levels. Chambers of Commerce are exhorted to abandon their racial character in practice as well as on paper. In Parliament there are complaints of organised opposition from businessmen of other races who hamper the entry of Africans into the executive ranks of industry and trade. The Government is constantly challenged from the floor of the House to enable Africans to share or take over the majority of non-African businesses.

At the present stage, the official view seems to be that the promotion of new small-scale light industries, owned and managed by Africans, promises more than African infiltration into larger enterprises owned by Asians and Europeans. The kind of products involved are transistor radios, battery-operated record players, plastic products, blotting paper, ironmongery, bakeries, saw mills, sisal decortication, stockfeed, dry cleaning, and so on. In most countries of the region the number of such small concerns is steadily being added to. The situation illustrates well how growth on racial lines is, as it were, enforced by the traditional structure of business.

All schools are now open to all races, as they were not in the colonial system. There is no doubt and no reservation about the policy. But ease of entry into schools is not the same for every race. For example, in the secondary boarding schools of Nairobi there have been since independence a number of unfilled places. European pupils had left, but their places had not been taken by African pupils, since African parents had decided they could not afford the fees. The fees struck African parents as high, mainly on account of teachers' salaries. The average salary for teachers in this particular category of school was £1,200 p.a., and most of the teachers were Europeans. In African primary schools, where teachers were mainly African, the average salary was £350–£400.

Here discrimination works through income, much as in the public service it works through citizenship. In neither case is it formally or intentionally racial. But it finds an expression which appears to be racial to those whom it excludes. One way round the difficulty would be to reduce fees to a point within reach of the African parents' purse, and to make up the difference to the schools by Government grants-in-aid. For the present, however, the Government takes the view that it is preferable to use the money for building new secondary schools.

A similar point is exemplified by the hospital services. Hospital segregation has been abolished. Anybody can now be treated in any hospital regardless of race. Nevertheless the income factor entails that the racial distribution of in-patients in the various hospitals remains much what it was before desegregation was decreed.

In Kenya, hospital treatment has never been and is not free. Some hospitals charge more than others. Asians and Europeans have long had contributory schemes for hospital treatment relief in which membership was not always voluntary. Africans hitherto have had no such schemes.

Government policy is to extend this type of insurance to cover all races, and to make the system as simple and inexpensive as possible. It will not, however, be easy to devise a scheme that is free from anomalies, partly because of income differences which are still closely correlated with race, and partly because of the differing social customs among the races. When the Leader of Government Business in the Senate moved the second reading of a Bill to extend to Africans medical insurance facilities previously enjoyed by Asians and Europeans, a speaker in the

5*

debate complained that in terms of the Bill as drafted only one wife of a contributing polygamist and her children would be entitled to benefits.

The other countries of the region (Rhodesia always excepted) have taken steps which, though not formally the same as Kenya's, produce very similar results, so that north of the Zambesi the legal dismantling of the system of racial discrimination is now substantially complete. The brief indications given above show both how far social life has moved from the old restrictionism, and how much racial (or race-linked) inequality persists that cannot be shifted save by structural alterations in the social fabric. Such alterations are already very much in hand.

All witnesses concur that the new citizenship scheme is a notable improvement on the old colour scheme. The observer finds it hard to persuade himself that anything so crude and tasteless as the old ever really existed. There are, indeed, still pockets, parts of the Kenya highlands, for example, or of the Zambia copper belt, where race relations remain poor because too many people are trying to hold them to the old pattern. But these are exceptions. The rule is that Africans manifest a new pride and dignity, Asians are more open and less aloof, Europeans manage without their old swaggering disdain.

The inter-racial comedy of manners is being played on an altogether higher plane of mutual respect and consideration. Today, by merely listening to the tone of a European voice, it is almost impossible to tell whether an African or an Asian or another European is being addressed. The snarl is no longer there. There was a time when a semblance of servility was expected in the mode of address of Africans to the higher castes. Today neither the deference of the one nor the condescension of the other is looked for or supplied.

A feature of the changes is that, although they would have been called unthinkable ten years ago, and although they often had to be fought for in a somewhat riotous fashion, their actual coming and their working-out in practice were almost entirely smooth and peaceful. The prophets of ruin have been much confounded. The most common feeling among all races at the collapse of those entrenched barriers has been one of release and relief.

What has happened is not simply that a number of deplorable mannerisms have been abandoned. Each race has actually undergone a modification in its basic attitudes towards the others. This is not to say that prickliness has by some quick-acting magic been turned into pliancy and *bonhomie* all round. But a wide hole has been torn in the great cultural blockage that colonialism built.

Reciprocity has for the first time been introduced into race relations at both personal and group levels. The messages passing between members of different races are no longer a mere one-way traffic moving down a line of authority. Orders of course still come from above. But now information, appeals, suggestions, also rise up from below, and the higher levels are able and willing to take delivery of them.

Secondly, the element of randomness is being progressively eliminated from both types of message. They are becoming more finished products, more worthy expressions of the minds that transmit them. At the delivery point the quality of reception is better attuned and more discriminating. The text of the messages exchanged is thus psychically more developed, charged with richer meaning, and (in the statistical language employed by communication engineers) much more improbable that it was even in the recent past. Since all transmitters are also receivers, and vice versa, receiver and transmitter alike are learning how to reduce distortion, interference, and meaningless "noise" by a continuous process of cross-checking and self-correction. The foundations are being laid for the growth of that warm and fluent mutuality, both of knowledge and of feeling, which is the mark of unimpeded communication.

Since people can co-operate only in so far as they can agree, and since they can agree only in so far as they can accurately communicate, communication holds the key both to constructive work and to social health. It is a good omen that we are able to note, as a prevailing feature of the new order in East and Central Africa, an astonishing improvement in humane communication of this kind.

It is natural that Africans who have long suffered under a system where race was everything should in their revulsion hasten to create one where race is nothing. A man stung by other men's brutal contempt for his race may well seek a remedy in discrediting the whole racial factor.

African Governments and ruling parties believe that the principle of non-racialism can put an end not merely to discrimination based on the race-factor, but to discrimination in all its forms. They are out to build a society in which a man's genetic composition may be treated only positively as the reservoir of his capacities, never negatively as a ground for wilful disqualifications. They therefore insist that all citizens should be equal in two senses; one as before the law, and the other as possessing in practice real equality of opportunity to demonstrate the real inequality of their native gifts.

This real inequality is the proper ground for distinguishing between individuals in respect of education, employment, and socially entrusted responsibility. Distinction of this kind, since it fittingly accords with natural necessity, is not discrimination. The essence of discrimination is to be arbitrary.

An order so designed tries to ensure that social preferment should directly correspond to personal gifts and attainments, with no weighting for membership or non-membership of this or that group, whether racial or other. Yet the aim by no means implies either any leaning towards a philosophy of individualism in the western sense, or any undervaluing of the benefits of close identification with a group. Many items in the African cultural tradition make it virtually impossible that the self-made, self-determined individual who customarily figures in western thinking, should appear as anything more than an abstraction from the concrete corporate life.

What the aim does imply is firstly that all individual demonstrations of real inequality of talent should be compatible with the advantage of the community. Nobody, however talented, is licensed to disavow public hope or to contract out of public care. There is no public endowment of private irresponsibility. The social taker is not accorded equal rights with the social giver.

The second implication is that there is one, and only one, group of which it is important to be an active, and fully paid-up member—the citizen body and the party. For ideally these, though distinct in function, are identical in composition.

After non-racial equality the main emphasis is on the virtues of solidarity, seasoned with African flavours and carrying overtones of tribal culture. In presenting the Tanganyika Five-year Plan to Parliament on 12 May, 1964, President Nyerere makes his culminating appeal in these terms: "Perhaps most important of all, we must also retain the values of brotherliness, of family-hood, which our fathers had. Our task is to widen these values, not to eradicate them. This, in fact, is the purpose of all our work and all our Plans; the creation—through African Social-ism—of a country in which we can all live proudly as brothers."

Here is the special African concept of the human family tree, where our brotherhood begins before we are born and goes on after we die, where living human beings own nothing in fee simple, but are temporary *ex officio* trustees for a total kin that includes all ancestors and all posterity.

Hitherto African solidarity has been grounded in kinship so understood. To this powerful bond is likely now to be added an occupational solidarity, the unitedness of people engaged in joint enterprises of great pith and moment. Feeling for personal rights and health and well-being and inner harmony may well grow more sensitive and more widespreal. But the qualities of individuals will be assessed in terms of the quality of their participation in the common effort. To the Descartes of Europe the fact that thought-processes went on in his brain guaranteed his reality as a person; the Descartes of Africa, should he arise, would amend the famous pronouncement to "I am, because I participate". Reciprocal participation first in a brother-bond and then in co-operative labour is the rock on which the growing African solidarity is being built.

Understanding well that the Europeans in their midst are there to make money, responsible Africans tend to concentrate on measures of self-protection with a view to using Europeans more cunningly than Europeans can use them. Current relations between the two races are best described as relations of mutual outwitting, not all of which goes on at a fully conscious level.

From the African side the top priority is to make sure that the Empire-builders, the mercenary mischief-makers, and the wildly costly pension-drawers are the first to go. This phase is now approaching completion. The old gang have been largely replaced by people on short contracts, who serve as consultants and bear little or no executive authority. They show a quick turnover and do not pile up pension rights, while if they turn out well, their contracts can be renewed for another short spell.

Moreover, African Governments have learnt to spread the load over a large number of European countries, at least twenty, and to avoid disproportionate reliance on any one. They have learnt to play off one country against another, especially when they are on different sides in the cold war. They have learnt to be highly discriminating in the selection of expatriate personnel, and they know now, as President Nyerere puts it, how to distinguish between "those who come because we offer very high salaries, and those who come because they basically sympathise with what we are trying to do".

A further lesson which African Governments have by now thoroughly conned is what jobs to keep expatriates out of. "We now know," to quote President Nyerere again, "what are the highly political tasks for which we must have local people in order to safeguard our own control of the nation." And finally a supreme effort is being made to set a term to the whole issue once and for all by speeding up the education and training of local citizens with a view to 100 per cent staffing by local citizens in both public and private sectors as soon as is humanly possible.

In all territories of the region there is general African consent that in the long run the only place for the European is as an equal and unprivileged citizen. The passing of the authority-bearing non-citizen European was essential if only because the race-pyramid could nowhere be unbuilt without it. Almost all Africans now alive will thank heaven that they are witnesses of it, and will see in it a prerequisite for the full human growth of their people. Meanwhile they are not inhuman. They do not gloat. They do not seek to hale individual Europeans to the stake as scapegoats for the sufferings that history has inflicted on their race. They know well that this passing has repercussions which are often truly tragic when looked at in terms of the individual experience and destiny of the displaced persons.

The African epitaph on the lost empire of the Europeans might be written thus. If on the whole record of their contact with Africa over the centuries the audited account shows a net credit balance, let Europeans be accorded their meed of praise. If the net balance is of blame, the harshness of the hour they now confront is reprimand enough. In either case the lamp of their dominion is snuffed out. The sneer of cold command, which too many of their faces were long used to wear and which was one root of their offence to Africans and Asians alike, has met its Nemesis and soon will be no more seen.

If the Europeans still on the ground are a necessary evil, they are also a temporary one. Few will take out local citizenship, few will stay indefinitely as foreigners. Their numbers will taper off. Only in Rhodesia are they likely to form a considerable permanent element in the population, and there the time is not yet ripe for settling their relationship with the other races.

The Asian population, on the other hand, everywhere constitutes an issue which is not a self-liquidating one. A good number of Asians have applied for citizenship already, undoubtedly more will do so when they come to think the future less obscure. One way or another the Asians are in Africa to stay. Their numbers are much greater than those of Europeans ever were. A permanent place in the non-racial society has to be found for them. From the standpoint of the African leadership, it is Asians rather than Europeans who present the long-term problem in race-relations.

Hemmed in, as they feel themselves to be, by the new African hegemony, Asians tend to suffer from an out-of-the-frying-pan-into-the-fire complex. They see that Europeans who used to be on top, are now in the wilderness so far as political power is concerned. They do not forget that they themselves used to form the middle layer in the race pyramid, and they suspect that now they may be gravitating towards the bottom. To them, independence has brought little sense of liberation, rather a foreboding that they may have exchanged a bad set of masters for a worse. Their fears seem very unspecific, except where jobs in the public service or the competition of African traders is in question. But they have an uncomfortable sense that they are to be handed out least-favoured-nation treatment all round. Their attitude towards the new Africa is a wary, even a suspicious, wait and see.

This attitude is understandable enough, but it is doing Asians untold harm. Equally understandably it strikes Africans as ungracious and unconstructive. Africans have for years borne the brunt of the political struggle, with little convincing support from Asians. They insist that they have a good deal to be ungrateful for. The implication is that Asians who did nothing to help them in their hour of need, when a measure of candid co-operation would have been invaluable, should not look for favours now.

All this leads to a bickering sort of deadlock in which the African pot calls the Asian kettle black, and gets answered back in the same strain. When Africans say "You must identify yourselves with the country, if you wish us to do anything for you," the Asian reply is "You must treat us fairly, if you wish us to identify." When Asians say "You don't really want us here. Why should we sweat to help you?" the African reply is "You didn't help us before when we needed your help. Why should you expect to be welcomed with open arms now?"

The consequence is serious loss to both sides. African Governments cannot enlist the Asian capital and manpower which they so much need, and development plans largely ignore the existence of either. Asians for their part send their liquid capital off to Geneva and London, cock a snook at the Government, and in effect taunt it with "Now induce us to fetch it back". The game may be amusing, but it places Asians in jeopardy. They would quickly find this out, if conditions of civil disturbance should recur where the cry goes up for a scapegoat. In the current phase of the new Africa, Asians are much the strongest candidates for the appointment; and if looting breaks out, the handiest shops for the purposes are always Asian shops. Both sides are aware of these possibilities and worried by them.

Asians themselves admit that they are not readily fired with creative dreams, and that the new Africa does not inspire them to creative effort. They like to be left alone with good opportunities for accumulating wealth in business and the professions. People committed to this kind of outlook, however, people so untouched by public hope, are not the people that African Governments are looking for, or indeed can usefully employ in their great schemes for regenerating half a continent. In their disappointment and frustration, official quarters are inclined to write Asians off as spiritless blacklegs and money-grubbers incapable of standing for any magnanimous cause—and to go on giving preference to Africans, even upon occasion to Europeans.

The position is, of course, absurd. In the whole distressing impasse two things at least are clear. One is that the Asians are a talented, industrious and adaptable people who have an unlimited contribution to make to any country which they wholeheartedly adopt as their home. The colonial system was calculated to stifle at birth any offering from them whatever. In the emerging new order means have not yet been found for providing a proper chance for them to make the best they can. Here is one of the big unsolved problems of East and Central Africa.

The second obvious point is that in an objective view the outlook for Asians who truly call Africa their home is rosier than it has ever been. The real threat to them would come from the failure of African development planning, not from its success. The helpful enterprise of Asians in achieving that success is the strongest safeguard of Asian interests at large.

Probably a third point is also valid. What would do more than anything else to release Asians from their present anxieties is a self-imposed psychological revolution, by which they cease to present themselves to themselves as a separate cultural bloc, a nation within a nation, and resolve to live as individual native citizens, Africans of Africa, whose flesh is made of African dust, to which at their death it will return. Then they might feel able to ask themselves, in a searching and positive spirit, what are the most vital gifts which they are fitted to dedicate to the motherland that needs their trust and yearns to cherish them.

For Asians it is hard doctrine. It is hard because it expresses the essence of non-racialism, the kernel of its difference from multi-racialism—which is also why in the last resort it must be accepted. For the non-racial society is what Asians are being incorporated into; they are inevitably becoming built-in components of it. By temperament they are natural multi-racialists. It is their misfortune that in Africa multi-racialism is dead.

Multi-racialism is the concept according to which distinct racial communities as it were federate into a single political society, living and working side by side (or, pyramidally, one on top of the other), but preserving each its own communal distinctness and its own cultural identity. Non-racialism is the concept according to which all citizens live and work together in an equal solidarity where distinctions are made solely in terms of personal qualities without regard to racial description. In all the territories of our region, Rhodesia apart, non-racialism is established as the basic principle on which the new order is to be constructed.

Sociologically speaking, there can be little doubt that non-racialism is the more mature and sophisticated concept, and the one which holds out better prospects for a smoothly integrated social system. But integration on a non-racial basis entails the disintegration of encapsulated racial groupings. This is rough on Asians, who are perhaps more attached than most people to their corporate manners and customs, and who owing to their minority situation will be called on for a more fundamental readjustment than the African majority. In particular, non-racialism implies the eventual abandonment by Asians of their geographical and occupational segregation. It will require that, no longer identifiable as residents of one quarter, and as nothing but traders, they should freely disperse and mix. Such a desegregation process, apart from its desirability on principles of non-racialism, is as it happens also their best insurance against the scapegoat risk.

However desirable, it cannot be easy. In addition, Asians have a number of other equally genuine reasons for feeling unsettled, apprehensive and aggrieved. They have been much shaken by events in the Congo and Zanzibar, the Sudan, and Nigeria. They have had a raw deal so far as the public service goes, both in being pushed out and in being passed over. Indian expatriate officers who had been recruited direct from India by East African Governments before independence were given early retirement terms that compared unfavourably with those given to European expatriates, and the United Kingdom made no contribution to their awards.

At the lower end of the manpower scale also Asians are being squeezed, partly for reasons connected with independence, partly for other reasons. In the palmy days of the race-pyramid it was virtually true to say that there were no poor Europeans and no rich Africans. But the Asian groups have always had their own rich and their own poor. They still have them. About half Kenya's 180,000 Asians in fact are poor or very poor.

The main assets of Asians who are at or near the poverty line are some primary schooling and some acquaintance with the English language. If they do not make as much of these as they might, the reason often is that their patrons and employers are richer Asians. They are, moreover, always in direct competition with the unskilled African mass. Again, it seems likely that the traditional Asian small trader is destined soon to disappear. His job is being killed in the towns by modern methods of retailing, including supermarkets (which are often Asian-owned). In town and country alike he is increasingly threatened also by African co-operatives and by individual African traders. To this extent he stands in the way of African determination to get an effective foothold in the private sector.

Such changes in the social structure and relationships they were used to amply account for some alarm and despondency in Asians who by tradition regard it as a virtue to scare easily and to sit on the fence till the iron enters into their soul. But the outlook for them is not all instability and want of promise. In an expanding economy (and whether the economy expands or not depends in no small part on Asian endeavour), Asians trained in business and the professions know well how to make new opportunities for themselves; and the middle ranks of the Asian community, the craftsmen of the construction and transport industries, together with the jobbing electricians, mechanics, plumbers and so on, look out on an assured future with rising prospects.

Outside the economic sphere, there is widespread agreement that in spite of all current difficulties independence has opened up a new era in race-relations. However unenthusiastic some Asians may feel about some recent developments, not one has a word of regret for the colonial order. Many allow that the phase of rectification in the public service was necessary. They express the belief that it is really approaching its end, and that henceforward African Governments will wish to use all man-power on a genuinely non-racial basis.

African and Asian schoolchildren, boys and girls alike, mix happily at work and play. The issue of educational integration is well on the way to being settled. Even the parents, many of whom are still blinkered by conventional taboos and by ideas more appropriate to a caste system than to contemporary Africa, are beginning to open their eyes to the need of adjusting themselves to the disposition of non-racialism. They begin to savour the public hope that is sweeping the continent, and to calculate how they might benefit by enlisting under its banner. They are aware how ironical it would be if they, who have complained so bitterly about enforced segregation in the past, were now to insist upon a self-inflicted segregation.

Many Asian businessmen agree that it is right for Africans to seek to enter the world of business. They acknowledge that they, as Asian fellow-citizens, have a duty to coach Africans in business methods and to be on tap to advise them on the running of their stores and co-operatives. Some Asian trade associations have drawn up formal schemes for promoting African participation in commerce. They see, of course, that they themselves will to a greater or less extent get crowded out of trading as Africans come in. But they also see that in gear with this process there will be a compensating movement of their own into the sphere of manufacturing industry, and possibly into large-scale agriculture as well.

At present both Asians and Africans are given to ostracising any member of their group who marries or looks like marrying into the other. But the determination to apply such sanctions already begins to seem dated. There may still be many closed minds on the issue, but the issue itself is very much open. Some Asian witnesses of advanced views actually put it that the future of Asians is to merge with Africans socially, politically, culturally and genetically. They hold this to follow of necessity from self-identification with the African homeland. In several places *avant garde* groups of Asians and Africans of the younger generation are springing up, who meet to discuss what is known to them as "total integration", i.e. social and cultural mergers of all kinds, including inter-marriage.

It should be said finally that those Asians who feel most of respect for Africans as such are the same who have committed themselves most fully to the new public hope and to the ideal of the non-racial society. They report their conviction that the most gifted Africans of their acquaintance are already disclosing, in their thinking and their feeling and their doing, a wisdom truly their own, and different from the Graeco-Roman, the Christian, and the oriental wisdom. Perhaps history has marked these Asians out as the channel by which a like conviction is eventually to filter into the minds of the Europeans.

Such, then, in the sphere of race relations, are the significant attitudes developing in what one might call the interior life of the new societies of Eastern and Central Africa. In point of constructive commonsense Africans evidently grade a good deal higher than Europeans do or ever did, and very much higher than Asians. If this interior life had a prospect of undisturbed evolution over the next two generations, the outlook for sane humanity in the race issue would be hopeful too. Unfortunately African interior life is not likely to be decisive here. There are more powerful outside factors which make for violence.

In the first place comes the offensive alliance between the South African Republic, the Portuguese, and Rhodesia. If, as seems possible, this alliance were to attempt to overthrow Zambia and to subject it to white supremacists, anti-white feeling throughout East Africa would at once become much more specific and much more intense. The already precarious balance would be upset by which some distinction is maintained between the whites of Southern Africa and those of the N.A.T.O. countries. The guerrilla war which black Africa is already beginning to wage against the triple alliance of the South would be speeded up and made more bitter, becoming perhaps the most potent of all means to a general unification of the new Africa.

In the second place, it is necessary to take into account both the swiftly growing revolt of the Third World against the N.A.T.O. countries, and also that other revolt (which is a part of the Third World's) of the American negro against his white overlords. Africa, at the moment of writing, does not yet feel itself intimately affected by either of these. But it soon will, for it is progressively getting drawn into both. Both are committed to violence.[1]

And the first at least involves the great Communist powers. U.S.S.R. has taken charge of the anti-N.A.T.O. front in the

[1] cf. "To shoot down a European is to kill two birds with one stone—to destroy an oppressor and the man he oppresses at the same time. There remain a dead man and a free man" (from the preface to *Les Damnés de la Terre* by Frantz Fanon).

Arab sector of the Third World, and China is developing a corresponding line of policy in tropical Africa. If the triple alliance of white supremacists were to embark on a reconquest of independent Africa, Chinese intervention would at once gather momentum.

In the third place, there is no doubt that race relations in Eastern Africa have been helped by African tribal animosities. The latter have served the perverse but in some ways useful turn of diverting violence towards false foes and away from the true ones. As Africans come to grasp the fact that their frustrations and disasters are rooted in the economic structure of the N.A.T.O. world, tribal dissensions will weaken and disappear. Then Africans will rationally direct their violence against the real authors of their distress. In doing this, and in proportion as the proper target is hit, African society will re-create itself in an extending unity.

But this unity will leave little room for liberal relationships between black men and white, whether in Eastern Africa or anywhere else. The white man's violence against the men of colour has gone too far and too deep for that. No gentleness can efface the marks of that violence, which has now been going on without intermission for five hundred years. Thanks to the white man, we all live in a world where it is too late for gentleness. The nigger's place is in the white man's keeping no more. The revolt of the Third World is a war that gives no quarter.

CHAPTER 12

DEBALKANISATION

THE STORY OF the break-up is a long and tangled one—the break-up first of A.O.F., then of the French Union, finally of de Gaulle's Franco-African Community. This is no place to retrace it. It is known that the end-result was to leave francophone West Africa a shambles of ten battered fragments of meaningless "independence", whose only hope of viability lay in a rapid re-union.

The question is Why has no re-union even begun, let alone come to completion? Every politician, every civil servant, every businessman between Cotonou and Nouakchott knows that all talk of development and modernisation is so much trumpery, unless politico-economic units are created on a scale capable of furnishing the motive power for development. Yet the trumpery talk goes on, and the prospect of neighbourly inter-state association fades to invisibility.

Julius Nyerere, President of Tanzania and an unusually candid man, when asked why the project for an East African Federation came to grief, replied: "It was our fault, the fault of the leaders. We are the guilty men—in the East as in every other part of Africa. It was we who refused to carry our people towards unity. The masses are too rational to turn away from unity on their own. The leaders merely mutter 'What would happen to me? Who would come out on top?' The masses don't ask that sort of question. But leaders in office simply will not run any risk of losing it."

This is eminently fair comment from the inside. It emphasises in a valid and valuable way that African separatism is primarily an expression of class-interest in African society as at present structured. And this is just as true of West Africa as of East. But in West Africa there are external causes of separatism as well as internal ones.

From the moment in 1960 when a gathering cry for independence made a dead letter of the Franco-African Community as President de Gaulle had envisaged it, the policy of the French Government has been to ensure that territories which declined the dish of community ungarnished with independence should be obliged to make a dish of independence without the sauce of community. This policy has been and still is strictly carried out through four main instruments:

(1) the French military presence in Senegal, Ivory Coast, Chad, and Madagascar,
(2) the monetary and financial bearing-rein of the franc zone,
(3) the commercial domination of the big French trading companies,
(4) a reliable political mouthpiece (necessarily African) on the spot.

The fourth requirement was met in the person of M. Félix Houphouët-Boigny of Abidjan. In 1960 he was both a minister in de Gaulle's Government and President of the Ivory Coast Republic. He it was who then assumed leadership of the drive to balkanisation, on the declared grounds (a) that it would be foolish to pay federal taxes levied from Dakar, and (b) that, using his hot line to de Gaulle, he could get more lavish aid out of France on his own than he could hope for from a mere slice of a collective cake shared with the rest of French West Africa.

President Senghor of Senegal was soon persuaded that here was an example to follow, and with his defection Sékou Touré's struggle to create a West African Federation collapsed. For the complex of French interests it was an occasion for rejoicing— especially the French commercial interest. Just as Houphouët-Boigny thought he could milk France best alone, so the big French firms thought they could milk many weak states more satisfactorily than one strong one.

Houphouët-Boigny's victory, as French go-between, over the federalists was a major disaster for all West Africa, a chief source of the sub-region's present troubles. And even at that cost it failed to confer any lasting benefit on the smooth operators of the Ivory Coast themselves.

He took six locust-eaten years to wake up to the blunder he had committed. In a New Year message for 1966 we can over-hear him forecasting that only countries wise enough to unite into larger regional communities would survive in the future. His puppets, the Entente States,[1] thereupon decided to trade in their second-hand Conseil de l'Entente for a regular con-federation, and to institute common nationality between them all. In the economic field they further agreed to make a reality of their nominal customs union, to harmonise their agricultural and industrial policies, and to examine their separate develop-ment programmes periodically with a view to avoiding rivalry over projects.

But by 1966 such wisdom was too late. Houphouët-Boigny's original mischief had worked more completely than he realised. The entire plan of closer association—political confederation, common nationality, co-ordinated economic development—made immediate shipwreck on the opposition of the white-collar workers of Abidjan (most of them in the public service), who feared that their jobs would be threatened by an inflowing brain-drain from adjacent territories. The reaction was precisely the same as that which Houphouët-Boigny had himself en-couraged in 1958, when riots in Abidjan resulted in the mass expulsion of Togolese and Dahomean personnel. In the inter-vening eight years the people of Ivory Coast, under their charismatic leader and in the sunshine of his economic miracles, had advanced not an inch towards African fraternity.

The whole atmosphere now was thick with vested interests in separatism. The French Government and French big busi-ness, specialists in keeping people out of economic communities, had *their* vested interest in continuing balkanisation. The vested

[1] Upper Volta, Niger, Togo, Dahomey (besides, of course, Ivory Coast itself).

interest of trade unions and the labour market in separatism
was as strong as ever. The subversive inner virus of tribal
separatism was spreading. Ethnic groups proved quick learners
of the lesson the nationettes had taught them, and prompt to
practise a balkanisation of their own.[1]

In West Africa this last factor has worked even more calami-
tously than separatism at the state level. And, though active in
francophone countries, it is far from confined to them. Ghana
is threatened with disintegration because of it.[2] The great
combine which could have been Nigeria has because of it
(and ironically enough in the name of unity) been reduced to a
mere heap of mutually destructive murder-gangs.

For those who do not really mean business the simplest way
of appearing to launch some kind of counter-attack on separatism is to leave political issues on one side and set up a customs
union. In our area several such attempts have been made, with
complete lack of success.

As early as 11 June 1959 Ivory Coast, Dahomey, Upper
Volta, Niger, Mali, and Mauritania entered into a full free
trade agreement, and formed the Union Douanière Ouest-
Africaine (U.D.O.A.). Except as between Senegal and Mauritania, the convention never came properly into force, and
therefore has never had any positive influence on inter-state
commercial relations. Its paper provisions, so far from trans-
lating themselves into practical effect, have been continuously
torn to pieces by *des entorses, dérogations, et infractions*. In a word,
the high contracting parties honour their engagements only
when it suits them. On 14 March 1966 U.D.O.A. turned into
the *Union Douanière des Etats de l'Afrique de l'Ouest* (U.D.E.A.O.).

---

[1] For nationettes who are too "nationalistic" to join up with their neighbours to reproach tribes with being "tribalistic" is simply a case of the pot
calling the kettle black.

[2] Brigadier Afrifa of Ghana's ruling National Liberation Council said
in a speech to the Journalists' Association in Accra in October 1967, "Our
society is tending towards disintegration, and the unity of Ghana is facing
its greatest challenge. The reason for this, as I see it, is that we are becoming
too tribalistic in our outlook."

Apart from this pregnant transformation, neither body has shown any sign of life.

A similar effort was put up later by the so-called West African Free Trade Area (W.A.F.T.A.)—which did not even get as far as being honoured in the breach. The countries agreeing (in 1964) to participate this time were Ivory Coast, Liberia, Sierra Leone, and Guinea, an interesting combination because francophone and anglophone states were equally represented in it. In 1965 a secretariat was established under the title of the West African Interim Organisation for Economic Co-operation. It had offices in Monrovia and a Sierra Leonean as Administrative Secretary. The function of the Organisation was defined as "promoting and elaborating a common policy of economic and social development" among the member states.

It soon appeared that in setting up the Interim Organisation the member states had exhausted the last drop of their co-operative potential. The Administrative Secretary spent two years striving with increasing desperation to convene even one meeting, either at ministerial or at some other level. At the end of that period he found himself no longer able to face the great and honourable challenge of serving the cause of African progress and unity. He resigned and the Organisation died, its Last Post echoing in his dry comment, "If four countries cannot agree even to meet, it is for decision at a level above mine whether, how, and between how many countries co-operation may be possible." Rarely do civil servants rebuke so plainly the frivolous irresponsibility of their political bosses.

Both U.D.O.A. and W.A.F.T.A. looked at the start like promising initiatives in an anti-fragmentation sense. Both were sabotaged before they got off the ground. Only one country was a member of both—the Ivory Coast. Some observers treat this as evidence that its leaders are not enthusiastic about putting humpty-dumpty together again, whatever verbal protestations they may make.

There is a second, and more ambitious, type of association between neighbouring states. This type bases itself on some striking geographical and ecological feature, shared by several countries and therefore capable of drawing them together in activities of mutual concern. Examples are the Committee on Trans-Saharan Transport and the Chad Basin Commission.

The Senegal river stands in such a relationship to the four riverain states of Mauritania, Senegal, Mali, and Guinea. A scheme is under discussion for using the river as a focal interest on which these countries might converge to form a regional grouping. It springs from a meeting of the Heads of State held in Nouakchott in November 1965, when an Inter-State Committee for harnessing the waters of the Senegal River Basin was asked to formulate a common programme of economic integration.

Between June and September 1966 the Committee carried out a series of surveys in the four countries, and in mid-1967 produced a prodigious report for consideration at a further meeting of the Heads of State arranged for November of that year.

In appraising the general economic condition of the region the Report notes (a) that there is an over-all deficiency of food-crops and that it tends to increase; (b) that agricultural production is not enough to promote industrial growth, or even to supply existing industries, except for cotton in Mali and groundnuts in Senegal; (c) the problems of the diversification of crops and the integration of stockraising with agriculture are still without any genuine solution; (d) there is no real lessening of the fragility of the economies in the face of trading and climatic hazards—a judgment that applies equally to food-crops and industrial crops.

It follows that a workable development policy is bound to base itself on an increase in agricultural productivity, partly because development requires internal financing which an agricultural surplus alone can provide, and partly because without such a surplus there can be no balanced rise in living standards.

In the years since independence all four countries have made a sustained endeavour to achieve a general rise in agricultural productivity. But they have each been working in isolation, and they have failed. It is time to try what sensible co-operation can do.

The joint improvement of the river basin would have three broad objectives, and they would be approached concurrently: first, the irrigation of the valley; second, the navigability of the stream; third, the generation of hydro-electric power.

The key-piece in the whole scheme is, in the Report's View, the building of a barrage at Gouina (in Mali), which would provide 1½–2 milliards Kwh per year. This barrage has been much talked of for a number of years, especially in the context of the establishment and siting of an iron and steel industry in West Africa. The Report recommends setting up an inter-state iron and steel complex in association with the Gouina barrage, as an *industrie industrialisante*, whose effects would make themselves felt throughout the economy of the region. A complex of this kind probably constitutes, so the Report urges, the one real chance of accelerated industrialisation open to the four states.

Stress is laid on the co-operative character of the entire enterprise. The *mise en valeur* of the Senegal Basin is not to be thought of as an operation concerning the river as a mere geographical entity; rather it is a prime engine of economic development of the whole 4-state region. From this standpoint the operation itself is less important than the maximisation of its effects.

The joint build-up of the Senegal Basin is not to cut its participants off from other adjacent states through whose territories the river happens not to run. Hostile economic fences are not to be erected at the perimeter. On the contrary, the perimeter is to be designed as a *frontière-filtre* which admits and organises constructive influences from without, and excludes only those that would hinder growth.

Evidently the authors of the Report are men of enlightenment and goodwill. And it would seem, on the surface anyway, that they and the Heads of State for whom they work have chosen a favourable time for preparing a new kind of draft instrument of inter-state co-operation.

President Senghor has emphasised that a joint river-basin development project is a central plank in his foreign policy. In

Mali the leaders insist that they are only too well aware of their need to form some sort of united economic front with their neighbours. The grouping they are working for consists precisely of these four states, and would do so even if the Senegal river did not exist. However, focus on the river basin, with a hydro-electric scheme at Gouina plus associated steel works, suits them well. They also reckon that inside a common market of 13 million people, which would also be an area of co-ordinated planning, the Mali economy might have a hope of viability.

Accordingly, the United Nations Development Programme is undertaking, at the request of the Inter-State Committee, five special studies to estimate how feasible and how costly the several components of the scheme as at present envisaged would be likely to prove in practice.

Beyond the customs unions, beyond the ecology-based projects, a plan is being worked out for an economic community comprising all the fourteen states of the West Africa sub-region. This plan falls within the framework of the Economic Commission for Africa's policy to promote sub-regional co-operation in all the four quarters of the continent—central, east, and north, as well as west.

E.C.A. has been pressing the policy with vigour and understanding for several years. It has succeeded to this extent. There is now a broad consensus throughout the new Africa that the realistic approach to African defragmentation is through regional groupings. One must not forget, however, the riddling character of such formulations. The so-called consensus does not imply that any African country has any intention of taking any practical part in any concrete enterprise of joint regional development. Its principal implication is merely that most African countries are opposed to the continental approach to development problems.

Still, the E.C.A. success does not stop here. At a meeting in Accra in May 1967, thirteen countries from Mauritania to Nigeria (Guinea alone holding aloof) signed Articles of Association for a West African Common Market, and agreed on transitional arrangements governing the means of co-operation between the member states, pending the formal constitution of their Economic Community. The W.A.E.C., when it comes, is to have a Council of Ministers, an Economic Committee, and a Secretariat.

It is agreed, further, that in principle the aims of the proposed organisation should be progressively to eliminate all barriers to the free movement of people, goods, and money anywhere within the sub-region. There should be continuous consultation on economic matters, and joint participation in as many projects as possible. There should be joint research and training. The last preliminary, the drafting of a Treaty binding on its signatories, is actually being undertaken by an Interim Council of Ministers.

Thus on paper the whole business looks to be pretty well tied up. The efforts of E.C.A. have drawn a well-considered blue-print and put up a firm scaffolding which indicates very clearly how a reality could be made of inter-state co-operation, if member states wished. E.C.A. cannot do more than this. It is in no position to influence the motives of West African Governments; and these alone have executive authority. The record of office-holders and business leaders in West African countries since 1960 overwhelmingly suggests that they would feel no interest in coming together in an Economic Community, except to the extent that it might create new high-salary jobs and enlarge opportunities for malversation, without curtailing the old ones.

When in 1960 the Mali Federation was torpedoed, the common services which had operated within A.O.F.—harbours, roads, airports, railways, posts and telegraphs, customs, taxes, investment, health, veterinary, control of plant diseases, etc.— all were systematically pulled to pieces, in the name of those very *volontés nationales de développement différentes* which for seven long years have made development impossible. If the idea was to prove that the members of what had once been A.O.F. could still combine to destroy, if not to build, the proof was elegantly conclusive.

There is no sign that the wounds inflicted by this disastrous triumph have begun to heal, or that the motives which brought it off have undergone any wholesome change. Apart from reducing the efficiency and increasing the cost of the fractured services, the main consequence has been to place the fractured economies more completely under a better-camouflaged domination by the great French corporations.

If the purview is to include the anglophone countries of West Africa,[1] as it does and must, the question at once arises how restrictions on the movement of money and goods can possibly be abolished, as stipulated in the Articles of Association, so long as the several currencies of member states are firmly tied to the currency of one or other of three non-African powers,[2] whose African interests are in more or less vehement conflict.

It is hardly practicable any longer to evade the challenge thrown out by the O.A.U. Summit Conference of 1963, when it called for a move towards setting up a Pan-African monetary zone. One understands, of course, why E.C.A. should shrink from grasping such a nettle. But not to grasp it may jeopardise the hope of any Economic Community that could really work. Yet again what reason is there for thinking that member states will prove more co-operative on the currency issue than on any other? Perhaps it is a mistake to ask which should come first— common currency or common market? For if either comes at all, surely both will have to come together.

Ironically, as if these troubles were not enough, they are crowned by the European Economic Community; which of itself, and because most francophone states of West Africa are associate members of it, vetoes any thorough economic community in the West African sub-region, as effectively (and as it were in the same motion) as President de Gaulle vetoes any thorough community in Europe.

It could hardly be more plain that the kind of schemes we have been looking at—U.D.E.A.O., W.A.F.T.A., the Senegal

[1] They comprise two-thirds of the population of the entire sub-region.
[2] i.e., dollar, sterling, or franc.

6

River Basin scheme, the West African Economic Community—
are made of nothing more substantial than paper and words.
Realistic and appropriate in the sense that they correspond with
the people's needs, they are wholly unrealistic in the sense that
the people's needs have no correspondence with the rulers' wants.

Nevertheless such schemes perform one useful function. They
expose the emptiness of "dialogue" between nationettes in
whom the emotional grounds for staying apart are more powerful than the rational arguments for coming together. They
prove once for all that economic community, in West African
conditions, is not to be achieved by double-faced Laodiceans
over cigars and drinks in conference-room bars. It will be
achieved in the arena by devoted champions of the cause, after
hard struggle and stark sacrifice.

Where, in that segment of West Africa which stretches from
Ivory Coast to Mauritania, are such champions to be found?
The answer is easy. They are to be found in Guinea (Bissau),[1]
in Guinea (Conakry), in Mali, and in the Sierra Leone of Siaka
Stevens. If there are others elsewhere, they are likely to be
exiles or prisoners.

It happens that these four territories adjoin one another.
Geography does not oppose their closer economic and political
association; rather it invites it. It may be that this area will
become the bridgehead of a real movement of West African
reunification.

If such a movement comes into being, one may surmise that
it will be confined at the start to the two Guineas. It could be a
congenial partnership. To some extent it already exists, for
Guinea (Conakry) has ever since 1962 been giving valuable
help to the freedom fighters led by Amilcar Cabral in Guinea
(Bissau). Both are countries whose politico-military strategy is
shaped by exceptional clarity of purpose. Both are commanded
with great determination by Parties resolved to build an entirely
new structure of social life.

---

[1] Portuguese Guinea, as it is still sometimes called, is about twice the size
of Wales and has a population of some 600,000. The combined population
of both Guineas is some 4½ million.

In both, the urban areas are secondary features. In Guinea (Bissau) indeed the Portuguese now hold no more than the principal towns and their rural outskirts, plus some forty beleaguered garrisons in the countryside which have to be supplied from the air. Rather more than half the villages and rural areas are held by P.A.I.G.C. (the African Independence Party for Guinea and the Cape Verdes), which is gradually taking over the rest. In both the Guineas the villages are the country's basic economic units which have been adopted as the basic administrative and political units also. Both therefore foreshadow a development broadly following the lines of the Chinese commune.[1] Both see themselves as organic parts in the revolutionary advance of the Third World, and for them African unity is vital not merely for the modernisation of that continent, but also for the global rebellion of the *plebs pauperum* everywhere.

That the Portuguese, after five years fighting, have lost the war in Guinea (Bissau) appears to be no longer open to question. It is the P.A.I.G.C. and not the Portuguese who are in a position to say when the eventual take-over will come. When it does, the repercussions will be far-reaching throughout the new Africa.

Most immediately it will put new heart into Mali. Mali is going through a frustrating period. Its struggle towards socialist development is at the moment threatened by the pythonic embrace of the C.F.A. franc and the gnomes of Paris who, spurred on by the spirit of Vichy and the O.A.S., manipulate it. Its ideological sympathies with Guinea (Conakry) are real. Both countries are fighting a rather desperate long-term holding action to keep open what they like to call their socialist "option". What Mali is willing to do in the interests of the Senegal River Basin, it might be readier still to perform if socialist solidarity as well were the prize.

And Senegal? Senegal, like Guinea (Conakry) though on a smaller scale, is already giving some rear support to the P.A.I.G.C. forces in Guinea (Bissau). It also claims to have

[1] See Appendix D.

made a socialist option of its own—*la voie d'un socialisme sans illusions et collé aux valeurs profondes de notre peuple africain.* Furthermore, it is in urgent need of a social solidarity of its own. Throughout 1967 there was increasing uneasiness in the ruling party (U.P.S.). Several incidents of political violence took place, the most serious of which was an attempt on the life of President Senghor, and of which the most frequent occurred in the Casamance region next door to Guinea (Bissau).

There is also the banned but by no means inactive Marxist party, and beyond that the continuing and well organised support for the ex-Prime Minister, Mamadou Dia, who was jailed for life in 1963 after an unsuccessful struggle with Senghor for political supremacy. A further element of uncertainty, not to say confusion, is added by the unremitting clan feuds of the present run of Senegalese politicians. In these circumstances, the Government has proclaimed a national reconciliation policy. Talks with Mamadou Dia's supporters have begun (November 1967), and it is said in Dakar that Senghor himself offered his prisoner an amnesty, but that Dia's conditions were too tough.

Hence it seems at least a possibility that Senghor may perceive a way out of his mounting difficulties, first by coming to terms with the Dia organisation, and second by adding a genuine socialist dimension to the comprehensive scheme for developing the Senegal River Basin. This would bring his country much closer to the two Guineas and to Mali than it has ever been, and it would impart to the mutual relations of the four countries a drive and a common direction such as they have never known.

If some such working alliance were formed, the Gambia could not stay out, and Mauritania would hardly wish to. We should thus be back at the Senegal River Basin group, but with Guinea (Bissau) added, and with the whole coalition radically reoriented towards revolutionary socialism of a distinctively African kind. This is precisely the mixture that West Africa needs to prod it out of its lethargy and stagnation.

It would not be difficult, and it would be advantageous both to the coalition and to Sierra Leone itself, to draw in that country too. The new forces in Sierra Leone which would know how to turn the rapprochement to the profit at once of their nation and of African unity, are for the moment in eclipse, by order of the military régime. But they are still led by the All Peoples Congress which, as evidence before the Dove-Edwin Commission has now proved, decisively won the elections of March 1967. Since then they have been far from losing adherents either to the rival party (also suspended) or to the soldiers-cum-police. It cannot be long before they come into their own.

It is not a very venturesome forecast that the next 5–10 years may witness the emergence of a West African axis Freetown–Conakry–Bissau–Bathurst–Dakar–Nouakchott–Bamako. Such a grouping would be a notable stroke against the separatist tendency which has so far ruined all hopes for the new Africa, it would represent a first clear triumph of African socialism, and it embodies a coalition which could readily be slotted in to any wider economic community that might come into existence.

It would not, however, find itself automatically freed from the troubles that arise from different currencies. To alleviate these, with a view to maintaining old trade inflows, developing new ones, and generally encouraging intra-coalition exchanges of personnel, goods, and money, would remain a vital issue for all member states. On the other hand, the affinity of their world-outlook and ideology, as well as the structural resemblances of their incipient social growth, would take them half-way to a solution. It would, for example, make it easy for them to take a leaf out of President Nyerere's book by carrying out a joint nationalisation of foreign commercial banks.

These banks, unhealthily dominant in West Africa at present, have their headquarters in North Atlantic currency centres whose lack of interest in inter-African trade leads to shortage of credit, obstructs the opening up of new trade circuits, and makes for difficulty in effecting financial settlements.

Decisive in this whole question is the principle of where

there's a will there's a way. It is certainly not beyond the wit of a coalition such as that foreshadowed to find some convertible currency of account through which to channel members' payment balances. And one can assume that the coalition may give proof of a will here that the mere scattered remains of A.O.F. are unable to summon up. It might be helpful to make a preliminary study of the banking institutions and practice of some Eastern European country, such as Jugoslavia, which has had to deal with difficulties in this field not unlike those of West Africa.

The alternative at least is plain. A coalition of small West African countries, out to manage its affairs on the basis of a genuine African socialism, has no hope of success as long as it is strapped to an international capitalist economy abroad, and struggling to earn a living by trading competitively across the world. That way lies only new failure, deeper humiliation.

CHAPTER 13

EXPANSION WITHOUT GROWTH:
IVORY COAST

THIS CHAPTER AND the next present samples of case-material concerning the problems of modernisation in the new Africa. In considering them we need first an operational definition of the term modernisation; and second an account of how a country's aptitude for modernisation or success in it, can be measured.

Here the term modernisation is taken to mean the application of science and technology to politico-economic and to social arrangements, with a view to increasing productivity of material and mental goods.

The degree and the pace of modernisation are measured in terms of two criteria, (a) economic expansion, (b) social growth.

Expansion is an economic phenomenon expressed by a rise in real income per head. Growth is a cultural phenomenon expressed by changes in social organisation which tend to diffuse real income evenly, and thereby to improve technical performance, among all sections of the population.

It follows that modernisation is possible only when expansion and growth occur together.

Failure to modernise, or unfitness for modernisation, on the other hand, are consequences of any one of three distinct sets of conditions, (a) expansion without growth, (b) growth without expansion, (c) neither expansion nor growth.

Here Ivory Coast is taken as an example of (a) ; in Chapter 14 Guinea is taken as an example of (b). Most other countries of the new Africa fall into category (c).

"The Ivory Coast is a peculiar market, with a population of

four and a half millions, of which only five hundred thousand
are spending consumers, and only thirty thousand are substantial ones. It is in many ways a very restricted market."[1]

The Ivory Coast is another economic miracle, like Liberia
and West Germany. Here are some indicators from the first six
years of independence 1960–65.

(1) *Gross Domestic Product (at factor cost) in milliard francs C.F.A.*

	1960	1961	1962	1963	1964	1965
Primary Sector (farming, fishing, lumbering)	70	69	70	81	92	89
Secondary Sector (manufactures, construction)	17	20	22	24	29	34
Tertiary Sector (transport, commerce, administrative services)	34	44	44	49	62	63
TOTAL	121	133	136	154	183	186

The secondary and tertiary sectors have increased, the
primary sector has declined, in relative importance for the
economy as a whole.

(2) *Investment.* For the six-year period investment totalled 190
milliard C.F.A. It rose from 20 milliard in 1960 to 44 milliard
in 1965. In 1965 42·5 per cent came from the State, 57·5 from
private enterprise.

(3) *Income per head.* At constant prices this rose by an average
of 4·8 per cent a year, in spite of a population growth of more
than 2 per cent a year.

(4) *Standard of living.* Consumption of goods and services rose
by 54 per cent between 1960 and 1965. Thus, though prices

[1] Remarks made in Lagos, during a West African tour in February 1968,
by the Chairman of the African Section, Birmingham Chamber of Commerce.

rose by 15 per cent and population by 14 per cent, the net rise in living standards remained substantial.

(5) *Balance of trade*. In each of the six years the trade balance was favourable. Between 1960 and 1965 imports rose from 36·5 milliard C.F.A. to 65·7, exports rose from 45·3 to 75·4 milliard.

Evidently we meet here an economy more diversified and more efficient than is normal in African countries. The picture that builds up in the mind as one studies *l'ensemble des travaux de Comptabilité Nationale* is impressive. If, however, the study is followed by a visit to the Ivory Coast, the observer quickly realises that the picture, which he had taken for one of African prosperity, is really just one of French prosperity in Africa—a rather different matter.

The point is made by Samir Amin in the following form. The boom conditions which the national accounts describe have been brought about by the employment, at very high rates, of foreign capital. Expansion has been purely dependent on outside factors whose dominance over the whole of the country's economy is exercised in the most absolute way. The boom has left the great mass of Ivoirians untouched. Non-Africans (almost entirely French) occupy the key posts. They alone are responsible for economic and financial policy, business management, and technical training. Amin notes that in 1965 private funds transferred abroad amounted to 25 milliard C.F.A., or more than twice the total of foreign aid and private capital which came into the country in the same year. The drain (Ivoirian aid to France) gathers momentum.[1]

Amin's view is corroborated when we take a look at the composition of the active population, which is said to consist of about 2,340,000 persons (52 per cent of the total population of $4\frac{1}{2}$ million).

First come the Europeans, some 35,000 of them, of whom 90 per cent are French. Their numbers, in contrast with the position in almost all other new African States, have increased threefold since independence—evidence that the Ivory Coast

[1] Samir Amin: *Le Développement du Capitalisme en Côte d'Ivoire* (Editions de Minuit, Paris, 1967).
6*

is pre-eminently a place to which Frenchmen come to get rich.

These 35,000 persons comprise the holders (plus their dependants) of some 10,000 jobs. The job-holders in turn comprise the whole leadership in the spheres of banking, industry, and commerce, and include numbers of high-grade technicians as well. Where their treasure is, there do their hearts lie also, and they have accordingly become fierce promoters of their adopted country.

Many of them, being closely concerned with agricultural production (rubber, palm oil, pineapples, bananas, coffee, cocoa, timber) and engaged in the related processing industries, are increasingly becoming their own best customers. They are, in fact, foreign buyers of primary produce who make some contribution both to production and to on-the-spot processing. This helps to make the drive for export sales effective. If the firm which produces or at least collects the coffee, or cocoa, or palm oil, is at the same time a European sales agent, the problem of finding outlets is eased. Such a firm becomes, as it were, its own Produce Marketing Board. Moreover, in seeking investors the Ivory Coast will always see a special point in dealing with firms which already specialise in trading in local natural resources.

This explains why so large a part of local industry is held by French trading companies, which often expand vertically as well as horizontally. A typical case is the firm of Blohorn. It originally came to the Ivory Coast before the war to establish a soap factory, drawing much of its raw materials from local sources, as a hedge against competition and falling sales. It soon found itself setting up its own oil processing plants, and later its own oil-palm plantations.

At the inter-governmental level the same principle takes shape as a commercial agreement, in which the trading partners tend to achieve a natural balance not only in respect of the merchandise involved but also in respect of their currencies. The position of French commercial interests, thus entrenched in most types of local business enterprise, ensures that France is far and away the Ivory Coast's best customer as well as largest supplier.

Next the Africans. In 1966 the labour market was said to comprise some quarter of a million African jobs, in three main categories:

public and administrative services	32,000
private sector (urban)	95,000
private sector (rural)	125,000
	252,000

It is a feature of the French system of control in the Ivory Coast that, without a murmur, it hands over to educated Africans the whole province of politics and administration. Other ex-colonial powers have made this transfer only as a relinquishment of control, not as a means to it. To be sure, there is an unpublicised admixture of French advisers in the Ministries, but little systematic attempt to use them for steering Government policy in conformity with French views. The indirect leverage provided by occupation of the commanding heights of the economy is, in the French judgment, enough. The more so, as in order to staff the civil service with Africans throughout, the country has had to mobilise practically all indigenous men of education. Consequently there are few left over for political agitation against the régime.

The policy of Mr. Ian Smith in Rhodesia and of President Tubman in Liberia which flatly excludes Africans from politics and government seems uncouth by comparison. The fact seems to be that, provided they may not tinker with the economy, it makes little practical difference whether Africans are politically in or out. But if they are in, they gain an illusion of authority which they find psychologically tranquillising. French big business has since 1960 played on the African politicians of the Ivory Coast much the same trick that the House of Commons has played historically on the British Crown. It has accorded notable accessions of dignity and pageantry and wealth as compensation for forgoing the reality of power.

The arrangement by which the National Assembly and the civil service between them soak up, like a sponge, all the trained African minds in the country has some odd side-effects. To begin with, the key-sectors not merely of industry and technology, but even of education have to be run by non-Africans. Although employers unanimously desire[1] to replace European supervisory personnel by Africans, they cannot do so because the Government offices monopolise the people with any relevant qualifications.

The quarter-million or so of African wage and salary earners can be broken down in another way:

Persons in posts of authority	12,000
Persons of subordinate rank in office or factory	45,000
Skilled workmen	35,000
Unskilled labourers	160,000
	252,000

If we wish to complete the tally of people who earn money incomes, we must add a further 40,000 or so, representing the self-employed group, who engage in the main in road transport, trade, and crafts.

Thus we have accounted for approximately 300,000 out of the active population of 2,340,000. The balance of 2 million odd, 85 per cent of the whole, are the peasant mass. The peasants are all subsistence farmers in the sense that they grow their own food. They are also to a large extent outside the money economy, in the sense that their cash sales and purchases represent a minute fraction of the country's total

[1] This springs less from a wish to train Africans to manage the country's affairs than from anxiety about the size of their own wage-bill. The total cost of a European supervisor averages about £500 a month including salary, housing, social charges, and repatriation. Africans, if available, could be had for a good deal less than this.

commercial transactions. True, coffee and cocoa and bananas are traditionally peasant crops, but the scale of the cash earnings they bring in is not significant. In 1964, for instance, the peasants shared 29 million C.F.A. (on average a few shillings per family) out of the 46 *milliard* which the Ivory Coast received for its coffee and cocoa exports.

This peasant mass is the sleeping (and forgotten) Titan, in the hollow of whose horny hand the future of the Ivory Coast lies. He, together with his counterparts in the rest of tropical Africa, is incomparably the greatest potential force in the continent.

If French big business and their subalterns, the African politicians, can devise a new way of life for him which will arouse him from his slumbers, harmonise with his instincts, and furnish the satisfaction of his needs, their system will survive, and they will survive with it. Social growth will march forward in step with social cohesion. Mischief-makers will not subvert its order from within, so long as the Titan, alert and well pleased, says No to mischief. External enemies will fail to overthrow it, because of its internal strength.

But if, on the contrary, the giant is left to lie in torpor and disregard; or if, being roused, he finds that the dwarfs who are his keepers seek to burden him with irksome or meaningless compulsions for the sake of their own supposed gain; why, then, they will be swept aside and the Ivory Coast will revert to the status of a Land of Fragments, until leaders with more sense and insight get thrown up.

In fact, agrarian policy has hitherto been directed only lethargically towards modernising the methods and the productivity of the subsistence farmer. Respectable efforts have indeed been made to improve rural housing, to diversify agricultural production, and to link new processing industries with the new crops. But the principal beneficiaries here have been not the self-employed peasant, but the European plantation-owner and the wage-earning African labour-force that he employs. Even so, the results have not been particularly striking as far as output is concerned. Agricultural production rose by 21 per cent from 1960–65, which is less than 3·5 per cent a year, and not much quicker than the population growth. It being clear that the plantations were responsible for most, if not all, of the rise, one has to conclude that the peasantry has, on average, been stagnating or slipping back.

The Agricultural Plan, whose present time-horizon is 1975, pays special attention to eight main goals in diversification, (1) oil-palms, (2) rubber, (3) cocoa, (4) pineapples, (5) timber, (6) cotton, (7) rice, (8) sugar.

Five of these (oil-palms, rubber, pineapples, timber, sugar) are grown, harvested, processed, and marketed without need of any peasant participation at all. Bulk-production is undertaken on large or medium plantations run by European concessionaires and worked by paid African labourers.

The case is different with cocoa, cotton, rice; and also, one may add, with two other traditional and still important crops, coffee and bananas. By long custom these five are all peasant crops, and their cultivation is still carried out largely by Africans on a family basis without hired labour. Before independence, for instance, there were no European-owned cocoa plantations, and 97 per cent of the coffee output came from African family smallholdings. The typical holding was of 1–3 hectares, and these little individual properties are still to be seen encircling the villages or strung out along the roads in parts of the country where conditions of soil and climate suit the given crop.

Changes take place periodically, of course, in the balance of planned targets for agriculture. The Government has recently called for increased output of cocoa. On the other hand, official policy discourages the expansion of coffee-growing; here reduction of the planted area is to be offset by rises in yield per acre, and by conversion to oil-palm, coconut-palm, or rubber, of land released from coffee. Decisions such as these are taken with an eye to comparative export prospects rather than to peasant development.

But on the whole there is no permanent or sharply defined

line between crops to be grown by expatriate planters and crops to be grown by African peasants. The frontier between the two methods of cultivation is continuously fluctuating, and both contribute, though unequally, to the output of most crops. French private enterprise in agriculture has much increased since independence, mainly by way of expansion of previously established non-agricultural businesses. On the other hand, there has not been and there is not now anything to stop the Ivory Coast peasant from growing oil-palms, rubber, sugar, pineapples, or anything else, in addition to or in place of the crops with which he is familiar. How far he takes advantage of this permissive situation depends on his own assessment of his own interest.

In the south of the country particularly, there is often a sprinkling of African outgrowers (as they would be called in places like Uganda) of predominantly European crops. In such cases the peasant outgrower is free to dispose of his produce through the same marketing channels, and grade for grade on the same terms, as are open to the European producer of the same crop. Moreover, in making this usually rather minimal contribution he can, if he wishes, get technical help from a variety of French service companies who operate as agents of the Ministry of Agriculture. Such companies, for instance, will for a consideration undertake certain more difficult parts of the cultivation routine, e.g. the initial clearing of virgin land, the renewal of established family plantations, the application of pest-control measures, etc.

As may be imagined, few African smallholding peasants are in a position either to meet the cost or to face the psychological challenge involved in such facilities. This fact is explicitly acknowledged in the current programme of oil-palm development. The State corporation in charge of the programme, the *Société pour le développement du palmier à huile* (S.O.D.E.P.A.L.M.), has had to decide between expansion by means of block-plantations (i.e. sizeable areas run by European concessionaires) and by means of village-plantations (i.e. entrusted directly to peasant-farmers). Not ruling the latter out, S.O.D.E.P.A.L.M.

has tilted the scale markedly in favour of the former. Block-plantations are to be established at the rate of 7,000 hectares annually for the 5-year period 1966–70; village plantations at the rate of 1,200 hectares in 1966 and 2,000 annually for the 4-year period 1967–70.

It would be idle to criticise the decision, and one can think of many reasons why, at the present juncture and on Ivory Coast premises, it may have been wise. The comment made on it by one of its knowledgeable French defenders carries a special significance, all the same.

"This distinction (sc. between block-plantations and village-plantations) arises from the fact that the material difficulties involved in creating blocks of plantations are considered less formidable than the psychological difficulties involved in creating village-plantations. In the first case it is a question of means and financing, in the second of education, which requires time and patience."[1]

Here M. Charbonneau puts his finger on the central attitude determining the whole economic and social strategy of the present régime and its French managers. Ivory Coast expansion is to continue to be confined to the 15 per cent of the population who understand about means and financing. The 85 per cent whose pressing need is education can safely, even preferably, wait while the régime builds up a buffer stock of time and patience. Not yet is Reveille to be sounded for the sleeping Titan. Time means nothing to him and his patience is inexhaustible. Does it? And is it?

If modernisation is the process of drawing out, and making the most of, the special human resources native to Africa, then the Ivory Coast, hand in hand with Liberia, is about the least modernising country of them all. This is a fundamental, gratuitous, and in the long term disastrous, failure which it behoves the student to explain. In point of expansion the Ivory Coast may be an economic miracle, in point of growth it is a sick and malformed society. It has gone astray in this fashion

[1] René Charbonneau, in *Marchés Tropicaux*, No. 1068, 30 April 1966.

because its African leaders have misread or ignored the law of their country's situation.

Owing to this perversity in their perception, the fact eludes them that the Ivory Coast is an African country and, whether they like it or not, a country of the new Africa at that. President Houphouët-Boigny and his colleagues and their party have somehow remained bogged down at the stage of the Brazzaville Conference of 1944. Already a quarter of a century out of date, they survive as increasingly anachronistic worshippers of the sacred cow of Great Colonial France (G.C.F.).

Under the leadership of General de Gaulle and his Free French, that Conference endorsed the principle proclaimed by the then Commissioner for the Colonies, René Pléven, in these words:

"We read at one time or another that this war must be ended with what is called a liberation of the colonial peoples. In G.C.F. there are neither peoples to liberate nor racial discrimination to abolish. There are populations which feel themselves to be French, and which wish to take (and to which France wishes to give) a greater and greater part in the life and democratic institutions of the French community. There are populations which we mean to lead, stage by stage, to personality, for the most mature to political freedoms, but which do not mean to understand any other independence than the independence of France."

That the Ivory Coast all these years later should still envisage its future as that of a *département* of the motherland, with G.C.F. spreading care and protection like a tent above, and stretching its everlasting arms beneath—this is, shall we say, a striking tribute to the efficacy of French cultural aggression. But it is quite out of gear with the central realities of the world today—with the stupendous effort of decolonisation which is raging throughout all the tropical and sub-tropical zone, with the entire tendency of the African renaissance, and with the accelerating phthisis of the North Atlantic bloc.

In the Ivory Coast not merely the economy but the social matrix itself is an annexe of the French business world and an expression of the French mentality. The "more mature" Africans referred to by M. Pléven, by which he means Africans who are *évolué* furthest away from *négritude* and closest to *francité* —in short, those glossy stall-fed Africans who throng the official world of politics and government—these people give an irresistibly comic impression of marionettes dancing at the end of strings jerked by the imagined requirements of French cultural norms. As marionettes without personality or freedom, they labour to represent entities which symbolise both; and they turn out to be equally *ersatz* whether judged as persons or as French or as African.

As monopolists of the plums offered by the public service, they substantiate the claim that the service is 100 per cent African-ised. As *fonctionnaires dénaturés et déracinés*, they illustrate the fact that the service is 100 per cent de-Africanised. They are living proof that, given the local conditions, Africanisation and de-Africanisation are correlative and concurrent processes. The "more mature" an African becomes from M. Pléven's stand-point, the more of a nonentity is he from the standpoint of true African development.

What dismays the observer is that, for the palate of quondam Africans recently risen from impotence, the native salt of Africa should so soon have lost its savour. They seem no longer to be aware that savour was ever one of its qualities. They do not ask themselves any more what public spirit, in the sense of an uncalculating pursuit of an African common good, ought to mean for real Africans in a real Africa. One is left nursing the wound of a bleeding contrast between something great and illimitable that calls for release in the African genius and the one-dimensional worm's-eye view by which these ex-Africans seek to steer their country's life. (This presumably is the angle of vision from which African independence and the indepen-dence of France appear indistinguishable.) One marvels that anybody should attach importance to what they are doing, or should expect anything durable to come out of it.

Certain more hopeful signs are, however, appearing on the

horizon. Ivoirians themselves begin to notice that the Houphouët way no longer brings in the old magical dividends, either in the home economy or in relations with neighbouring states. The bowing down before the graven image of G.C.F. has damaged the prospect of African unity not merely since independence, but even since Brazzaville fifteen years before that. It is now obvious to all that it is a major factor in the disarray of the whole strategy of African development, and that in practical terms a definitive choice will have to be made between the shadow of G.C.F. and the substance of O.A.U.

This implies that even ex-Africans such as the current Ivory Coast politicians will be driven to acknowledge that within the continent of Africa the African interest should enjoy primacy over external interests, including the French. The present situation is in essence not unlike that of 1962 when the Algerian insurgents attained their victory. Until then the twelve states members of the Brazzaville group had backed the French cause in Algeria while the rest of the new Africa was bitterly protesting against it. It was only the Evian agreements which made possible some rapprochement between the Brazzaville group and the other African states, and so led to the creation of O.A.U. in 1963.

Today the organ of the Brazzaville group, now functioning under the alias of *Organisation Commune Africaine et Malgache* (O.C.A.M.), backs the French supply of arms to South Africa, just as in its earlier guise of *Union Africaine et Malgache* (U.A.M.) it had backed the French army throughout the Algerian rebellion. Throughout a protean career O.C.A.M. has revealed its basically anti-African attitudes by adulation of Moise Tshombe and his supporters in the protracted Congo crisis. All these policies—on Algeria, on Tshombe's Congo, on South Africa—can only be seen as deeply mischievous in the context of African unity and African independence.

In the local context of West Africa, the Ivory Coast and its four fellow-members of the *Conseil de l'Entente*, acting as agents of O.C.A.M., have been no less successful in preventing any constructive regional grouping either in the spirit of economic community or across the francophone-anglophone line. It is a record by comparison with which those of a Nkrumah or a Sékou-Touré shine out as beacons of sweetness and light.

The Ivory Coast will not, of course, move far towards abandoning such lamentable postures, so long as it remains under the economic coercion of the franc zone, and while the spiteful jealousy of the French outlook on African affairs remains unchallenged. The most effective step open to those genuine Africans who believe in independence and unity (and they exist in far greater numbers than the zealots of francophone separatism) would be to establish a convertible African currency on a regional basis. To be sure, the Ivory Coast will take no initiative in such a matter, but it is not inconceivable that it might go along with an effective scheme worked out by others more sensitive to the penal discomforts of the French stranglehold.

As recently as 1966 this assessment would have seemed merely fantastic. But the Ivory Coast boom is no longer what it was in 1965, and the Government has now some inkling that even in its heyday it was simply the kind of boom which makes the rich richer and the poor poorer. Second thoughts are emerging, some of them carrying implications critical of the French *mainmise*. The countries of the Entente, too, rely less on the Ivory Coast than they did. The feeling spreads that perhaps there is less to this decorative country than meets the eye.

It is instructive to note the language used by politicians when matters like these are raised in public. We are much helped here by a speech made in Abidjan on 16 May 1967 to the *Jeune Chambre Economique de la Côte d'Ivoire* by M. Mahomed Diawara, *Ministre Délégué au Plan*.

"We are to move," he declared, "from the *Plan-fétiche* of earlier years to a novel *Plan-populaire*." How are we to interpret such esoteric terms? A fetish is taken to be an inanimate object worshipped by savages for its magical powers or as being inhabited by a spirit. Perhaps, therefore, we may conjecture that a fetish-plan is an inert and lifeless sketch which has been, and is being, irrationally reverenced. By contrast, a popular plan would be not only the reasonable business of each and all, but it would also mean business in the sense of expressing policies which are seriously intended to be carried into effect on the ground.

If this construction is correct, it implies recognition on the part of the Ivory Coast authorities that economic expansion cannot be spontaneous and harmonious at the same time. If you want harmony, you must supply *un instrument d'impulsion, de cohérence, et d'independance* (sc. from external pressure).

Here, indeed, is an important shift of emphasis. The Ivory Coast has ever since 1960 been working to a Plan of a kind, but a kind which made no effort to *dépasser l'empirisme parcellaire et l'horizon forcément limité de la gestion quotidienne.* Its *raison d'être* was not to inspan the totality of development activities as means to defined social change, but rather to procure for the Government the collaboration of private capital, in the faith that this is only of effect within the framework of some consistent public programme. In practice planning so understood signified a series of separate programmes for separate sectors, any one programme being capable of speeding up or slowing down without throwing the rest out of gear.

Or, put another way, the Government's job was to provide a footing and a scaffolding (roads, ports, buildings, telecommunications), the job of private enterprise was to contribute the initiative for and the carrying out of productive works. Three phases were foreseen in this collaboration:

(a) 1960–70: intensive investments in productive facilities,
(b) 1970 onwards: accelerating yields from the system,
(c) 1975: the turning-point where real economic independence begins.

No special meaning, beyond a vague *décollage* of the economy, seems to have been attached to the term "real economic independence". One may guess that it hints at a stage where expansion becomes to some extent self-generating.

It is this conception of the planning process and this time-schedule which M. Diawara now seems to be calling in question. Popular planning and *public* initiative, he explains, are a necessary counterweight to the country's dependence on foreign trade, and they furnish a principal tool for building a truly national economy. At present the essential parts of the modern sector are in the hands of economic agents *non-nationaux*.

Evidently it is the French who are so described, and the phrase suggests that, after all, Ivory Coast prosperity can properly be distinguished from, and preferred to, French prosperity. It is a mistake, M. Diawara adds, to have counted so much on increased exports from a low-productivity traditional agriculture at a low standard of living, and on an industrialisation which has been almost exclusively the work of the *secteur expatrié*. "This is why we have experienced economic expansion without social growth."

Such lopsidedness at once reflects and perpetuates a serious *déséquilibre ville-campagne*. Abidjan, which had 125,000 inhabitants in 1955, now has more than 400,000. It is likely to have 800,000 by 1975 and 1,100,000 by 1980. Expansion has been essentially concentrated in Abidjan, whose growth has been and is too rapid. This raises disquieting problems of urban equipment, housing, school provision, technical training, employment, etc. What is worse, the growing disparity of incomes in town on one hand and country on the other can jeopardise the whole unity of the nation.

Such, M. Diawara concludes, are the reasons why it is no longer possible to dispense with a coherent strategy of national development. That strategy will have to deal with three issues:

(a) the level and distribution of public investment,
(b) the uneven growth of different regions of the country,
(c) the *ivoirisation* of the economy.[1]

In a single phrase, the new keynote in rural reconstruction. "Besides tackling the work of integrated agricultural development, we wish to create a rural commerce and a small-scale

[1] i.e. its de-Frenchification.

rural industry of modern type. This in turn will lead to a network of semi-urban centres, designed and equipped in up-to-date style, and hence capable of counter-balancing the meretricious allurements of Abidjan."

It does not do to over-estimate the practical consequences of one address by one man, even if he is a member of the Government. But if M. Diawara's affirmation bears any relation to what the Ivory Coast is actually going to do, it represents a promising change of heart. We hear in it a tinkling of the knell of G.C.F. We perceive that it embodies a wiser diagnosis of West Africa's troubles, and a truer feeling for the interest of Africa, than have been available so far in the Ivory Coast.

CHAPTER 14

GROWTH WITHOUT EXPANSION: GUINEA

"I HAD TO agree with Touré: he hadn't changed: he was still earnest, intense, sincere—still a dreamer, living his dream and articulating his own quasi-religious philosophy. It was Africa that was changing and passing him by. Touré was becoming anachronistic—a talker in a continent where the doers were taking over. He was no longer in the main stream of African evolution, and I felt sorry for him. For he had been a trail-blazer whose defiance of de Gaulle in 1958 gave Black Africa a sense of pride and confidence in its own destiny; and now he was just a nice but erratic guy who was beginning to look as if he might finish last."[1]

"Mais la Guinée de Sékou Touré, là, on peut en parler. Ça, c'est une expérience pour nous tous, une expérience qui n'est pas très heureuse aujourd'hui. Mais ce qui nous plaît dans Sékou, c'est l'effort qu'il fournit, sa fièvre de chercher, de dominer, de vaincre ses difficultés.

"Et seul, surtout ça : seul.

"La pauvreté de la Guinée, le vide du *Printania* de Konakry, c'est une question quand même un peu secondaire. Parce qu'on ne peut pas comparer le rendement de la Guinée aujourd'hui à l'effort moral qu'elle fournit."[2]

Is Guinea a back-number, as the former U.S. Ambassador in Conakry supposes? Or is it a beacon for all Africa for its steadfast moral endeavour, as the radical French-language journal believes? This chapter seeks to provide evidence on which the issue can be decided.

It is undoubtedly true that the nine years since the present

[1] William Attwood: *The Reds and the Blacks*, p. 323. (Hutchinson 1967). The Author was U.S. Ambassador to Guinea April 1961–May 1963.
[2] *Jeune Afrique*, 1967.

régime was established on 2 October 1958 have been disappointing, when measured by the yardstick of economic expansion. Mr. Attwood judges that, because of that, all else is failure—which could have been avoided if only Touré had had the sense to throw his country open to foreign private investment with the freedom of a Houphouët-Boigny or a Tubman. The question, however, is more complex than this, as will become clear when we look in detail at the state of the economy.

In respect of social growth, on the other hand, Guinea's record is outstanding. This is largely due, as *Jeune Afrique* rightly surmises, to the resolutely maintained integrity of the Parti Démocratique de Guinée (P.D.G.) under Touré's leadership. In another large part, it is due to the order of the French evacuation of Guinea at de Gaulle's direction.

The French Government in the autumn of 1958 put before its territories in West and Equatorial Africa proposals for autonomy within a so-called French Community. On 28 September a referendum was held in which the choice offered was of accepting either these proposals or immediate independence. By Touré and the P.D.G., grieved as they were at the failure to create a West African federation, and perceiving as they did that the new Community was a cloak for continuing French dominance, the proposals were declined. Everybody else said Yes.

"De Gaulle angrily decided to make an example of Guinea. He ordered all French administrators, teachers, doctors, and technicians out of the country. Before leaving they destroyed documents, ripped out telephones, smashed light bulbs, and stripped the police of uniforms and weapons. Touré's Guinea had been condemned to death."[1]

Paradoxically, de Gaulle's vengeful petulance, for all its first appearances of disaster, turned out to be the best thing that could have happened to Guinea. For several crucial years, while the country was finding its feet after the initial shock, French meddling was reduced to a minimum, so far as Guinea's

[1] Attwood, op. cit., p. 21.

internal development was concerned. Indeed, French meddling was confined to periodical plots to topple Touré himself. Not only that, but other N.A.T.O. countries, including even the U.S.A., held off from meddling too—for fear of annoying the French. If all N.A.T.O. countries had applied France's Guinea-treatment to all independent Africa from 1960 onwards, the prospects for peaceful African growth would be far rosier today than in fact they are, so wretched have been the consequences of those tortuous machinations which go by the misnomer of "aid".

In face of the capital punishment which de Gaulle hoped to inflict, the P.D.G. was obliged, willy-nilly and literally as a matter of life or death, to ask itself what on earth was to be its strategy, first of public survival, then of recovery and development. Utterly alone and forsaken, beset by crisis and confusion, yet buoyant with the sparkling excitement of millennial expectations, Guinea took its stand where death would pass.

It set out to evolve from first principles its own solutions to its own real problems. No other African country, except Algeria, has had this merciful necessity so cruelly forced upon it. Genuine French spite, however petty, has proved a truer benefactor than spurious international benevolence, however glossy. Yet no other African country, again except Algeria, could on its own have withstood so brutal an ordeal. The first thing to realise about Touré's Guinea is that, like Algeria, it is a miracle of survival. Aside from all questions of expansion and growth, just to be alive and kicking constitutes a signal, a historic victory.

The first principles from which the P.D.G. proceeded to work out its preferred kind of salvation for the country, were two. The new social order was to be such as would (a) cancel the self-estrangement of victims of colonial oppression,[1] and (b) exclude divisions of tribe or social class.

It is highly characteristic of Touré's outlook (and of his morality) that the first step of all towards this dual objective is to lay stress on the Pan-African and global responsibilities of

[1] *"créer un système de désaliénation de l'homme ex-colonisé."*

his small and struggling land. From the dawn of independence, Guinea presents itself to the world as a humble but trusty musket-bearer in the ranks of world revolution. This is a never-flagging theme in the never-flagging exhortations of the party.

The *Rapport politique et de doctrine* presented by the *Bureau Politique National* (B.P.N.) to the 8th Party Congress of 1967 was set out in twenty sections, of which the first was headed The Revolution as Global and Permanent Necessity. At least nine others treated of one or other aspect of the anti-imperialist movement. Guinea is not alone, the public are constantly assured; she stands shoulder to shoulder with two-thirds of the world, with all countries everywhere who are laid low, as Guinea is, with the crippling affliction of under-development. We have to enlarge the intellectual, moral, and material capacities of our people *pour créer ce qui lui manque*. We must make ourselves worthy of our allies. Seek truth therefore, forgetting private gain.

Guinea proclaims, alike in its constitution and its practice, the equality and solidarity of all its nationals without distinction of class, sex, ethnic group, or religion. Accordingly the P.D.G. is not merely a mass party, but a whole-people party. It is not an organ of particular factions or sections or interests. In the western sense of the term, therefore, it is not a party at all. On the contrary, it is the entire nation organised for its political and economic duties. Everyone of suitable age is invited to join it, and the paid-up membership is said to amount to 55–60 per cent of the population.[1]

The purpose of all social arrangements in Guinea is to exclude the class struggle. The P.D.G., though it knocks incipient bourgeois tendencies hard, fights not so much against a local bourgeoisie as to prevent the emergence of one. The sole advantage of under-development as basic as Guinea's is that there is nothing much yet for any bourgeois to batten on. Whole-people democracy seeks to make possible a social framework not pyramidal but cubic, the expression of a balanced and

[1] Bernard Charles: *Guinée* (L'Atlas des Voyages, Editions Rencontre, Lausanne, 1963).

an even growth in which one and all raise themselves up in one and the same motion.

The Guinean leaders have perceived that the class struggle has become internationalised and expanded to global dimensions. It is in fact none other than the current relationship between the N.A.T.O. countries (the international bourgeoisie) and the Third World (the international proletariat). The two-class structure, while still vestigially identifiable within a number of countries, now appears mainly in the form of over-developed countries on the one hand standing against under-developed countries on the other. Marx's increasing misery of the workers has turned into the widening A.L.A.A. Gap.

Realising that Guinea is and must be wholly committed to the international class struggle, Touré and his colleagues are the more determined not to find an internal one on their hands as well. If such a domestic rift were to develop (in the shape of the Onitiri Gap), Guinea would be fatally weakened as a fellow-combatant with the rest of the Third World.

Touré is no stranger to the hatred and contempt, the pity and love, which overwhelmed Marx and Lenin as they contemplated the industrialisation of 19th century Europe in all its offensive realism. An exact echo of theirs are his own feelings when he confronts the facts of modern under-development, whether in Guinea or anywhere else. He regards it as an obscene and degrading disease with which the entire Third World has been surreptitiously, but systematically, infected over the last five centuries by the countries of the North Atlantic enclave. These countries now, as is manifest, cannot or will not offer any cure. The cure therefore must be discovered and applied by the Third World alone—through the co-operation of all the Third World's component parts.

Such is the appraisal by reference to which Guinea's every attitude towards international affairs is determined. In regard to the N.A.T.O. countries, all is plain sailing. They are the bourgeois, Guinea is a proletarian. The class war (not of Guinea's choosing) is on, and must be fought to a finish. But what of the Communist countries? They bear no blame either for the slave trade or its successor, the widening A.A.L.A. Gap. Hence they have not, as N.A.T.O. has, put themselves automatically out of court as allies and even friends. But whose side are they on in the Third World's struggle against N.A.T.O? There is no room for non-alignment here. Guinea judges the U.S.S.R., Eastern Europe, and China in terms of their concrete behaviour, year in and year out, on this issue; and in the long run in terms of the consistency of that behaviour.

To spread these attitudes and to popularise the appraisal on which they are based, the P.D.G. was constructed. The party is now more than twenty years old, and has been in office for the last nine of them. It would be hard to exaggerate the importance of its unresting activities in the field of ideological and administrative training. In village or in town ward its 7,000 local committees hold each its own weekly meeting, at which every aspect of party and national interest is discussed. Even the smallest hamlet of a dozen huts in the deep bush has its Party committee composed of the headman and nine elected militants (4 men, 3 women, and 2 youths).

The multitude of ground-level committees are brought together at the level of town or district (as the case may be) into 163 sections, each section having its own directing council. At the peak of the pyramid is set the B.P.N. of 17 members, three of whom are women. This body, which constitutes in practice the country's responsible Cabinet, is in *prise directe* with all Party committees. Hence the sections, while occupying a useful intermediate position between summit and base, cannot become a bottleneck in the line of communications. Touré's method of consultation with all levels of the Party structure has nothing spasmodic about it. It has been called *démocratie pendulaire*, in view of its continual swing from centre to circumference and back again.

The P.D.G. under Touré's leadership has been effectively at the head of affairs in Guinea since March 1957, when at elections held in that month it won outright control of the

Territorial Assembly, and Touré shortly afterwards became Vice-President of the Council of Government in terms of a French-drawn constitution providing for autonomy in internal affairs. His first act on assuming office was to press for measures to deal with the urgent problem of inter-tribal conflicts. These had reached a point where Foulah seemed endlessly at violent odds with Soussou, Malinke with the people of the forest zone, and so on. Guinea was, even before full independence, becoming the symbol of the new Africa's fatal curse.

On 27 July, 1957, accordingly, a momentous conference of *commandants de cercle* was held at Conakry. The outcome was a really revolutionary step which went straight to the root of the whole issue of the *groupes ethniques*—namely, the suppression of tribal chieftainships in the rural districts, and the dissolution of racial and tribal organisations in the towns. The chiefs were replaced by administrative officials, appointed and paid by the Government, and charged with bringing rulers and ruled, centre and circumference, as close as possible together, through the machinery of the Party organisation.

This difficult and vital reform, which leaders in no other African country have yet found the nerve to promote, entailed a complete reorganisation of the countryside on the economic as well as on the administrative plane. It was necessary to dismantle the feudal modes of action customary within the tribal system, yet obstructive at the same time of all movement towards modernisation. The reciprocal spongeing arrangements of tribal tradition were replaced by a new frame within which the peasant could work under conditions making for a better correspondence between effort expended and result obtained. Hence the establishment at Government level of the Ministry of Rural Economy, at ground level of the co-operative societies, at the intermediate level of the Sociétés Mutuelles de Développement Rural (S.M.D.R.).

Alongside the emancipation and pacification of the tribespeople, overlapping it on one side and linking up with the development of the Party organisation on another, goes a third cardinal reform, the enfranchisement of women. To confer on women the same political and civil rights as men is a relatively straightforward matter. It is a necessary but not a sufficient condition for ending the age-old inferiority of womanhood which has dogged the footsteps of African nationalist movements from their first beginnings. It has to be followed up by a review of the institution of marriage itself. This is the key, in P.D.G.'s belief, not merely to the advancement of women to the equal status which is their due, but also to the balanced evolution of African societies in general.

Several tentative steps have been taken already. The duration of the tribal initiation schools has been reduced from 6–12 months to two. The minimum age of marriage is officially fixed at 17, which, low as it may seem, is a big improvement on traditional practice. In a broader context Touré, as a student of the comic dramatist of ancient Athens, understands well how to use his country's sexuality as an instrument of Party policy. Aristophanes built his play *Lysistrata* around the fancy that if women were to go on strike and down their sexual tools, the procedure would have the opposite effect on the opposite sex; and that, in face of their own nagging and mounting discomfort, men would soon abandon even war in return for the restitution of conjugal rights.

Touré puts the point in the form *Chaque matin, chaque midi, chaque soir, les femmes doivent inciter leur mari à adhérer au P.D.G.; s'ils ne veulent pas, elles n'ont qu'à se refuser à eux; le lendemain, ils seront obligés d'adhérer.* Such measures and such quips appear to be popular among Guinean women, from whom Touré is known to derive solid political support. The women's movement plays a militant and influential part not only in the public life of Guinea, but also as a member of the Pan-African Organisation of Women.

The P.D.G., with a kind of circumspect audacity, is moving towards the suppression of polygamy. Since Guinea is 90 per cent Moslem, and since the average number of wives per husband (1·9) is higher there than in any other West African country, the need to be at once bold and wary is obvious. The youth movement has for some time been encouraged to campaign actively in favour of ending polygamy. At the Party's annual congress in 1967 Touré came out strongly against this marriage-form. Henceforward, he told his audience, any officer of party or government at any level would be debarred from taking more than one wife. Those who now had several wives would not be obliged to put any of them away; those with one wife would stay as they were. The purport of the speech was that a point had been reached where men would just have to choose between sex and responsibility.

It is not hard to foresee that from the attack on tribalism plus the pressure towards monogamy the nuclear family will gradually emerge. Family planning programmes, or at any rate practices, will not be far behind. Steadily the relationships between sexuality, marriage, procreation, and the form of the domestic unit will be harmonised, both among themselves and with the public interest, by means of a population policy. Such is the road on which P.D.G. has already set out.

The new Africa is facing two capital problems, and two alone. All other problems derive from them. One is population, the other is *la question ville-campagne*. Guinea is the only African country so far to arrive at some inkling of this.

In sum, then, we may say that Guinea is, politically and socially, the best organised State in West Africa. Its Government is probably as close to its citizens, and on terms of as much mutual trust with them, as any Government in the world. The ruling Party is quite genuinely a party of the whole people. The citizen body itself is not rent by animosities of tribe, class, race, or religion. It has a common consciousness of being Guinean, an awakening sense of a kind of nationhood, and is proud of it. Some local observers say that the man in the street, though with inadequate support from the figures of G.D.P., has an all-round feeling of being better off today than he was five years ago.

Party and country are led by resourceful, long-headed, and determined men who have gathered over many years a comprehensive experience of all conceivable troubles of leadership short of international war. They practise the self-denial they preach at least as well as Christian priests and votaries commonly do. For a decade they have steered their people through minefields of foreign intrigue and underground aggression which would have blown a less sure-footed society to pieces. Whatever they have tried to be, whatever they have engaged in, they have always found themselves repulsed by the world's knavery and falsehood, which blocked every path of action. Yet their hope and their resolve have never faltered, they always know how to find their way back to the springs of spiritual resource, how to renew there the old *élan*, and even how to draw on them to accelerate the rhythm of their revolution.

Nor is the land of Guinea less well endowed with natural resources, especially for agriculture and stockraising. Great also, therefore, is the potential of the industries that will in time be built on these. Guinea has enough bauxite to supply the whole world's aluminium needs for fifty years. Its many rivers furnish it with large and well-distributed possibilities of hydro-electric power and irrigation. It possesses in Conakry a natural deep-water port, which has been much improved in recent years by additional deep-water docking facilities. It has an important international airport.

Its road network, though still inadequate (especially in the five months of the rainy season), is getting steadily better. At many points in the country's infrastructure developments small or large are going forward all the time, and in their aggregate appear to be approaching a new critical threshold. A beginning is being made with the great task of rural electrification. Guinea's hitherto inaccessible forest area now enjoys a workable outlet, via the highway built across Liberia, to the port of Monrovia.

Whether one looks at Guinea from a political, a social, or an economic angle, what one surely sees is a young state splendidly equipped for dramatic progress, actually poised, indeed, to embark on it. How, then, comes it that in fact the country still ekes out a precarious living from day to day, from hand to

7

mouth, with recurrent interruptions in restocking even with such basic requirements as fuel and food? Bread is rationed, black markets flourish in every type of commodity, except those whose supply has dried up altogether. The menace of economic breakdown now here, now there, one day everywhere, hovers in the air, like a flock of Conakry's own vultures. Why does the economy not flow into the frame of social growth that has been made ready to receive it?

The state of the Guinea economy can be briefly sketched in terms of conventional indicators:

PRODUCTION

(a) *Agriculture*	1957–59	1961	1962	1963	1964	1965	1966
Total Production Index	100	107	114	110	104	112	111
Per capita index	100	98	101	96	88	92	88

(b) *Agriculture* ('000 metric tons)	1961	1962	1963	1964	1965	1966
Rice (paddy)	320	319	320	250	330	300
Millet	130	134	138	142	146	150
Citrus fruits	76	76	78	81	83	85
Coffee	14	13	10	9	9	9
Cassava	393	430	420	420	420	433
Bananas	58	86	81	87	85	88
Palm Kernels	20	20	23	24	25	26
Palm-oil	11	11	11	11	13	13
Meat	13	13	14	14	14	14
TOTAL	1,035	1,102	1,095	1,038	1,125	1,118

(c) *Mining* ('000 metric tons)						
Bauxite	385	55	175	167	288	200
Aluminium (F.R.I.A.)	400	458	480	484	520	525
Iron ore	526	702	558	767	678	510
TOTAL	1,311	1,215	1,213	1,418	1,486	1,235

(d) *Electricity*

Total Production (million KWH)	135	147	156	168	174
Per capita Production (KWH)	43	45	47	49	49

GROSS DOMESTIC PRODUCT

(at current market prices)

	TOTAL (milliards C.F.A. francs)	PER HEAD (C.F.A. francs)	PER HEAD ($)
1956	53·5	19,814	81
1958	48·9	16,300	65
1962	64·7	19,606	81
1965	63·5	18,000	75

These tables paint the portrait of an economy in stagnation. Neither agricultural nor mineral production keeps pace with population increase, and power production is only just doing so. It is also a fact (not exposed in the tables) that the trade balance is in chronic deficit, amounting to some 30 per cent of imports, which is held in check only by the exports of a foreign bauxite enterprise wholly insulated from the Guinea economy proper.

The big international firm of F.R.I.A. exports more than half a million tons of alumina a year; but the proceeds go to swell national income in U.S.A. and France; all Guinea gets out of it is a dollop of wages for unskilled labour and $11 million[1] a year in royalties. Such mineral exports of foreign firms account for 70 per cent of all exports. Future prospects of mineral earnings are, however, somewhat more cheerful, because production from the bauxite deposits at Boké, which are richer and more extensive than the F.R.I.A. deposits, is now beginning. The producers are a joint stock company in the equity of which the Guinea Government has a 49 per cent interest—much more favourable terms than those offered by F.R.I.A., even though the majority holding is still foreign.

Of the balance of payments the less said the better. Foreign

[1] Figure given by U.S. Ambassador, Conakry.

debts and the cost of servicing them steadily increase, while the internal expansion for the sake of which they were incurred still makes no visible start. Well may Touré ask publicly, as he has asked more than once, "What shall we do when the friendly countries stop giving us advances? We shall be paralysed. The hold-up will be complete." He might well have put the supplementary question also, "And if they go on giving them, how shall we ever pay back?"

In general, the whole business of foreign aid has been full of troubles, although Guinea is much more cautious about taking on aid commitments than most West African countries, and there have been none of the scandals of contractor finance which were factors in the downfall of a Nkrumah or a Margai.

Between 1959 and 1962 foreign aid totalled $100 million, and it rose to nearly three times that amount by the early months of 1964. Its sources were as follows:

	$ million
From U.S.S.R., Eastern Europe, and China	183
From U.S.A. and West Germany	81
From Ghana, Morocco, U.A.R., and Jugoslavia	31
	295

Most of it came on fairly easy terms, as foreign aid goes; from U.S.S.R. 2½ per cent interest a year and repayment over 12–22 years, from the Chinese interest-free and repayment over 10 years. And much of it was completely wasted, owing to lack of common sense in the donors and sheer ignorance and inefficiency in the recipients.

William Attwood quotes a comment on Russian aid made to him by the Soviet Ambassador in Conakry. "We gave them what they wanted, and they didn't know what to do with it. Of course, our mistake was to send them stuff without showing them how to use it." Large quantities of transport vehicles, farm-machines, road-making machines, and machine tools have been reduced to scrap (a) by mechanics who drive their machines without engine oil and then complain that the design is all wrong for African conditions, (b) by managers who are surprised to find that stocks of spare parts gradually get exhausted, and cannot be replaced if there is no foreign exchange to pay with.

In spite of a substantial influx of technical experts and instructors to assist in the administration of aid programmes, Guinean feeling is that the economic consequences over the last seven years have been much less bright than the Government had a right to expect. Guinea has had nothing like value for money. The best appreciated help has come from the Chinese. They work hard, live like the Guinea people, make no attempt to throw their weight about, and turn out a good technical job. Next in esteem come the East Germans, followed at a decent interval by Russians and Czechs. But on the whole Guinea, like Mali, is in a cleft stick. It hates taking foreign aid, and would give anything to be able to dispense with it. Yet Guinea's life, at any rate its expansion, depends on some measure of aid— properly given and properly received.

The Guinea people cannot be charged with not helping themselves as best they could. They have understood perfectly well that every under-developed country has to start from nothing. That is the definition of under-development. They have watched the scorched-earth policy of the French removing all traces of equipment that might have served Guinea's interests. They realise that to create any industries, small, middling, or large, one must have skilled workers, trained management at middle as well as higher levels, means of transport and communication, exploitation of sources of energy, investment finance, technical teaching institutions both theoretical and practical. They knew how short they were of all these things and even of the means of acquiring them. Large-scale manufacturing by power-machinery would have to wait until they could borrow capital or earn it by trade.

Meanwhile, small-scale beginnings have been made, well

suited to current needs and not marred by over-ambition. Some typical examples are:

(1) A plastic goods factory, which, at present using imported material, performs the useful function of providing almost all the footwear and waterproof garments needed by the Guinean population, together with a good proportion of the packing for fruit. The organisation is excellent, and can be compared with similar establishments in Europe.

(2) A small works producing standardised steel constructions and interchangeable parts for shops and workshops.

(3) A factory making prefabricated concrete, especially building blocks and reinforced pipes.

(4) A quinine factory.

(5) A well-equipped brewery.

These and other similar enterprises have crossed the dividing line between the craftsman's workshop and small industry by way of machine-tools *assez évolués* and a very good organisation. Now that manpower with adequate training is in better supply, some larger enterprises are in operation, though not yet at anything like full capacity, e.g.:

(a) A large printing plant equipped with the most modern machines whose potential is much bigger than present needs. (Soviet aid.)

(b) A broadcasting station (100 kw) which can be heard all over Africa and in Brazil. (East German aid.)

(c) New runways at Conakry airport to fit international standards. (Soviet aid.)

(d) A Polytechnic Institute, which can take 1,500 students and is already supplying Guinea with its professional-level manpower. (Soviet aid.)

(e) A large brick factory. (Jugoslav aid.)

(f) An abattoir and cannery, including cold-storage. (Soviet aid.)

(g) A match factory. (Chinese aid.)

(h) A cigarette factory. (Chinese aid.)

Alongside such developments as these, the Guineans have earned fame by showing what their own unaided sweat could do. Here was a form of investment capital of which they had plenty. Sweat is always a key-factor in development, a pre-requisite of every advance and of all proper utilisation of assistance from outside. By sweat they could build works which do not demand large financial and technical resources, but whose usefulness is directly perceived by the groups that under-take them.

A proud endeavour in such human investment was made over several years, on the principle that everyone contributes his work-strength free of charge for some collective construction, while the local authority provides materials and transport. By means of self-help so organised 20,000 kilometres of country roads and 2,500 bridges and culverts were built in the first three or four years of independence—not to mention large numbers of school buildings, dispensaries, sports grounds, etc.

This was the more to the credit of those who took part in it, because human investment, valuable as it is in improving basic amenities in the countryside, is not all sunshine. In Guinean conditions it is bound to go on chiefly at the infrastructure level, where it is not directly or immediately productive in terms of the national accounts. Moreover, it has its own com-plexities of operation, it can only work in areas where population is fairly densely settled, it runs into difficulties of its own, it has its own abuses which crop up when the organisers are off guard or at odds with one another.

In agriculture and stockraising, again, for both of which Guinea is by nature particularly well placed, a start can be made without large finance capital, or costly mechanical equipment, or elaborate technical training; at any rate with much less of these things than manufacturing industry requires. In view of the outpouring of energy in human investment, one might have expected to find a corresponding surge forward on the farming front. It has not happened. Why not?

The summary answer is, Because Guinea has not managed to

offer effective incentives to the peasant farmer. It has half-ruined itself in trying to do so—even paying special rates for farm produce in order to get increased production, and then finding itself obliged to sell in overseas markets at prices lower than those originally paid to the local growers.

But the prices obtainable for agricultural exports continue to dwindle. The prices paid to growers, though still subsidised, become less and less adequate as a stimulant to productivity. There is evidence of some demoralisation among peasant producers.

Basically this comes about because increased peasant earnings cannot be matched by more imported consumer goods to spend them on. Such consumer goods are just not there. Guinea has been troubled all along by a persistent epidemic of generalised smuggling. It began with the re-export across Guinea's land frontiers by a swarm of petty private traders of goods bought from the State importing enterprises. These goods, which were meant to be used for establishing a healthy *ville-campagne* relationship within Guinea, are in fact carted into Senegal for C.F.A. francs, Sierra Leone for sterling, Liberia for dollars.

Watching this racket with interest, the Guinean peasant embarks on some compensatory smuggling of his own. He too works a "tuppenny tube" for his cattle and coffee to Liberia, Sierra Leone, and Senegal. He then exchanges them there for the consumer goods previously smuggled out by his black-marketeering compatriots, and finally re-smuggles them back home to his own compound.

Leaving the re-exports of consumer goods aside, the illicit trade in cattle and coffee (with some diamonds thrown in) has been valued at $10 million a year. The volume of neither the re-exports nor the exports appears to be affected by Touré's stinging public abuse of "betrayers of the revolution" or by making such smuggling a capital offence. From the P.D.G.'s standpoint it is a tragic let-down. The Party has done so much to train the people of Guinea in social responsibility and in accepting public and private austerity as a national duty. Nothing could be more galling than to have to watch these disciplined troops reverting to an orgy of looting, to the ruination of their country.

The motive behind this generalised fraud is not, of course, just to evade customs duties. It is to sell the Guinea franc short, and acquire illegal foreign exchange. Its importance is not so much that the dodgers do well, rather that farmers are so busy dodging that they do not tend their fields properly. Thus the agricultural front crumbles. The solution lies less with the *Collèges d'Enseignement Rural* (though their technical merits are high) than with well-judged currency reform in which neighbouring countries are included.

Here the rulers are up against two deep-rooted propensities in the unregenerate African temperament, which it will take many generations to educate away. In the first place, all Africans are petty traders by nature; that is to say, they much prefer distributing goods produced by the efforts of others to producing goods by their own. They will go to enormous pains and show themselves models of industry, when there is question of enlarging their profit-margin on a sale. When the question is of *creating* some new good of ten times the value at one-tenth of the effort, they will not lift a finger. In the second place, when two equal gains are in prospect, one straight and the other crooked, the attraction of the latter is invincibly stronger.

Such are the reasons for which much of Guinea's farming potential is being frittered away. It is no longer simply that outdated methods, grass fires, shortage of trained personnel in the farming world result in poor output. The area under rice shrinks year by year, because the irrigation canals are neglected. The production of rice, as the staple food, ought to get top priority of all, in the interests both of domestic self-sufficiency and of export trade. In fact, rice-production per head of population falls rather sharply, and the smugglers ensure that not all even of the production there is finds its way to the Guinean consumer. Hence increasing and excessive rice imports.

The quality of Guinean coffee is remarkable. More than 90 per cent of exports are graded as *extra-prima, prima, and*

7*

supérieure. But coffee production falls, and coffee exports fall sharply, because the measures required to control tracheomycose are not taken. In some districts 25–30 per cent of plants are affected.

Even the new plantations of dwarf oil-palms, the high-yield variety, are poorly cared for. Thick underbrush is allowed to grow up between the trees. It throttles them and reduces their output, while at the same time making it difficult to harvest what crop there is.

In general, bananas, coffee, pineapples, groundnuts, and oil-palm products are all of good quality. Their production could be pushed up to make useful exports. But while total output, except in the case of coffee, keeps steady or slightly increases, exports tend to drop, partly because the marketing machinery in Guinea is not efficient, partly because export prices sag, partly because population growth means more mouths to feed at home. Hence the increased imports of fertiliser required to raise output do not come in, since they cannot be paid for.

It is easy to trace all these troubles back to the smuggling fiasco, and that in turn to the currency question. And lamentably true it is that the weakness of the Guinea franc, worthless abroad and to a large extent rejected by the local people, is a painful handicap in dealing with all development questions. The F.G. is not linked with any large monetary zone, and it cannot in its restricted framework constitute a sufficient support for the local economy.

But this is by no means to say that it was a mistake to set up the F.G. at all. The Guinea Government really had no choice. If they had not left the franc zone of their own accord, it is likely that de Gaulle would have thrown them out of it. If he had not done that, it is pretty certain that he would have used his franc-zone leverage to destroy Touré and the P.D.G. If, on the only remaining hypothesis, he had done neither of these things, and if Guinea had stayed in the franc zone, running, like Senegal, on the C.F.A. franc, it might possibly have had more economic expansion. It would quite certainly have had less social growth.

Guinea's basic social situation today is appreciably more favourable than Senegal's, and income per head is about the same in both countries. Guinea's present difficulties are not an argument for trying to get back into the franc zone. They are an argument for creating a common West African currency, as part of an all-African currency zone.

Potentially Guinea is one of the most prosperous of African countries. Actually it is still a disoriented agricultural economy with 85 per cent of the population scratching a living on the land. That is the standard European comment on the present state of the Guinean nation. And the standard European implication is that everything in Guinea's garden would be lovely today, but for that misguided socialist option. The comment, true enough a decade ago, is now a decade out of date. The implication is and always was pointless; whatever the causes of Guinea's troubles may be, they have nothing to do with socialism.

Comment and implication alike ignore every constructive thing that has happened on the spot since Touré's No to de Gaulle. To any observer who recalls where Guinea stood when the French walked out, the unrelenting hostility the country has since withstood from everybody it was entitled to think of as a friend, the enlightened social reconstruction the P.D.G. has successfully carried out in a fifth of the time that most West African countries will require for it—to such an observer the achievement of Touré and his supporters will seem striking indeed. To be sure, the difficulties still to be surmounted remain formidable. But a Guinea which has weathered without disaster the storm of the first ten years will not scare easily at facing the second.

Touré's fundamental problems are the harshness of the untamed African habitat and the ignorance and superstition of the untutored African peasant. All living things in Africa, men and beasts and plants, are at once friends and enemies to one another. Even sun and rain, without which there can be no life, are also life's great destroyers. The very earth, mother of all harvests, teems with innumerable pests and diseases against which no harvest can stand. Men and their non-human neighbours wrestle and groan in an internecine symbiosis. The only parts of the continent still undamaged by man's devastations are those from which the trypanosome or the malaria germ have beaten him back. Timbuktu is the one human settlement of any antiquity which the habitat has not smothered or engulfed. And Timbuktu is extant still, only because desert sands encroach more slowly than jungle flora.

Those therefore who seek to build a new civilisation by drawing out Africa's resources inevitably find not only that gains material or mental are sadly hard to make, but also that, once made, they are wickedly hard to hold. Every wholesome growth in human resources is pounced upon at birth by a virulent degeneration, which the statesman must ward off or cure. Every building, every machine starts to rot before it is properly put together; their care and maintenance in the West African setting is a major problem that only responsible vigilance and high skill can solve.

That the first decade of independence (and *such* independence) should have any gains to record is great credit to Guinea's rulers. That most gains have been consolidated is a triumph. In the same circumstances it is unlikely that any alternative leadership could have made either claim.

III

THE LONG RUN

III

THE LONG RUN

CHAPTER 15

THE REAL PRIORITIES

THE POSITIVE POLICY—the drawing out of African resources—
is not an objective shared by ruling groups in all the new States
here surveyed. In Liberia and Rhodesia, for instance, the first
aim of national policy is to perpetuate the privileges of a settler
minority; in Nigeria it is to ensure that political control should
remain in the hands of the Moslem north; in Senegal, Ivory
Coast, and Cameroon, it is not to shake off the *mainmise* of
France in the interests of local sovereignty, on the contrary it is
to shelter under it, while basking in a measure of autonomy
and much lavish French aid.

Two generalisations can perhaps be made. One is that, apart
from the clear exceptions of Biafra and Guinea,[1] independence
and modernisation mean more to East Africans than to West
Africans, and in West Africa more to anglophone countries
than to francophone. The faintly animated mini-smithereens
which are all that remain of A.O.F. and A.E.F. resemble a
clutch of cross-bred day-old chicks huddling under the bored
wings of France, the broody mother—and lacking the heart
(not to mention the sincerity) to raise a cheep of protest, even
over the French supply of arms to South Africa, their Racial
Enemy No. 1.[2]

The other generalisation is that, in East and West Africa
alike, of the two aspects of modernisation, economic expansion
is thought to be of more moment than social growth, though
here too there are exceptions like Tanzania and Guinea. While

---

[1] Before 1966 two other exceptions would have had to be made, Ghana
and Mali.

[2] If Britain had done this, doubtless the bulk of francophone Africa would
have punished the delinquency by breaking off diplomatic relations, as in
the Rhodesian affair. At the hands of de Gaulle all francophone Africa
swallowed it without a murmur.

everyone, of course, wants higher living standards, few can see that modernisation is like a Seidlitz powder which will not effervesce unless the white packet (expansion) is mixed in water with the grey (growth).

Ruling groups in the new African States, as might be expected, vary greatly in their insight into the real nature of their own problems. A clearer appreciation of what they are up against is undoubtedly spreading, however slowly. When one considers the conditions in which "independence" came upon them, and how little preparation they received for it, it is not surprising that at first they could cope only in a confused manner. Its challenges still pass over the heads of many of them, and the smaller the state, the higher overhead they fly. It is also true that the more crucial an issue is, the more difficult it looks to handle, and the more evasive and irrelevant therefore is the action taken.

Objectively speaking, however, the great gain, amid all the disasters, of the first decade of "independence" is this. It has become manifest beyond all cavil that the whole complex melting-pot of Africa's current troubles boils down to two cardinal issues, which needless to say are intimately connected —population and the relation between town and country. When Ghana set up on its own in 1957 at the start of the independence era, no one in Africa, or in the United Nations, or for that matter anywhere else, had any inkling of this central fact. Less than nine years later the First African Population Conference was being held at Ibadan University. By February 1967 the Arusha declaration of President Nyerere of Tanzania had introduced the first real attempt by political leadership in the new Africa to deal with the division between urban élites and the peasantry. And three months after that, in capitalist Ivory Coast of all places, the Ministry of Planning was issuing a three-line whip to emphasise the serious *déséquilibre ville-campagne*, and calling for a coherent strategy of national development to rectify the uneven growth of different regions of the country. The real priorities were emerging into the light of day.

No country in the world yet has a population policy in the proper sense of the term. African countries can scarcely be blamed for being as far as any others from framing one. For a real population policy is hard to frame, and harder still to execute. It has to concern itself with the relations between the current generation and the unborn on one side of it, the dead on the other. It has to disabuse the living of their brash conceit that they constitute the weightiest element in this working trinity. It has to convince them that only as modest collaborators with the other two elements can they hope to conduct their own brief lives well.

Their eyes must be opened to the fact that the new generation has not merely to be cherished and reared after its entry upon our scene; it has also to be selected and recruited before that. Correspondingly, as the old generation makes its exit, such worthy contributions to the arts of humane living as it has made are to be stored and organised and kept generally available as a current account for their successors to drawn on.[1] The efficient discharge of these tasks, plus the making of contributions of their own to the common fund, encompass all the duties and all the rights that the living can own.

No African state yet thinks along such lines, still less founds policy upon such thinking. But there are several countries in whose official circles the notion dimly dawns that there is such a thing as overpopulation in relation to available resources, and even the more advanced notion that while your biology is wrong, you will never get your politics or economics right. Some Africans can be found to ask what precisely is the point of procreation if you lack the equipment to rear, train, and employ offspring. Many more see that a population growth rate of 3 per cent a year is on any reckoning far too high. They start shrinkingly away from its consequences, without distinctly comprehending what these are.

In principle, the first steps most pressingly required are (a) a fully informed decision as to the optimum growth rate in the particular circumstances of the given country, (b) concrete

[1] In principle a straightforward matter in the computer age.

measures to ensure that the chosen optimum is not exceeded.

Until these steps are taken, substantial modernisation in tropical Africa is out of the question, since neither balance nor league of economic expansion and social growth can be brought about. In all the new Africa the only two countries where such steps are even imaginable yet are Guinea and Kenya.

How long will tropical Africa condemn itself to the stagnation, the crumbling, the waste, the unmeaning violence which are the inevitable results of ignoring this issue? To judge by the present state of African public sentiment, a 20-year sentence is the most lenient that can be hoped for. Truly this is harsh enough; for if the social problems which chastise the body politic in the torture-chamber of population growth are whips today, those chastising it a generation hence will be scorpions.

The demographic question, because it is fundamental in an absolute sense, is quite a-political. It affects every state system, no matter what its ideological complexion, in exactly the same way. Not so its great partner in mischief, *le déséquilibre ville-campagne*. Any attempt to cope with the latter leads straight to a hornet's-nest of competing class-interests. And the rivalries are of a complex kind, since they are active at three distinct levels of feeling and action.

The first level is global, and concerns what we have called the A.A.L.A. Gap—the broad difference in living standards between the over-developed and the under-developed countries of the earth, between the North Atlantic world and the tropical world, between world-industry and world-peasantry.

In a logical view one might expect all the countries of the new Africa to share a common attitude here, since they are all on the same side of the Gap. They all suffer from its organic consequence, the dreadful disease of under-development. For them all the source of infection is the same. Over many generations they have all been the victims of North Atlantic aggression and oppression. Actually, however (and illogically), the new African states, though all belong and are inextricably tied to the Third World, are still a long way from feeling a common loyalty to it, or even from envisaging a common policy for it. No doubt the spirit of Bandung will return one day to dwell among them, but for the moment it has no power upon their consuming love for their consuming hatreds.

True, there is good agreement among them that the terms of trade between the over-developed and the under-developed countries are inequitable. They do not differ, therefore, at any rate in principle, as to the need for joint Third World pressure on the N.A.T.O. countries to rectify the position, both directly by modifying the terms of trade and indirectly by "development aid".[1] But what is the ultimate aim of such pressure?

The answers given to this question vary over a wide range. It is curious to find two neighbouring countries, both francophone, marking opposite ends of the spectrum, on the one hand Guinea, on the other the Ivory Coast.

For Guinea the aim is to put an end to commercial and financial dependence on the over-developed countries by building an African economy not wholly self-sufficient indeed, but based primarily on inter-African exchange of goods, capital, manpower, and services. Emphasis is placed on the country's Pan-African and international responsibilities, on the fact that it does not and must not try to stand alone, on the promise of salvation through Third World solidarity against its centuries-old exploiters. The foreign aid that Guinea cares to accept comes mainly from its companions in the Third World and from communist countries, because these are all free from the taint of N.A.T.O.'s ancient tyrannies.

For the Ivory Coast, on the contrary, wisdom consists in the pursuit of a strong domestic economy which retains strong links with the colonising power. Sovereignty as distinct from autonomy is regretted as a fate forced on it by adverse circumstance. The African ruling group has therefore given French private enterprise its head through an investment policy of maximum

[1] The intransigence of the N.A.T.O. countries at the second U.N.C.T.A.D. conference held in New Delhi February–March 1968 showed that such pressure has little effect. In contrast, the President of the conference in his closing address, observed that "the Socialist countries have fulfilled our expectations".

attractive power. E.E.C. countries, in recent years adding their participation to France's, have been welcomed, but the Ivory Coast will take no communist aid even with a disinfected barge-pole.

Lip-service is sometimes paid to the need for closer economic co-operation between African states (provided they are not anglophone), but operative policy is directed to sabotaging any attempt to bring it about. The attitude to the rest of the Third World is one of indifference; indeed, the Ivory Coast has no feeling of forming part of it at all.

The Ivory Coast proposes to emerge from under-development not in company and in solidarity with the Third World, but by brushing the Third World off and leaving it behind. The Ivory Coast will leap the A.A.L.A. Gap alone, by virtue of its own internal expansion. If the expansion is bought at the price of turning the country into a backyard of European capitalism, well and good. That may well be a passing phase. A gradual transformation into Ivoirian capitalism is mildly hoped for, though not strenuously sought. Meanwhile, the Ivory Coast hopes to have caught up with the European Joneses, and won acceptance as a member of the N.A.T.O. club.

If Tanzania stands with Guinea, Malawi, using the white racialists of Southern Africa instead of France, lines up with the Ivory Coast. The rest of the new Africa takes up one or another of the many locations intermediate between these two poles. In each case the actual stance adopted is largely a response to the behaviour of the richer countries outside Africa.

Like the Third World in general, Africa, in its relation with the North Atlantic world, exemplifies after its own fashion what Henry George towards the end of the nineteenth century was fond of calling "the great enigma of our time", namely the association of poverty with progress. Affluent people, in contemplating the active presence of others' destitution in the midst of their own riches, are never able to acknowledge that the contrasting tendencies are reciprocal functions of one another. They do, however, as a tacit substitute, sometimes develop a mid-Victorian sense of sin (not for attribution). A favourite cure for a bad conscience about the poor has always been to buy it off by giving them money, while leaving their role and status otherwise unchanged. Hence the proliferation of charitable societies in Victorian England. Hence also, on the international plane, the current proliferation of agencies for "aid to under-developed countries".

Naturally enough in these circumstances the reaction of most African countries is not to draw out the resources of their continent by their own energies, with a view to creating a wholesome and satisfying social environment for themselves. Nor is it to follow the Ivory Coast example of using the old colonial power as a springboard from which to leap the A.A.L.A. Gap. It is the simpler reaction of exploiting bad consciences about African poverty wherever they can be found, and tapping richer countries for all the hard cash they can be shamed into parting with.

They soon learn, like any professional beggar, how to play on ideological susceptibilities so as to promote a keen competition in which capitalist countries and communist countries outbid one another in efforts of charity. Of course, Africans insist with some complacency that it is less charity than compensation, just a small step towards the righting of old wrongs. They fail to perceive, or they perceive without regret, that by inuring them to habits of settled mendicancy, it turns their countries into almshouses and their citizens into pensioners of the very authors of their poverty.

Counting on other people's bad consciences, however, cannot furnish a trustworthy footing for African development, since the bad consciences themselves are quickly dispelled. Rich countries, like any professional social worker, soon find it both useless and wrong to give to all who ask, especially if the asking and the receiving are accompanied by a multitude of pitiful little frauds. A kind of repentance for their earlier remorse sets in. They reproach themselves for seeking a sense of virtue on the cheap, by means which actually injure the community and the almsfolk alike.

Thus they form themselves into a kind of Charity Organisation Society to co-ordinate one another's "aid" activities. Policy becomes based on a sharp distinction between the deserving poor and all other varieties of down-and-out. The temperature of charity sinks to zero. The cringing almsfolk, now written off as not worth helping, are harshly told to try living on cake if they find breadwinning too difficult.

Finally, charity is frankly renounced in favour of the mere gain-seeking of merchant and money-lender. The tide of "aid" from the rich countries is not merely stopped, it is reversed. It ebbs from the poor, and flows from them to the rich. In the Ivory Coast during the 1950's 60 per cent of all investments went into the public sector. Since 1964 it is the private sector which has accounted for two-thirds. In 1965 private transfers out of the country to Europe amounted to more than twice the amount of foreign aid and private capital which came into the country in the same year.[1] According to Le Monde of 8 March 1967, the developed countries as a group have to date made profits from their trade with the under-developed countries as a group rather greater than the $8 billion which they have "granted" them as "aid". Old-model colonial exploitation resumes its sway. The wheel has come full circle.

The parallel with the organisation of charitable effort in Victorian England can be taken further. The permanently valid lesson of that period was that charity, whether organised or not, has no part to play in solving the problem of poverty. Destitution in England at the peak of the country's wealth and power was not checked by any condescension of the well-to-do. It was checked by self-help and mutual aid among the victims—by the network of non-conformist chapels, by the far-flung friendly societies, by the trade unions, and by that odd kind of shop, the co-op store. The generalisation, indeed, can fairly be made that poverty in the midst of riches has never given way to anything except the non-conformist conscience moving with instinctive inevitability towards socialist order.

[1] Samir Amin: Le Développement du Capitalisme en Côte d'Ivoire. (Paris Editions de Minuit, 1967.)

Once upon a time this generalisation might have been regarded as partisan. There are still backwaters where doctrinaire capitalists maintain the fiction that it is controversial. Their case was disproved long ago by the overwhelming evidence of practical experience. The pretence that the issue is even now an open one shows nothing but the power of misplaced desire to detach belief from fact. Africans deceive themselves if they suppose it "objective" to keep an open mind on a closed question. Actually it is easy to discern that, whatever may be the witting attitudes of Africans, Africa and all the Third World today is, with the same instinctive inevitability, groping its way along the trail blazed by the British working-class movement three generations ago.

In the English case the non-conformist conscience methodically overhauled the machinery of government, and re-tooled it for social welfare. The prospect is that, acting from similar motives, the Third World will gradually relieve the N.A.T.O. countries of their burden of world-authority, and proceed by a variety of routes to build world-socialism. African countries which are in any sense alive to this probability, and seeking to accelerate it, are not yet many. But some exist, and their existence cannot but leaven the lump of their less alert neighbours. The latter group may be little more than analogues of the "sturdy beggars" of the Elizabethan Poor Law—mere able-bodied but pauperised unemployed. The point is that an African mind is already emerging in which there begins to crystallise a realistic view of how the African population will have to settle its own problems for itself.

CHAPTER 16

PEASANT TRUTH

THE SECOND LEVEL of the town-country dilemma is national; that is to say, internal to each African country. Precisely as our current world-disorder springs from the total estrangement on a global scale of urban industry from peasant agriculture, so Africa's current internal disorder springs from the severance of peasant production and consumption from the modernising sector of the domestic economy which is located in the trading ports and other urban and industrial centres. In other words, the macro-chaos of the human race is rooted in the A.A.L.A. Gap, the inward micro-chaos of the new African states is rooted in the Onitiri Gap.

It is an easy inference that there can be no world-peace till the A.A.L.A. Gap is closed, and no social unity within or between the new African states till the Onitiri Gap is closed. Easy, but also sterile and otiose. For it is impossible in practice, and undesirable in theory, to close either Gap. As we have seen, what the Third World is up against is the need to build, in divorce from the ·N.A.T.O. countries, a new civilisation of its own that fits its own proper talents and the tropical habitat. Equally the job of the African peasantry is to discover and develop a new rural culture uncontaminated by the aims and values which inform the forces of African urbanism.

The Onitiri Gap is a legacy of a colonial system that felt nothing but contempt for the tribal peasantry. And the political leadership still in power in the new Africa, therefore, which thinks of itself as the legatee of the colonialists, by no means wants to see the last of it.[1] This is especially true of the many countries whose "independence" was thrust upon them or

---

[1] There are, to be sure, the usual exceptions—primarily Guinea and Tanzania, secondarily Mali, Kenya, Zambia.

reached through mini-struggle. For there the mild course of events threw up as leaders not decolonising statesmen, but those know-all, slap-up, wily, overdressed intellectuals, dusted over with expatriate culture, whom the street-crowds still cheer as, heralded by motorcades, they purr by in glossy limousines.

"We find intact in them," observes Frantz Fanon with his typical well-judged violence, "the manners and forms of thought picked up during their association with the colonialist bourgeoisie. Spoilt children of yesterday's colonialism and of today's national governments, they organise the loot of whatever national resources exist. Without pity, they use today's national distress as a means of getting on through scheming and legal robbery, by import-export combines, limited liability companies, gambling on the stock-exchange, or unfair promotion."[1]

Fanon might well have added that these leaders are direct spiritual descendants of those African middlemen, indispensable partners for many centuries in the slave trade, and often even more heartless and venal than the Europeans or Arabs to whom they sold their stolen youths, women, and children. Admittedly the kind of slavery into which they sell their compatriots today is a modernised one, and their trading methods are shrewdly depersonalised.

Shortage of alternative personnel may keep wasters of this type in office a little longer, but not much. Having revealed themselves as quite unequal to leading their countries along any new and worthy road, they already begin to float out of history on their own emptiness and the heat of their people's anger at their ravages. Not by such as them will the problem of the Onitiri Gap be tackled. It will be tackled by the peasant community itself, reinforced by a backward surge of genuine (i.e. decolonised) intellectuals towards bases of thought, feeling, and action grounded in that community.

For the native intellectual, self-decolonisation and insight into his own real situation are one and the same thing. In the moment of this process he again makes touch with his peasant folk, and puts his shoulder alongside theirs in concrete exertion

[1] *Les damnés de la terre.* (Paris, Marpero, 1961.)

towards social growth. In that moment he grasps, and marvels at, their good faith. It is not merely that they are honest in themselves and with him. It is that they embody the truth, all of truth that Africa can boast, all the truth that the intellectual has never met before.

Thus the intellectual, in discovering his peasant neighbour, at last finds himself. From now on "the danger that will haunt him continually is that of becoming an uncritical mouthpiece of the masses, a kind of yes-man who nods assent at every word coming from the people, greeting it as if it were considered judgment".[1] He is rescued by the peasants themselves, who have no interest in an echo, or even in a public relations officer to give them a good image. They ask one thing only—that all resources should be pooled.This, their dumb subjective demand, is also their silent objective contribution to reconstruction.

For the intellectual the dumb demand defines his own articulate answer. His relation to the peasantry becomes a kind of organic problem-solving reunion, in which the peasant intuits the end and the intellectual elaborates the means. The peasant plays poet opposite the intellectual's scientist. Peasants, just because they alone have nothing to lose and everything to win, are engined by the great driving force of all social growth—instinctive inevitability. The intellectual, as their map-reader and technical consultant, becomes an active and essential partaker in a revolution of which, without them, he could only have vainly prattled.

The third level at which the imbalance of town and country calls for action is the level of organisation and methods. These, we have argued, must be collectivist in principle, both because no approach to solving the problem of poverty in the midst of wealth has ever been made except by means of socialism of some kind,[2] and also because the peasant cry "Pool all resources" is itself a demand for some kind of socialism. Capitalist

---

[1] Fanon, op. cit.

[2] The genuineness of any professed socialism is measured by the degree of practical success in handling this problem.

procedures, being designed rather for maximising spoils and sharing them among an élite, rule themselves out of court in this context. Africa's main instrument is manifestly an apparatus of development planning one of whose principal guidelines is equality of opportunity for all citizens. For the disequilibrium to be treated is a joint product of unregulated demographic forces and unregulated market forces.

The objective fact constituting the point of departure for development planning in the new Africa today is that urban expansion, since its consequences are largely negative from the standpoint of modernising a country as a whole, is not a rational way of using economic resources. It is impossible for any country in tropical Africa to create city services fast enough to cope with an urbanism that increases at its present rate, unless the claims of rural development are effectively ignored, and probably not even then.

All the new African Governments will cheerfully agree verbally that top priority must be accorded to rural reconstruction. In practice, however, no such reconstruction takes place, and the countryside together with its peasantry continues to be degraded to a mere utensil of rampant urban centres. Whatever line of policy official quarters may proclaim, there are deeply ingrained tendencies for development impulses to flock together, by unthinking routine, into the towns. No one is yet able to forestall or neutralise them. Yet neutralised they must be, if social order is not to collapse.

The six essential steps towards this end were detailed in Chapter 9, and need not be repeated here. They are all concerned with keeping the size of the urban population in phase with the development of rural production and with productivity in the totality of rural enterprise. They represent a task of complex difficulty which, in the case of the N.A.T.O. countries, has proved far too much for the available political capacity. In consequence these countries, it appears, are no longer able to attain any rural-urban balance at all, nor therefore to make any general adaptation of a constructive kind to the changing conditions of their world.

In Africa there is perhaps still time to escape such evolutionary inadequacy. Indeed, this is one major point where it is better to be underdeveloped than overdeveloped. Africa is still free to choose undistorted modes of development, if it has the wisdom to do so. The muscle-bound N.A.T.O. countries are so fettered by such multitudes of past maladaptive choices that now they can scarcely move. Having overshot the mark at which current amendment may cancel earlier blunders, they can only sit and wait for whatever is coming to them.

In Africa as a whole urbanisation is still no higher than 10–12 per cent, compared (for example) with Britain's 78 per cent and 54 per cent in U.S.S.R. The continent retains a vast rural hinterland available for development as genuine countryside so as to exhibit the full range and richness of rural culture. Hence Africa alone among continents still has something like a clean slate, where the question of town-country balance is concerned. Degeneracy has unmistakably set in, but it can be reversed if the proper treatment is applied; whereas in N.A.T.O. countries and some others (e.g. India) it is already unstoppable by curative measures of a politically acceptable, or feasible, kind.

Yet again one must repeat that even in this specially favoured Africa, no proper urban-rural balance can be achieved until population growth itself is subjected to the logic of development planning. This is the ineluctable precondition for all African modernisation.

These things, one must also repeat, are all matters of socialist order. No system grounded in individualist "free enterprise" can make any impression on them. For a major weakness of capitalist method in its present decadence is that, while it can have a go at *restrictionist* planning for the differential advantage of a sectional interest, it has no motive for *development* planning in any general public interest. However, the question remains "What sort of socialism?" There exists in the world today a wide and increasing range of variant socialist systems.

All of them have been devised to meet non-African conditions; hence it is unlikely that any can be taken over, lock, stock, and barrel, as a standard model for African countries. Africa has good grounds for critical eclecticism, the more so as, in spite of all the chatter, no African form of socialism exists either as viable régime or even as coherent idea. Hints will no doubt be taken from U.S.S.R. and Eastern Europe as well as from China and Cuba. They are all rich mines for the development planner.

A careful study of the Chinese experience since 1950 may well be the most rewarding, since China alone so far has founded its whole development strategy on the rural domain as the crucial point of departure for a balanced modernisation. And this is the broad approach that all the new Africa will be obliged to follow, if not out of admiration for the Chinese example, then in obedience to the stringent law of its own situation. That is why this book includes a skeleton account of the Chinese system.[1]

[1] See Appendix D.

CHAPTER 17

SUB SPECIE EVOLUTIONIS

POPULATION POLICY AND policies for establishing a valid town-country balance are long-term affairs. Even if all Africa were to embark tomorrow on all the wisest measures under both heads, beneficial results could not begin to manifest themselves on any sizeable scale much before the end of the century. The modern politician will certainly, therefore, invoke the Principle of Unripe Time as a reason for inaction indefinitely prolonged. But to choose inaction now in these two crucial areas is to render nugatory all action in all other areas. This is the real African dilemma, and a very painful one it is.

However, nothing could be plainer than that wise measures are not going to be embarked on tomorrow, or in any near future, even if some leaders of insight might wish to take them. The diagnosis is not yet even understood in Africa, let alone accepted there. Come the day when it is both, the lag between diagnosis and prescription is likely to be protracted. Building up the will to apply the prescription and the machinery for doing so can be no quick job. Also implementation depends for success on some concurrent economic improvement and on some continuing social growth.

What are the chances of such improvement and such growth in the new Africa over the next thirty years? No one who has recently been over the terrain and kept his eyes open could possibly reckon them as better than slender. It is much more likely that the confused routs of the Congo, the Sudan, Nigeria, to mention only the most horrific examples, will spread until in many parts orderly living collapses, and a war-lord period sets in propped up by gangs of foreign looters and mercenaries.

There is a mass of evidence that Africa is now in a phase in which "the niggers beat each other up", as Fanon puts it, speaking as a man of colour himself, but using in bitter jest the language of the colonialists; a phase of collective auto-destruction at the level of communal organisations. Fanon explains it as a pattern of avoidance behaviour, a death reflex in the face of danger, which enables large numbers of Africans to plunge into a fraternal blood-bath as a simplified substitute for grappling directly with the real authors of their insupportable frustrations.

Africans, Fanon thinks, are in general long-persecuted persons whose enduring dream is to become the persecutors. Provided they can steep themselves deeply in outrage, they care little on whom it is committed. Not the target, but the release of frenzy is the important thing. In the African situation the handiest outlet is another tribe, another clan. This psychological device will be employed, and therefore this phase will last, until Africans learn to identify, by the discriminating use of an adequate conceptual apparatus, the stumbling-blocks and booby-traps which imperil their social advance, and to evolve rational political principles for removing them.

Even if home-grown African chaos is kept under some sort of control, there is still the prospect of widening chaos in the non-African world, and the question of its influence inside Africa. In June 1967 the World Food Panel of President Lyndon Johnson's Scientific Advisory Committee issued a warning that a world food crisis of staggering proportions was likely to occur by 1985. Generalised famine, brought on by the A.A.L.A. Gap and involving large populations in Asia and Latin America, may well antedate this prediction by five years, as Dumont has urged.[1] It is quite on the cards that the great war in Asia may in a flash spread without limit; and China knows, or thinks it knows, that it has been selected for a joint military attack by U.S.A. and U.S.S.R. The Mediterranean and Middle Eastern crisis will certainly re-erupt in many unforeseen ways.

We are, in short, already in the presence of a wide, though not well organised, rising of the Third World against the N.A.T.O. élite, which in its turn is already in the very act of

[1] René Dumont: *Chine Surpeuplée* (Editions du Seuil, Paris, 1965.)

taking all measures to put the rising down. From the effects of this conjuncture few bolt-holes will remain open for long in any part of the world.

So comfortless as well as so ubiquitous, indeed, do these effects promise to be that statesmanship is obliged to re-think the whole issue of world war. People have tended to regard nuclear war, together with its apocalyptic partners chemical and biological war, as the ultimate disaster which those incompetent triflers known as men could call down on themselves. This view manifestly underrates human resourcefulness. The A.A.L.A. Gap is now cleverly presenting us with a less eligible alternative.

If peace might mean a general harmony and friendship in human relations, some, perhaps even most, men would still choose it; though this must remain doubtful, in view of the growing company of hate-addicts to whom enemies are more necessary than friends. Present conditions of human living are on average, however, so unwholesomely congested that peace can no longer bear any such construction. Thus the disjunction "either peace or war" is emptied of current significance in the life of nations. Today peace is definable only as non-war. Non-war is definable only as a state in which a large majority of the human race, a majority increasing at unmanageable speed, cannot be kept in health, or educated, or trained for any occupation, or provided with any employment, or even soundly nourished.

When the choice between war and non-war is presented in such terms, reasonable grounds for preferring non-war are much to seek. The grounds on which in former times nations held days of prayer for peace simply have no meaning here. Neither the most devout nor the most sinful nor anybody in between could be moved to pray for the blessing of non-war as just described. This is a dilemma which has not hitherto arisen in human experience. Hence it is hard for the current generation to make an assured approach to it. Our descendants, if we have any, may understand it better. Meanwhile it is perhaps the part of grave wisdom to greet war, with all its modern knobs on, as our deliverer from non-war.

What a fall is here. And what a theme for a modern Aristophanes. How man, the sui-genocide, is offered a choice of weapons, a rough one of mindful violence and a smooth one of mindless lechery; how, calling on his reserves of logic, humour, and good sense, he weighs up the pros and cons; how he takes pains to process the data through his computers; and how, so advised, he settles at length for violence as the more stylish and less boring executioner.

The new Africa cannot stand outside this common human impasse. Along with the rest, it has to take a common punishment in the shape either of war or non-war. This is unjust, since Africans have done nothing to fix such alternatives or to merit such punishment. But this is the common abyss to which the N.A.T.O. countries have driven the world. We are all, with no exemptions, involved in it.

We may say with a sigh that were Africa only to be blessed with thirty steady years of growing prosperity and peaceful social construction, it would stand a faint chance of making a faint dent in the problems of population and town-country balance by the year 2000. In practice, however, looking to the A.A.L.A. Gap and the bomb-syndrome, that blessing is not likely to be vouchsafed. Without it, the outlook is deepening degradation (self-inflicted) or enormous devastation (imported) or both. It is within a broad context of this kind that the realist is obliged to consider Africa's future.

He may find some comfort in the reflection that nothing can be done yet from inside Africa to modify the world context, and that Africa's only possible policy meantime is to do the best it can with the demographic and the urban-rural issues.

In this case, what sense is there in speaking of an African renaissance? Would not the dark night of the dark continent be an honester label for the coming years? It certainly looks as if a dark night is being and to be lived through. But this need not mean that the early stages of re-birth do not overlap with it. After all, in that New Start which we call the European renaissance the artistic and intellectual triumphs of the Tuscans

8

and their neighbours took place in a general social setting of much turbulence and disorder. Then also re-birth was tricked out with an *obbligato* of passionate vice and dumb bewilderment. The combination of war and non-war in which we are already so deeply involved today is indeed more destructive than the battles between Florence, Pisa, Lucca, Siena. But the differences are largely in the scale and the method.

It is often said that our current global war, when its full resources of undoing are deployed, must once for all denude the earth of life, at any rate of human life. The better the probabilities are weighed, however, the harder it becomes to suppose that, even in that extreme event, no life-protecting nook, no crevice anywhere in mountain or in valley, in cave or in sea or hollowed out of ice, would evade the miasma of annihilation. The point can only be settled experimentally. Meanwhile, it does not do to underrate the organic stubbornness of life. And if it should turn out that even real sophisticated war cannot be equated with total extermination, life will build up again step by step, and the problem of what to do about it will again raise its ugly head. Survivors will then have to re-ponder the old familiar theme of post-war (and post non-war) reconstruction. Africa's big job is to prepare for that moment, for when it comes a special responsibility will be laid on Africans.

Basically all that has happened is that man's first attempt to invent civilisation has failed. This need surprise no one. To pass from the savage to the civilised state is a highly complex operation. It would be astonishing if the first attempt, necessarily based on random trial and error, had succeeded. From our present vantage-point it is obvious that the cause of failure was over-reliance on war and slavery as constitutive principles. The ocular demonstration of our time that cultural machinery worked by such motive power quickly and irretrievably breaks down, enforces a useful lesson. Consequently the seven thousand years or so during which the attempt has been going on, have not been altogether wasted. No doubt the lesson would have been more promptly absorbed if the leaders of the movement had listened to the best advice on offer. But to anyone who looks at the matter *sub specie evolutionis* (which is the right way), a mere seven millennia seems a remarkably, even a creditably, short span.

When, by reason of changes in their environment, the dinosaurs lost their power of biological adaptation, the species became extinct. And this is a fate, of course, which has overtaken multitudes of other species too. *Homo lupus*, wolf-man of our present type, is like them a failed evolutionary product. But he is not quite in the same boat. Their evolutionary unfitness, being physical, was also final; they got no second chance. But man's evolutionary unfitness is not physical; it is of the mind, cultural. He can look back over the record and, if he spots where he went wrong, it is open to him to return to Square One and try all over again.

Theologians call the procedure repentance. To the social psychologist, and to the lawgiver, it is the search for alternative solutions to intractable problems. Admittedly, in the case we are discussing, the repentance is not very voluntary, since the contemporary world-experience of combined war and nonwar, pressed home to the hilt, is needed to compel the strategic alteration. Yet the compulsion is not quite absolute either, nor is man wholly passive in its hands. It arouses in him a response, albeit ambivalent, and a teachability, albeit rudimentary.

Hence in man's case, which seems to be unique in this respect, what becomes extinct is not the species but the civilisation. The old cultural moulds are smashed that formed man's mentality and made of him the creature he became. But the race persists, no matter how drastically self-destruction may reduce its numbers. Man recovers his biological adaptability by dismantling the social environment he could not adapt to, and by substituting for it one to which he can adapt. He cures his evolutionary impotence by pitchforking out of the window the morbid culture that induced it.

In the loss of a *raison d'être* by the white man's civilisation, there is nothing for tears. Regret is not a fit emotion for hailing the last bang and the last whimper of a régime which, out of all possible policies, selected the policy of annihilating all living things on the face of the earth. To have made this choice is the very top, the height, the crest, the crest unto the crest of murder's arms. All murders past do stand excused in this, the desperation of wholesale and irredeemable failure. Here brutal self-will has wrenched, for a brief moment, the cosmic process out of the true. Nature itself exacts the inevitable penalty.

It is not easy for white men to make a general confession that the civilisation in which they have been reared, which by their daily deeds they fondly seek to sustain, and towards which they feel a strong, though alarmingly irrational, loyalty, is today quite pointless and unnecessary. That conclusion, however, is readily and logically drawn from the plain facts by non-white men in all parts of the world. Hence white men are not brought to the temper of total contrition and unreserved amending solicitude which alone could become them. Hence also non-white men halt prematurely at the notion that, once N.A.T.O. has been evicted from the world arena, their troubles will be at an end, the road to heaven unmissable.

In truth, their real troubles will be just beginning, though happily they will be *real* troubles, the honest strain of building a new civilisation to a new design, not the mere vexation of anxious *débrouillage* in a savage world they never made and would never have dreamt of making. Among non-white men, as was said above, the survivors will look in a special sense to the black people of Africa. After America, Europe, and Asia have completed their act of mutual extirpation, whether by war or by non-war, those Africans who have not been laid low in the general holocaust will comprise humanity's main strategic reserves.

This is important, partly because, in the context foreseen, physical devastation may well be less in Africa than elsewhere. People eager to destroy Africa are fewer than those who yearn for the destruction of the other continents. Many interests that cherish generally destructive aims are under the delusion that they will in any event be able to control Africa. They therefore incline to leave it relatively unscathed. Moreover the African habitat, for climatic and ecological reasons, is exceptionally capable of shrugging off any work of man, including maybe the work of chemical, biological, and nuclear warriors. Thus there is some prospect that a sufficient contingent of African survivors might emerge from the climax to form a viable society. And Africans have unrivalled experience of how to keep going, especially as peasants, even when by normal standards they are not viable. Urban types, whatever their racial breed, will have much lower survival capacity and survival value in the post-climax world.

There is a weightier reason still why the post-climax lawgiver should extend a particular welcome to Africans as recruits for and builders of his non-urban civilisation. For civilisation of any kind there is but one organic starting-point, the neolithic revolution and its cardinal invention of food-production. From here all humane culture and all productive technology derive. Our lawgiver's task is to get back to the peduncle-base, the neolithic point on the main evolutionary stem whence the first civilisation once hopefully branched out, to encompass all the globe yet come at last to such stupendous grief. Lopping off the cankered wood that had carried the aberrant *homo lupus*, he finds close at hand a new cultural bud, whose divergent growth moves towards a new variant, later to be named *homo bene volens*, man of good will.

During the seven thousand years in which western civilisation has been pushing out from the tree of life, this other bud has remained dormant, patiently awaiting its evolutionary opportunity—which comes at length with the die-back of the *homo lupus* branch. Africans are this bud, or a main element in it. They feel at home in the neolithic, for their feet are still firmly planted in it. African peasants, who comprise four-fifths of all Africans, live a daily life whose pattern closely resembles that of neolithic man. The neolithic outlook, based on ties of kin, has found in them a decent immortality.

When modern Europeans meet the African peasant, they stand, culturally speaking, in the presence of their own first ancestor. If they have good feeling and an eye for their own condition, they know themselves to be his prodigal sons—those crazed self-opposites who lost sight of nature's unity, rebelled against her guiding hand, and then sneaked off, sunk in vile fears and pleasures, to feed the swine in a far country. In this way they sometimes learn to fetch up into awareness that hatred of themselves for being what they are, which at all times forms in their hearts so powerful a subconscious motive.

The African peasant is a man who, so far as concerns his insights, beliefs, and desires, that is to say his civilisation, quietly outspanned at the proto-human stage, and let the great trek go on without him. The white man, for his part, after a frenzied journey of alternating promise and disaster, now reaches the odd destination of a subhuman stage. After seven thousand years of toil and trouble, he ends up lower than he started, able to make no better claim than that his subhumanity is of superhuman dimensions. He embodies, that is to say, a civilisation which, possessing the gifts to transcend the human, misuses them to negate it.

The African is in a real sense underdeveloped; his flaws are all deficiencies which can be made good. The white man is in an equally real sense overdeveloped; his flaws are all excesses too deeply ingrained to be unlearnt. In the post-climax world the African may re-live, in a new growing fashion of his own, all yesterday's seven thousand years, and so put the species back on the straight path. The white man's old wood cannot flower again. Humanity's chance of a second shot at civilisation, if it gets one, may be due in part to Africa's consistent refusal through the centuries to yield to the cultural aggression of the west.

Africans have other assets besides the key-asset of recalcitrance to the precepts and example of *homo lupus*. Among these is their secure possession of the characteristic psychological equipment of neolithic man. In this equipment lies their capacity to lead a new and healthier expansion of the human force.

We should greatly err in thinking of either African peasants or those spirited food-producing pioneers as feckless starveling nomads shoved by buffets of misfortune from pillar to post, all their wealth a dead buck and a small heap of millet or palm-huts, "their old age sores and leprosy, their religion a few stones in the centre of the village where the dead chiefs lie, a grove of trees where the rice-birds build their nests, a man in a mask with raffia skirts dancing at burials."[1]

When neolithic man first scattered a handful of barley on the wet silt, or dug a strip of garden with a stone hoe in hope that punctual rain would start the seed, he opened the most momentous revolution our species has ever known. He bridged the gulf that divides the hunter's life from civilisation. He invented mind—and so enabled the tragi-comedy of *homo lupus*, who rose by using his mind and fell in abusing it.

In their uncouth way the early food-producers waxed and prospered in a richly expressive life. They filled it with laughter and beauty that held deep meaning for them, and now seems the most courageous thing in nature. They decked it out with feasts, with drum-beats of involuted, shoulder-shaking metre, with mimetic dances. They carved with high accomplishment in wood and stone and bone, their art now exalted in serene expression, now twisted by the bugaboos of shameful sorcery. Masters of cunning woodcraft, readers of the skies, lovers of children and of the dead, well tuned to the virtue of the common life, they wore in figure and carriage such rhythm and such symmetry as delights one in a stanza of fine verse.

Theirs is the life which still flows, magically preserved and only superficially corrupted, in African veins today. It is the life which, in its simplicity and its limitless potential, qualifies them better than many other sorts and conditions of men to restore our race's broken home. Africans themselves are half-aware of this. It is this they half-grasp when they yearn after their own negritude, when they reach backward to a past they can take joy in, far back beyond the degradations of century upon century of slavery—to an era of Africa's untainted nature.

Unformulated as yet, they know in their bones and in their muscles an endowment of qualities and values which the west

[1] Graham Greene: *Journey without Maps.*

has never had or has long lost. They strive passionately to dig it out, as if it were some earthquake-victim buried under the debris of the wolf-man's prison house. Their instinctively inevitable resolve is to rescue it for life in the timelessness, the spontaneity, the free discipline, the creative brotherhood which are proper to Africa and to *homo bene volens*.

APPENDICES

APPENDIX A

FIGURES OF AREA, POPULATION, OUTPUT

Country	Date of Independence	Area (,000 sq.Kms.)	1964 Population (millions)	Population Growth per cent per yr.	Gross Domestic Product per head at current market prices 1959	1964
Kenya	1963	582·6	9·1	3·0	£27·2	£30·9
Malawi	1964	119·3	3·9	3·0	£14·9	£12·9
Rhodesia	1965	389·4	4·1	3·3	£80·2	£88·4
TANZANIA:						
Tanganyika	1961	937·1	10·0	2·2	£20·6	£26·1
Zanzibar	1963	2·6	0·335	1·9	£35·0	?
Uganda	1962	236·0	7·4	2·5	£22·9	£27·1
Zambia	1964	752·6	3·6	3·0	£62·5	£69·2
Gambia	1965	11·3	0·324	2·4	£30·0	£33·0
Ghana	1957	238·5	7·8	3·0	£90·0	£90·0
Liberia	1847	111·4	1·1	1·4	£82·0	£100·0
Nigeria	1960	923·8	50·0	2·0	£19·4	£20·7
Sierra Leone	1961	71·7	2·2	2·0	£48·7	£54·6
Cameroon	1961	475·4	5·1	2·9	£36·0	£44·0
Chad	1960	1,284·0	3·3	1·5	£25·0	£27·0

Dahomey	1960	112·6	3·0	3·0	?	£26·0
Guinea	1958	245·9	3·7	2·8	£23·0	£28·0
Ivory Coast	1960	322·5	3·8	3·3	£69·0	£93·0
Mali	1960	1,201·6	4·5	2·3	£23·0	£26·0
Mauritania	1960	1,030·7	0·9	2·2	£26·0	£48·0
Niger	1960	1,267·0	3·3	3·4	£25·0	£30·0
Senegal	1960	196·2	3·4	2·3	£68·0	£70·0
Togo	1960	56·6	1·6	2·8	£33·0	£34·0
Upper Volta	1960	274·2	4·8	3·2	£17·0	?

APPENDIX B

		Page
§1.	The Current Predicament	238
§2.	To Develop the Tribal Areas	239
§3.	Industrial Labour	241
§4.	African Education	244
§5.	The Practical Results	245
§6.	The Curse	247

RHODESIA STORY

§1. *The current predicament*

One of the earliest acts of the first Conservative Party Government in Britain after World War II was to collude with the then Government of Southern Rhodesia in preparing a Central African Federation. The component parts of the Federation were Southern Rhodesia (now Rhodesia), Northern Rhodesia (now Zambia), and Nyasaland (now Malawi).

The policy had a double objective. First, to bar the southward spread of black nationalism by creating a large bloc of territory under the political control of a white minority, mainly located in Rhodesia. Second, to place in the hands of the Federation so controlled the economic advantages deriving from the rich copper mines located in Zambia.

From the moment the Federation came into existence (in 1953), it was manifestly inadequate as a vehicle for the policy. Throughout the ten years for which it managed to survive, civil disturbances among the African populations of all three territories grew in intensity, leading to the final collapse of the Federal structure in December 1963.

Twenty-three months later, on Armistice Day 1965, the white Rhodesians unconstitutionally declared independence, as the first phase of their revenge for the torpedoing of their federal scheme. It is not hard to foresee that the second phase will be the toppling, in collaboration with the South Africans and the Portuguese, of Zambia's African government and the diversion of the copper revenues from Lusaka to Salisbury. The tactics bear a broad resemblance to those of the Nigerian North in its dealings with Biafra.

There is not much likelihood that the revised tactics will lead to more stable or lasting results than the Federation did. The white Rhodesians, in choosing them, have incurred the settled hostility of all black Africa, and increasingly of all the Third World. Rhodesian resistance to the pressures which these forces will be able to bring to bear can only be relatively short-lived. True, the African guerrilla fighters are not yet very skilled performers. But they quite soon will be.

As the movements of the Third World become better co-ordinated, forcing the Americans out of Asia and the Zionists out of Palestine, Southern Africa will pose rather a minor problem. And the white populations there will get no massive help from western nations smarting from painful reverses in the Far East and Middle East.

The composure with which the white Rhodesians have ignored the flutterings of the British Government and the U.N., has led some observers to suppose that their position is a strong one. Actually it is distinctly hazardous—not because of sanctions (which in any case are not effectively applied), but for the simple reason that more than 90 per cent of the Rhodesian population is African. The problem is not to find foreign customers and suppliers; it is to get enough domestic output to trade with. This is hard, so long as a mere 10 per cent of the total population is in a position to produce for the external market at all.

§2. *To develop the tribal areas*

Politically and financially the Rhodesian Government is giving high priority to its "unified programme" for the development of African tribal areas. It knows that by such development alone can its basic problem be solved. Its sense of economic urgency has, as a preliminary, brought about the integration of European and African agriculture within the province of a single Ministry. This step, a departure from the practice of the Federation, acknowledges that in regard to agricultural extension and research services, to marketing opportunities, and to credit facilities, African and European interests are best treated on one and the same basis. Community development (the name given to the programme of local government reform) is likewise officially expounded as applicable to the whole population and is intended to be applied to all races (though not necessarily to populations some of whose members are African and some European).

Until 1964 the difficulties of extending credit facilities to African farmers in tribal areas were regarded as insuperable. But at that time a special Commission made a determined attack on the problem, and recommended innovations by which an African farmer, without having to show title to his land, might borrow, on his own credit-worthiness, as assessed by local loan committees, to meet the costs of fertiliser, spraying, etc. Such loans are channelled through co-operative credit societies wherever possible.

The scheme for African local self-government in rural areas is distinctive for its ingenious attempt to construct local authorities out of the procedures of community development. Beginning, as community development programmes normally begin, with small local groups or associations that undertake to identify and formulate local felt wants, it goes on to combine these largely spontaneous groupings into a much smaller number of local government councils, each large enough to justify an office and a secretary, and to assume the responsibilities of a grant-receiving body that deals direct with the Ministry.

The councils are trained in "black-board" budgeting. On one side a list is drawn up of the services they would wish to provide, noting the estimated cost of each. On the other side are set out their various items of revenue. If outgoings total more than incomings, they must strike an equal balance, either by cutting costs or by raising the difference from a levy on themselves. The guiding principle is that, within the framework of available finance, public affairs of local scope should be managed by local people in their own way, in accordance with priorities settled by themselves. The principle covers local African courts of law as well as social services such as clinics and schools, and environmental services such as roads, bridges, and village water-supplies.

Certain licence revenues are earmarked for the councils, and some forms of provision, such as schools and clinics, qualify for Government grant-in-aid. In certain cases councils may receive a block grant for their general purposes.

§3. *Industrial labour*

On 1 July 1958 the Division of Labour, Social Welfare, and Housing was set up to carry out a new policy in respect of industrial labour. Employers had had it brought home to them that the old one was hampering the growth of the manufacturing sector.

The old policy had in fact grown up almost by accident to meet the increasing demands of European farmers and mining enterprise for labourers. By the middle fifties, in terms of agreements entered into with neighbouring territories, more than 100,000 migrant African labourers were entering Southern Rhodesia each year on free transport services especially provided for them. An equal number made the return journey in the same way. The system indeed supplied labourers to employers who needed them, and it kept wages down. But it also involved a labour turnover of 100 per cent a year, and made it impossible for the migrants to undergo continuous training or acquire any but rudimentary skills. Moreover, it gave rise to an acute social problem by separating men from their families for long periods.

If these features of the situation had remained veiled in the obscurity of the countryside and the mining areas, they might have passed without comment. But the attraction of wages in secondary industry and commerce and the social magnet of urban life itself, set up an unmanageable influx to the towns of unskilled migrants seeking work.

The kind of manpower the migrants had to offer was not the kind of manpower that industrial employers wanted. The employers wanted, not unskilled migrants, but a stable labour force of Africans trained or trainable for semi-skilled and skilled work. In effect their requirements entailed the integration of a settled African labour force into the European industrial economy. And since secondary industry was located in the

towns, it further entailed that African industrial workers should
be resident in the towns.

In human terms, integration of this kind was bound, at least
at first, to be an uneasy process. Language, law, manners and
customs, social habits, racial presuppositions, educational back-
ground, general knowledge, the entire reading of life, all were
at variance between the two races. Neither shared any
significant cultural experience with the other. There was
virtually no communication between them, save at the most
superficial level.

Such integration, moreover, was repugnant to European
sentiment and convention, and forbidden by European law. By
long tradition the races were used to working in segregated
spheres, Europeans doing skilled work, Africans unskilled, with
the Asian and the coloured people somewhere in between. The
very jobs themselves had taken on a pigmentation, and were
classified as black or white.

All this was endorsed legislatively by the Industrial Conciliation Act of the time, which applied only to European, Asian and
half-caste workers. Administratively it was endorsed by the
existence of two public works departments, the Federal P.W.D.
employing European labour in defined European areas, and
the Southern Rhodesian Engineering and Construction Department doing the same kind of work with African labour in
"native areas" at much lower rates of pay.

As regards urban residence, the law did not countenance
permanent residence for any African, even if he had been born
in the town and had lived there all his life. It required that if an
African could not find employment within a few weeks of his
arrival in town, or if he lost his employment, he must thereby
forfeit his eligibility for accommodation, and return to his tribal
reserve.

Meeting the needs which pressed on manufacturing industry
in 1958 therefore involved driving a coach and six through a
complex entanglement of racial discriminations long sanctioned
and sanctified by convention and law alike. The main changes
were these:

(i) In 1959 a new Industrial Conciliation Act was passed. It marked the formal end of the old Native Labour Boards (which had previously governed the conditions of African workers) and of trade unionism based on colour.

(ii) In 1960 the Land Apportionment Act was amended to give Africans the right of obtaining freehold title to their homes in any of the African townships contiguous to European towns.

(iii) The flow of migrants from outside the Federation was reduced by terminating both the migration agreements with neighbouring territories and the free transport service, and by declaring areas in which foreign Africans were barred from accepting employment.

(iv) Efforts were made to increase African wages to a level at which a married man and his family could afford to live in the town on tolerable minimum standards. The average wage in 1958 did not permit of this. The minimum wage for all undertakings in urban areas was £6.10.0 a month on 1 January 1958, having risen from £4.15.0 a month in January 1954. Industrial Boards were therefore set up under the new Industrial Conciliation Act to fix minimum terms and conditions of employment industry by industry. This led to further increases, though uneven ones, the highest minimum wage reaching £11 a month in 1960 and the lowest over £8.[1]

(v) These results being, in the Ministry's view, still unrealistic in relation to the current value of money and the basic needs of African workers, the Services Levy Act of 1960 was passed with a view to raising a levy on employers in respect of all employees, in order to subsidise the earnings of married Africans. The greater part of the money thus raised is spent in the form of a subsidy to a privately owned bus company, which has the transport monopoly within a 16-mile radius of the larger towns. The company in return keeps African bus fares down to a

[1] A Commission appointed in 1956 after a bus boycott protesting against high fares, commented that it was not reasonable to expect men earning £5 per month to pay £3 per month on transport between their homes and their jobs. The Minister of Social Welfare in 1959 and 1960 often insisted that the poverty line for the African urban family of average size was at that time expressed in money terms as £14.10.0 per month.

maximum of 1s. 2d. per day regardless of distance travelled.
The fares are decontrolled at week-ends. In practice there is
little left over for the major purpose of subsiding the housing of
married Africans.

§4. *African Education*

In the sphere of African education plans have been worked
out which envisage full eight year primary education for all
by 1974. There would in addition be an output at the levels of
Junior Certificate and School Certificate commensurate with
the estimated absorptive capacity of the labour market.

The pattern of enrolments for 1962 was as follows:

		% of age-range
Lower Primary ($6\frac{1}{2}$–$11\frac{1}{2}$ years) Std. 3 and below	491,000	95·1
Upper Primary ($11\frac{1}{2}$–$14\frac{1}{2}$ years) Std. 4–6	70,000	26·5
Junior Secondary ($14\frac{1}{2}$–$16\frac{1}{2}$ years)	8,000	4·1
Senior Secondary ($16\frac{1}{2}$–$18\frac{1}{2}$ years)	2,200	1·4

The results aimed at by current plans are:

For 1972

Of 163,000 first enrolled in 1968 142,000 will be in Std. 3.
Of 157,000 ,, ,, ,, 1967 131,000 ,, ,, ,, Std. 4.
Of 143,000 ,, ,, ,, 1965 101,000 ,, ,, ,, Std. 6.
    (Places in Form I of Secondary Schools 11,000)

The programme represents an assessment of the needs of
Rhodesia in the light of proposals for the development of
African education set out in the final report of the Conference
of African States which was held in Addis Ababa 15–25 May
1961. If carried out, it will keep the country somewhat ahead
of the Addis Ababa schedule, so far as the provision of school

places is concerned. It certainly corresponds with what African parents want and are willing to help pay for. For the primary schooling at present provided for African children their parents already contribute the school buildings, furniture, and books, together with housing for the teachers, at a cost (in respect of rural Lower Primary Schools alone) of £17,500 per 1,000 pupils. For every genuine improvement in African education, they will no doubt be ready to dig deeper into their sadly shallow pockets.

§5. *The practical results*

The four examples of African agriculture, community development-cum-local government, manufacturing industry, and education have been chosen to illustrate the scope of administrative thinking in Rhodesia on matters which touch the racial question. How does the thinking work out in practice? It is impossible to escape the impression that the entire offensive is held up on all four fronts. The movement of African farmers into the cash economy remains painfully slow, and they do not seem to do much better when they get there than they did before. In the new credit scheme, which in many ways is the linch-pin of the whole operation, the loans which actually get through to the African farmer are still a mere trickle that meets but a fraction of the need. His average net returns are still hardly higher than a labourer's wage.

Where community development is concerned, the stumbling-block is more clearly traceable to the racial factor. Here it is not too much to say that, in the current climate of race relations, any recommendation thought to originate from Europeans generates so resolute a negativism in the Africans at whom it is aimed that its rejection follows as a matter of course. On the official side the response tends at once to be to fall back upon compulsion. *The Community Development and Local Government News Bulletin* (a Government broadsheet) observed as long ago as April 1964 that the administrator's role would be authoritarian. "Though he may be able at times to put his orders in the form of suggestions," it said, "let no one be deceived into thinking the suggestions are not in fact orders." There is a note of desperation in that comment which, one would surmise, sounds the death-knell of the policy for African rural self-government. It certainly is a negation of every principle of community development as previously expounded by the Ministry of Internal Affairs.

For the same kind of reason the Native Councils Act of 1957, which some years later was so favourably assessed in the Report of the Magwende Commission, did not in practice fulfil its early promise, as the Commission also clearly indicated. Later reports reiterate regret that "the present Native Council system has further deteriorated". There is reason to think that the community development schemes, conceived as a means of repairing the situation, are likely to go the same way as the Native Councils.

An expansion of manufacturing industry would be of advantage to Rhodesia for a variety of reasons. Yet the advantages have little bearing on African development. Indeed, viewed in that context, industry at best seems to offer only relatively dwindling prospects. In the years 1957–62 the proportion of the total African population working in the money economy declined by 2·5 per cent. Yet these were years over which the Gross Domestic Product increased by 19 per cent.

Since 1962 the proportion has fallen at an increasing rate. The actual number of Africans employed in early 1964 was 581,000. If the capital-labour ratio had stood fast at its 1946 level, there would have been employment openings for well over a million Africans by 1964. Doubtless it is right and proper from the viewpoint of private enterprise that the ratio of capital to labour should rise, and business efficiency has risen with it. The point here made is simply that as industrial output increases, so African employment opportunities per unit of output decline.

At the same time, the number of indigenous male Africans aged 15–59 is increasing by 18,000 a year. It seems impossible that the money economy should accommodate the increment. Moreover, a well balanced economy would provide opportunities for a growing number of African women as well as men. So long, however, as present trends continue, there can be no increase in the employment of women, unless they take the places of men. Yet African development sorely needs the gainful employment of women for cultural as well as economic reasons.

These considerations leave us with two lessons from the working of the new industrial labour policy to which recourse was had in 1958. One is that the effect of industrial development on African development will remain marginal, unless and until increases in African purchasing power create a home market of major significance for industry. Such increases can come about only through the economic development of the tribal reserves. The other is that deep-rooted racial prejudices in the European population can be set aside, when the prosperity-requirements of the European economy are clearly seen to demand this. It remains to be discovered whether there is an equally powerful solvent in the economic necessity of the African reserves, linked as they are with all prospective increase in prosperity for Europeans and Africans alike.

The mere fact that the Addis-beating programme of African education is the product of a Ministry of African Education, segregated from the Ministry of European Education, is in the present state of race relations enough to make Africans believe there is something fishy about it. To this extent, the Government have forfeited the interest of Africans from the outset, and without that no such scheme can get far. And indeed even in the towns, where in many ways its educational prospects are more favourable, the Government is falling behind its own planning schedules.

§6. *The curse*

On all these plans, then, alike in agriculture, in rural local government, in industry, and in education, a kind of curse is laid. The curse is a function—this conclusion cannot be escaped —of the pattern of relations, both psychological and material, between the two main races. It is thus firmly embedded in the very edifice of Rhodesian society. What can lift it? If one tries to comprehend in a single vision the history of central and eastern Africa over the last fifty years, if one strives to identify in it any relevant lessons to which it unmistakably points, one would be driven to reply—only the ending of the political hegemony of Europeans. While that lasts, all races are doomed to sterile bitterness among themselves, and to poisonous enmity with their neighbours and the world.

It cannot be that political power is worth this price. Yet the retention of power at all costs is part of the basic creed of many, probably of most, Europeans in Rhodesia. The creed is held, not only with uncritical tenacity but also with true sincerity, as the most adequate intellectual position which they have been able to reach for maintaining their balance in social circumstances of disturbing difficulty. It therefore has to be treated with sympathy and respect as an honest conviction.

Historically it is an elaboration of the slogan attributed to Cecil Rhodes, *Equal Rights for All Civilised Men*. None but the wilfully wrong-headed would cavil at this affirmation. Difficulties arise, however, as soon as it is asked by what tokens a civilised man is distinguished from the rest. They multiply when it transpires that no European in Rhodesia is ever relegated to the uncivilised category.

The practical interpretation is that while all Europeans are *ex officio* civilised, and cannot be or become uncivilised, Africans are *ex officio* uncivilised, but can become civilised if they learn to conform to European customs and conventions in a measure which Europeans judge to be sufficient. European acceptance of Africans as equal citizens, regardless of colour, is made conditional on African acceptance of European value-systems as second nature, regardless of any violence they may do to African first nature. All the criteria by which Africans are to be rated as fit or unfit for equal rights and non-racial treatment are arbitrarily settled by Europeans in accordance with European preconceptions.

Having cleared his mind on these points, the observer begins to wonder whether the ideology compressed into Rhodes's slogan is really anything more than a rationalisation of the

European preference for the racial status quo, of their reluctance
to dilute their political power, and of their fear of social change
—in short, a device for controlling the entitlement of Africans
to equal standing. He finds evidence in support of this possibility
as much in what the ideology omits as in what it contains.

Omitted, for example, is the thought that civilisation may be
something wider and deeper than those items of popular
European culture that happen to be in vogue at a given place
and a given moment. Also omitted is the thought that if
Africans are to be justly assessed, it is their potential that has
to be measured rather than their attainment. From the nature
of the case, their attainment can scarcely be less meagre than
the educational opportunities that their European rulers have
accorded them.

In practice, what an African might become in other conditions than those which actually hedge him in is not considered.
Nor is it usual to judge him even by his attainment. The most
common method of rating is by reference to the things he cannot
do—which guarantees, as a foregone conclusion, his being
found wanting.

At the Rhodes National Gallery in Salisbury and at the
Sculpture Centre in Bulawayo African Township both potential
and attainment are made visible at one time and in one process.
Here for all to see and admire are the works of a school of
confident African artists, who are doing something new and
vital for Africa and for the world, and who reveal a depth of
spiritual resource beyond the scope of those non-Africans who
fancy them unfit to manage their affairs.

Perhaps the saddest feature of the white ideology is the insistence that relations between European and African are, as
it were by natural necessity, non-reciprocal. It is this which
cramps the European's style of humane dealing to a point
where he takes pride in not communicating with Africans. It is
this which treats as merely laughable the notion that the
African people might conceivably hammer out a distinctive
contribution of their own to a global civilisation, or even that
they might have some wisdom to impart to the European which

has not reached him from any other source. Like all forms of privileged exclusion, this one most injures those whom it is designed to protect.

Here is the reason why the Rhodesian interpretation of the non-racial principle is so different from that expounded in the other countries of the region. True, the full citizen everywhere, Rhodesia included, is accorded equal rights without regard to race or colour. In the other countries the full citizen is anyone who satisfies certain conditions as to birthplace and residence. In Rhodesia the full citizen is one who satisfies a means test and an education test fixed at levels that exclude the massive base of the racial pyramid, and thus the majority of Rhodesia-born Africans. Rhodesian non-racialism is in fact rooted in the soil of racial discrimination,[1] or if the phrase be preferred, of a discrimination which is 100 per cent race-linked; and its operation is localised at the apex of the pyramid. One result of the arrangement is that those who conduct public affairs regard themselves as free at all times to ignore, and when deemed expedient to quash and supplant, the beliefs and desires of the unenfranchised.

Few Europeans in Rhodesia are able to see why their ideology might appear to Africans as a ground of offence, and as fallacious even to sympathetic observers from outside. In common with all irrational attitudes built on strong feelings, it wears for those who adopt it a primary certitude so overwhelming that any challenger must seem insane. The tragedy is that it is this ideology, so held, which in the last resort is making further development of either human or natural resources in Rhodesia impossible.

If the white Rhodesians had chosen to come to terms with the new African States to the north, their higher average level of manpower and their more developed industrial plant would

[1] An illustration is the Land Apportionment Act. Much controversy has fastened on this measure, which forms in effect an essential part of the organic law constituting the present Rhodesia. It divides up the land of the country between the races. It is scheduled for early repeal as soon as a majority Government takes office. However it may be defended, it cannot be defended on grounds of non-racial principle.

have secured them access to all markets between the Limpopo and the Congo rivers, between Kinshasa and Mount Kenya.

This in turn would have furnished them with a base from which to modernise the economic life of Rhodesia's own 4 million peasants. White Rhodesians could have played an honourable part in building up a great internal market in tropical Africa. They would have come in on the ground floor of the long-term development of the continent they call their home.

Instead they have chosen the pottage of a narrowly localised white supremacy, brief, precarious, poverty-stricken, with no long-term prospects whatever.

APPENDIX C

		Page
§1.	Count-down to Federation 1945 to 1960	254
§2.	Fudging the Census 1962 to 1964	255
§3.	The Wrecking of the West 1962 to 1965	256
§4.	The Army Take-over January 1966	258
§5.	The Ironsi Régime January 1966 to July 1966	260
§6.	The North's Revenge May 1966 to ?	261
§7.	End of the First Republic October 1966	264
§8.	October 1966 to May 1967. A Southern Front?	267
§9.	The Second Republic. 27 May to 6 July 1967	270
§10.	Why?	274

NIGERIA STORY

§1. *Count-down to Federation 1945–1960*

In 1946, as a measure of post-war reform, the British Government divided Nigeria into three regions, Northern, Western, and Eastern. Each region was given a government of its own (still, of course, under British tutelage). Each government, after elections, came to be controlled by a different political party.

The National Council of Nigeria and Cameroon (N.C.N.C.) won in the Eastern region. In the Northern and Western regions the winners were two parties, previously non-existent but now known respectively as the Northern People's Congress (N.P.C.) and the Action Group (A.G.).

N.C.N.C., founded in August 1944, was the earliest Nigerian political party. As its name implies, it was set up not merely on an all-Nigerian basis, but on one which covered the neighbouring territory of British-mandated Cameroon as well.

Its success in the East revealed that region, in which the Ibos were the most numerous ethnic group, as in favour of Nigerian unity. Its defeat in North and West revealed those regions as preferring regional particularism.

There followed some years of public discussion, not always non-violent, about the date for independence. In April 1953 A.G. introduced a motion in the central House of Representatives urging that it should be fixed for 1956. N.P.C. fiercely opposed this, and the House adjourned in deadlock. In May 1953 bloody riots and virtual civil war broke out in Kano, the chief city of the North, following a visit by an A.G. campaign team which sought to present its case.

After conferences convened by the British Government, a new constitution (still not providing for independence) came into force on 1 October 1954. It was federal in character in deference to the alleged fear of the Northerners that their region, owing to the comparative inadequacy of its modernisation, would be dominated by East and West, should Nigeria come to independence as a unitary state.

In the allocation of powers as between the regions and the federal centre, finance, the public services, the judiciary, and the state corporations were reserved to the regions. The federal solution, acclaimed by N.P.C. and A.G. alike, was accepted by N.C.N.C. for the sake of harmony, in spite of its consistent preference for a unitary constitution. The position of the three main parties, each entrenched in its own region and in control of the regional government was confirmed.

From the early fifties onwards it became increasingly clear that political power in each of the regions was devolving upon a majority ethnic group, Hausa-Fulani in the North, Ibo in the East, Yoruba in the West. Minority ethnic groups within each region began to show anxiety about their prospects after independence. By 1957 A.G. was sponsoring their cause, and calling for the establishment of three or more new regions or "states" in the minority areas. A Minorities Commission, however, reported to the British Colonial Secretary that no fresh creations of the kind were needed, and the recommendation was accepted by him. N.P.C. and N.C.N.C. insisted that no new states should be carved out of their regions, and A.G. perforce fell into line.

A federal general election was held at the end of 1959, as a result of which a coalition government of N.P.C. and N.C.N.C. took Nigeria into independence on 1 October 1960. A.G., which had won only 75 seats out of 312 in the Federal Parliament, became, in name at least, the official Opposition.

§2. *Fudging the Census 1962 to 1964*

By the independence constitution, seats in the Federal Parliament were earmarked to the regions on a basis of population. The North received more than half of them, because it claimed to comprise more than half of the total population of the Federation. Thus N.P.C., powerfully backed by the traditional

Moslem authorities of the region, became the dominant partner in the first Federal Government. It was able to reserve for itself the office of Federal Prime Minister and to occupy most other key-positions within the central authority.

The North used this dominance with marked effect after the results of the population census, carried out in May 1962, became known. The census figures disclosed that, if the population of the Northern region had ever been greater than that of the other two regions combined, it was so no longer. The constitutional vindication of Northern dominance was overturned.

N.P.C. did not hesitate. Acting through its representatives in the Federal Government, it declared the census null and void. A new census was ordered and took place in 1963. This, having been conducted to N.P.C.'s satisfaction, added on some 10 millions to the total population, and shared the surplus between the regions in such a way as to show once more an overall majority for the North.

The fraud was pregnant with calamity for Nigeria.[1] But it was far from being the only sign that the country was in bad trouble. During 1963 there took place a protracted general strike, which in less than a year was followed by a second. Both were well organised and determined operations, aimed at the Government and inspired basically by disgust at the cynical and callous dishonesty with which the Federation was being run in every department of policy.

§3. *The Wrecking of the West 1962 to 1965*

In May 1962, the Federal Government declared a state of

---

[1] Full details of this unprecedented transaction are set out in a paper read to the First African Population Conference, University of Ibadan, January 1966. The second census led directly to a political and constitutional crisis of the first magnitude, which the President of the Republic sought (without success) to resolve by taking over the government of the country. It also led directly to an enormous N.P.C. majority in the Federal elections of 1964.

The knavery of that result accounts for the bitterness of U.P.G.A. when they found themselves victims of the same tactics all over again in the Western region election of October 1965. (See below.)

emergency in the Western region, and assumed direct control. Some leaders of A.G. (the region's ruling party) were placed in detention, others driven into exile.

The pretext for the take-over was a rift between Chief Obafemi Awolowo, the A.G. President, and Chief Samuel Ladoke Akintola, for many years Awolowo's trusted lieutenant, but now a rival claimant to the regional premiership. The party split, and there were outbreaks of violence within the precincts of the Western House of Assembly.

During the emergency, which lasted until 1 January 1963, Awolowo and some other A.G. leaders and organisers were put on trial for sedition and conspiracy to overthrow the government. A federal commission also inquired into A.G.'s handling of the region's finances, and cleared Akintola, among others, of blame. He resigned from A.G. and formed a new party, the United People's Party from A.G. dissidents. At the lifting of the emergency he was placed in power as regional premier at the head of his rump U.P.P.

It is thus not surprising that Akintola came to be widely regarded as the nominee of the North. A frequent theme of press comment during 1963 was what the commentators took to be the tyrannical and feudal domination of N.P.C. in the whole ordering of Nigerian (not only Western) affairs. Apprehension was expressed that this was intended to become both absolute and permanent.

Akintola remained in office until September 1965, when the House dissolved. General elections were held on 11 October. Akintola's party, now re-named the Nigerian National Democratic Party (N.N.D.P.) and still strongly helped by N.P.C., was declared[1] to have won 71 seats out of the 94.

The result was at once disputed by the opposition party, the United Progressive Grand Alliance (U.P.G.A.), as the alliance between A.G. and N.C.N.C. had been christened. U.P.G.A. claimed that, but for widespread irregularities in the conduct of the elections, it would have won 68 seats.

Disturbances, which were prolonged, now broke out all over

[1] By the Western Nigerian Electoral Commission.

the Western region. By the end of 1965 many hundreds of lives had been lost, and many thousands of people injured.

Five weeks after the election the chairman of the Electoral Commission (Mr. E. E. Esua) wrote to the Governor of the Western region, saying that the Commission had been reduced to impotence during the polling because the returning officers neither owed nor showed it any loyalty. He was therefore obliged to disclaim all responsibility for the conduct of the elections.

By these steps the West had now become the cockpit of Nigeria's regional rivalries. The declared winners in the election were backed by the ruling party in the North (and as a corollary by the Federal Government). The declared losers were backed by the ruling parties in the East and the Mid-West.[1]

During November the Federal Prime Minister refused a public inquiry into the elections. He also announced that no amount of violence would by itself induce him to declare an emergency and run the regional government as he had done in May 1962.

At the same time Akintola's N.N.D.P. issued a statement that there would be no fresh elections until the new Assembly had completed its five-year term (i.e. 1970).

This reluctance in the highest quarters to look even for palliatives in the threatening situation gave rise to an impression in the public mind that constitutionality did not matter any more.

A crisis was clearly at hand.

§4. *The Army Take-over January 1966*

On Friday, 14 January 1966, a meeting took place in the Northern capital between Akintola and the Northern region premier, Sir Ahmadu Bello, the Sardauna of Sokoto. Also present were Brigadier Sam Ademulegun and certain other senior army officers.

The meeting decided to proceed to a ruthless extinction of

[1] A fourth region (called Mid-western) had been established in 1963, with Benin City as its capital. It was carved out of the original Western region.

the Opposition in the Western region. Units of the Nigerian army, under the command of Brigadier Ademulegun (himself a Westerner) were to carry out the military campaign. An officer was despatched to Lagos to inform the G.O.C. Nigerian Army of the decision.[1]

Before this officer could report to the G.O.C. (he was picked up and shot on the way), his information had leaked out to Major Chukwuma Nzeogwu and four other middle-grade officers who were themselves planning to overthrow the civil authorities. They acted at once. On their orders small army detachments moved against the Federal Government and the Governments of the four regions in the early hours of 15 January.

The Federal Prime Minister, Sir Abubakar Tafala Balewa, and the Federal Finance Minister, Chief Festus Okotie-Eboh, together with Ahmadu Bello and Akintola, were taken and shot, as also was Brigadier Ademulegun. An attempt, which in the event miscarried, was also made to lay hands on the G.O.C. In the Eastern and Mid-western regions the Governors, Premiers, and Deputy Premiers were held in their residences by troops. Ministry buildings were also occupied. No one was injured.

On 16 January Radio Kaduna announced that the army had formed a revolutionary council in the Northern region, and that martial law was in force. In Lagos the acting President of Nigeria. Dr. Nwafor Orizu, broadcast to the nation that the Council of Ministers had unanimously decided to hand over the government of the Federation to the armed forces.

On 17 January the G.O.C. held a press conference in Lagos. He stated that Major Nzeogwu had offered him assurances of his loyalty and that these had been accepted. There had been no fighting between opposed sections of the army. The military government was determined to suppress the disorders in the Western region.

Popular relief at the wholesale casting-out of the politicians was immediate and general. Very large numbers of organisations at once declared themselves in favour of the new military

[1] Major-General Johnson Aguiyi-Ironsi.

government, among them, rather oddly, all the main political parties, N.C.N.C., A.G., and even N.P.C. and N.N.D.P. The new government, indeed, was spontaneously hailed as the first real expression of Nigerian unity that the country had known.

In view of later events, the statement issued in Lagos on 18 January 1966 on behalf of N.P.C. by Alhaji Hasim Adaji, Minister of State, should be specially recalled. It read as follows:

"The N.P.C. regards the transfer of authority as the only solution to the many recent problems facing this country. The party gives its unqualified support to the military régime and to Major-General Ironsi in particular. . . . We call on all the peoples of Nigeria irrespective of tribe origin or political persuasion to rally round the new military government so as to make easy its great and noble task."

§5. *The Ironsi Régime January 1966 to July 1966*

Ironsi, now styled Supreme Commander, had to all appearances been auspiciously launched. He had had no responsibility for the coup, but the coup had thrown him up as the symbol of true Nigerianism. The country, reassured that the coup was not a tribal matter, that the North was not likely to rise, and that no Eastern politician had been involved, was solidly behind him. The disorderly West was non-violently pacified with remarkable despatch. Within weeks Nigeria was enjoying such a calm, and such a devotion to the public interest, as she had not known for years.

One of Ironsi's first steps was to suspend Parliament and the offices and apparatus of civil government, except for the judiciary, the civil service, the Nigerian Police and the Special Constabulary. These remained untouched. Military governors, responsible to himself, were appointed for each region as follows:

North	Major Hassan Katsina
West	Lieut.-Col. Fajuyi
Midwest	Lieut.-Col. Ejoh
East	Lieut.-Col. Ojukwu

Thus, by compulsion of circumstances rather than by preferred policy, Nigeria was transformed in a day from a federation with a "constitutional" President into a unitary state with an "executive" President. It was on this central fact that the general approval felt by the people was grounded.

By mid-February a number of study groups had been set to work to advise on the form of a new constitution. The groups were not tied to any particular type, though the military Government did not conceal its own preference for a unitary state.

Two other vital and related subjects were also placed under review:

(1) the delimitation of new (and more numerous) administrative units to replace the old regions,

(2) the unification of the five civil services (1 federal and 4 regional) into a single all-Nigerian service, and a corresponding unification of the five judicial services.

In due course, after the reports of the study groups had been assessed, decrees abolishing the regions, and instituting a unitary government and a unified civil service, were announced.

While this constructive work was being vigorously and hopefully pursued, a small cloud appeared above the horizon, which was quickly to swell and swell until it engulfed all Nigeria in desolating catastrophe. Already by the end of January Cairo Radio was croaking for war in a stream of broadcasts in English, Hausa, and Arabic. "The military take-over," screamed the message, "was a Kafferi onslaught on the very citadel of Islam in Nigeria."

Hardly less premonitory was the news, released in the second week of February, that Ironsi had appointed Lieut.-Col. Y. Gowon to the Supreme Military Council and the Federal Executive Council.

Less than six months later, on 29 July 1966, Ironsi and the cause of Nigerian unity were both assassinated.

§6. *The North's Revenge May 1966 to ?*

The North's revenge was a much more elaborate affair than

Major Nzeogwu's coup. It came in three waves, the first in May, the second in July, and the third in October. Its effects, in contrast with those of the coup, were permanent and negative.

It quickly became evident that the N.P.C. statement of 18 January in support of Ironsi (see §4 above) was mere prevarication designed to gain time. By April an article published in the *Daily Times* (Lagos) noted the sound of no good music issuing from the North. "The intelligentsia is slowly rising in hostility. The old song of Ibo domination is recklessly driven home with increasing venom."

On 24 May Ironsi made a speech setting out his policy (as outlined in §5 above) and announcing that his military government would hand over to civilians within a 3-year term. The country's constitution would be decided by a constituent assembly and a referendum. The speech was welcomed in the Western, Midwestern, and Eastern regions, where the feeling was that it was right to create machinery which would encourage the development of a sentiment of Nigerian nationhood, and above all favour national, as distinct from tribal-regional political parties.

In the North the speech was followed by disturbances with a death roll of 92 (official estimate), plus over 500 wounded. It was officially stated in Lagos that they had been incited by "some Nigerians in collusion with certain foreign elements. The Government sincerely hopes that these foreign elements are not being backed by their respective governments."

A high-powered tribunal was set up to inquire into all aspects of these events. Its first meeting was to have been held on 2 August, but was forestalled by the second wave of the Northern revenge-programme. On Friday 29 July, in a *putsch* engineered by Northern army officers,[1] Ironsi and other members of the military government were murdered.

[1] The Northern provenance of the *putsch* which Gowon and his collaborators had laboured to conceal, was first given away by the pilot of a B.O.A.C. VC 10, impounded at Lagos airport on 28 July. On his eventual return to London he revealed that he had done a deal with the *putsch* leaders, who agreed to let him leave on his home flight, if he would first take their wives and children to Kano.

The country was without a central government for three days. Then on 1 August Lieut.-Col. Y. Gowon, who had been negotiating on behalf of the *putsch* group, announced his assumption of power in succession to Major-General Ironsi who had been "kidnapped, whereabouts unknown". He had assumed power, he explained, "with the consent of the majority of the Supreme Military Council." He did not mention that two out of the four regional governors did not attend the meeting, Lieut.-Col. Fajuyi of the West because he had been assassinated, Lieut.-Col. Ojukwu of the East because the government now headed by Gowon could not have guaranteed his personal safety had he tried to attend.

A day or two later, seeking to attract support from the Yoruba for his régime, Gowon released Chief Awolowo, the Western A.G. leader who had been in prison since 1962 (see §3 above). A few other Western notables were also let out at the same time.

Much later (in January 1967) Gowon published a list of senior officers of the army who had been killed (a) in the coup of 15 January 1966 and (b) in the *putsch* of July 1966. The figures he gave were seven for January and twelve for July. Ojukwu's evidence was that 200 Ibo officers and men were massacred in July. Be that as it may, it is curious that Gowon should allow the mere seven for January to stand as sufficiently horrific for his purpose.

The two months immediately following the *putsch* were spent in Gowon-led discussions about a new constitution for Nigeria. Signs of the disintegration of the old Federal structure were piling up throughout this time. On 1 October, the sixth anniversary of independence, came the third wave of Northern vengeance. It took the form of an organised pogrom of Easterners, and looting of their property, in all the main population centres of the North.

The starting-signal was a report, broadcast over Kaduna radio and published in the *Daily Times* (Lagos) and the *New Nigerian* (Kaduna), to the effect that mass-killings of Northerners had taken place in the Eastern region. The report turned out at once to be a fabrication with no basis in fact. The pogrom, however, continued for several weeks. By the time it died down, some 30,000 Easterners (by no means all of them Ibos)[1] had been killed, many more had been physically mutilated, and two million Eastern refugees had begun their trek home from all parts of Nigeria in which Northern troops were stationed.

A well-known technique of massacre was used. It is the method by which Moslem troops, with their arms but without their officers, are turned loose in commercial and residential areas. They are given no orders, merely a general understanding that they are free to shoot "anything in trousers", and no questions asked. The method was employed with success over a number of years recently in the South Sudan, where wandering Moslem troops from the North have painstakingly destroyed some four-fifths of the African population. It is the same method as was lately favoured by Indonesians to kill a quarter of a million Chinese residents in their islands. Or, somewhat earlier, by Pakistanis in their confrontation of Hindus at the time of the partition of British India. And of course it goes all the way back to those massacres of Armenians at the hands of the Turks, about which Mr. Gladstone used to feel so badly.[2]

§7. *End of the First Republic October 1966*

By October, then, the Eastern region and its inhabitants had been expelled from the Federation with every circumstance of atrocity. The executive agents were Northern troops, the policy was N.P.C.'s. Constitutional lawyers naturally argue about how much of the original legal framework can be deemed to have survived this enforced walking of the plank by one of the Federation's chief components. But, whatever the *de jure*

[1] The only Southerners spared were those with Western (Yoruba) tribal markings.
[2] The method is convenient in that it allows one first to describe the killings as the work of "mutinous" troops; next, when the troops are recalled to barracks, one can claim that the mutiny has been quelled; and, finally, as a few men come up for court-martial, it is plain to all that the ringleaders are being correctly punished.

position, the Federation had *de facto* ceased to exist after the third revenge-wave.

From then onwards the one sensible policy was to leave the East alone to lick its wounds, and to make the best it could of its new situation. The one issue of practical importance was how much further the North would seek to press its destruction of the East's human and material resources.

The East's case was parlous. The North had demonstrated in ferocious terms its refusal to look on Easterners as equal human beings. No Easterner was any longer able to move freely outside his own region or seek employment or set up business in any part of the old Federation to which Northern troops had access. The military governor of the East himself was obliged to stay away from meetings of the Supreme Military Council because its chairman, Lieut.-Col. Gowon, could not or would not guarantee him safe-conduct.

After the North's October massacres Ojukwu deported all non-Easterners under armed escort from Eastern territory. But contrariwise the East had on its hands the tremendous problem of its own returning refugees. In respect of public finance it was still called on to pay over revenues to Lagos in accordance with the old formula, though it had lost all assurance that Lagos would in turn continue the previous central government grants.

Nigeria had never possessed more than two institutions which embodied an all-Nigerian outlook. These were the universities (there were five of them) and the army. The former had by now reverted to purely regional bodies, unable to claim any all-Nigerian concern or loyalty or influence.

As to the army, all personnel of Eastern origin had now returned to the East without any proper organisation or equipment, and had no contact with non-Eastern units. In West and Mid-west the locally recruited personnel had simply melted away. As late as 30 November Gowon was explaining in a broadcast that, if Northern troops were returned to their own region (as he had promised), Lagos and the West would be left with virtually no troops at all. This was Gowon's way of expressing the fact that West and Mid-west, including Lagos, were under military occupation by the North. So long as this remained true, it was plainly impossible to resurrect any genuine form of Federation.

We should note that the term North, which has been constantly employed in these notes, necessarily undergoes some shift of meaning, with the demise of the First Republic. Strictly, it can no longer cover the leaders and supporters of N.P.C., since N.P.C., qua banned political party, now has no formal existence. Nor can it cover the Government of the Northern region, since the 4-region structure, as we shall see in a moment, is about to give way to a 12-state structure. But "the North" goes on unchanged, for the forces once assembled together in N.P.C. remain active and still dominant over the Northern army and the so-called Supreme Military Council which Gowon chairs on the North's, not on Nigeria's, behalf.

These forces comprise the old N.P.C. leaders, a number of influential Emirs, a strong group of Permanent Secretaries in the "Federal" Ministries, other civil servants and intelligentsia still sighing for the days of the Bello-Akintola alliance, and of course the foreign Moslem interests mentioned above (§6). It is always worth remembering that Ahmadu Bello was Vice-President of the World Moslem League.

It is not yet possible to specify those interests in detail. It stands to reason that they like to keep anonymous. But some indication of their broad nature can be given. The present writer was in Lagos from 13 December to 19 December 1965, and he toured all four regions of Nigeria between 9 March and 13 April 1966. During that time it was put to him by several witnesses of good authority[1] that the Bello–Akintola coup, planned for January 1966 (see §4 above), had in view much wider objectives than the mere subjugation of the Western region.

There was, in addition, to be a military attack on the East, including the mopping-up, after bombardment from the air, of the university institutions of Enugu and Nsukka. The United

---

[1] Among them Dr. Janet Hartle, Department of Anthropology, University of Nigeria, Nsukka.

Arab Republic and Algeria were to be strategically associated with the operation in the interests of Moslem solidarity. Once the subjection of the pagan-Christian East, and of the non-Moslem groups in the West, was assured, Nigeria's name was to be inscribed on the scroll of Islamic Republics. The conporary historian who could confirm or falsify these suggestions would be performing a valuable service.

§8. *October 1966 to May 1967. A Southern Front?*

It might be thought that the North, having flogged the Eastern region out of the Republic, would call it a day. The East apart, the whole of Nigeria was under Northern military control. There was a tremendous job of work crying out to be done in the way of building a viable economy and a viable polity out of the 3-region rump of the First Republic.

But the men of the North have little stomach and less heart for construction, and no head for it at all. Moreover, the events of 1966 had marvellously whetted their wrecking appetites. After October they were in no shape to resist the lure of Operation Overkill—the full destruction of the East.

To remove the Eastern region from the map of Nigeria and to liquidate the highest practicable proportion of its 14 million inhabitants, was an undertaking which called for careful preparation, both militarily and diplomatically.

The logistics of an invasion of the East from the North posed formidable problems of reorganisation and re-equipment o₁ the Northern army, involving protracted shopping around the world for arms, which at best it would take many months to solve.

The diplomatic problem was even trickier. How to formulate a case against the East which would justify in the eyes of the outside world[1] what was intended to be, and what must sooner or later be seen as being, a war of extermination waged by one set of Nigerians against another?

In grasping this nettle the North decided, probably shrewdly, that the best chance of meeting all the conditions was to

[1] Especially O.A.U. and U.N.

represent the East as championing the further balkanisation of Africa. Here was a point on which all the new African states, particularly those (the majority) with guilty consciences about their own failure to debalkanise themselves, were sensitive. The cry for closer political association between neighbouring countries, the setting-up of economic communities, etc., had been ringing unanswered in their ears for years. If the Eastern region could be shown up as another Katanga and Ojukwu as a second Tshombe, most African states would think extermination a proper punishment for them.

It was certainly a bright idea, and from the standpoint of the North it has worked out admirably in practice. The East today is universally execrated as the enemy of Nigerian unity, indeed of African unity too. That this reading of the situation stands all the relevant facts on their heads does not, it seems, raise any doubt about its validity, either in Africa or internationally. No African state cares to dispute the Northern claim that for the North to drive the East out of the Federation was a gesture of genuine Nigerian patriotism; and that for the expelled East to set up house on its own was a treasonable act. To distinguish between being flogged out and breaking away in rebellion is held to be a trifling quibble. It was the hounded East, they say, not the hounding North, which torpedoed the First Republic.

But since the First Republic *was* indubitably torpedoed, and since the East *had been* indubitably extruded from it by the North, a Second Republic had to be floated and its new constitution imposed on the East. The East, in short, had to be flogged back into a refurbished Federation, before a charge of secession from it could be made to stick.

This topsy-turvy necessity accounts for the North's extraordinary preoccupation with the constitutional question throughout the period October 1966–June 1967. During these months enormous tracts of time were wasted in meandering argument about what the provisions of the new constitution should be. It served presumably as camouflage behind which the North's stockpiling of foreign arms could go forward unobserved.

In general, Gowon insisted on holding these talks in places where Ojukwu and his colleagues could only appear if they were prepared to expose themselves to the "kidnapping" fate which had overtaken Ironsi. However, in January 1967 a full meeting of the Supreme Military Council was held in Ghana "to clear up outstanding questions". Ojukwu refused to make the journey in any Federal plane, but agreed to travel in a special aircraft lent by the Ghana Government. This meeting was much boosted as a real get-together of all four former regions.

Nothing whatever came out of it. Nobody even tried to carry out the decisions said to have been reached; indeed, nobody could agree what the decisions were. In this kind of slipperiness three more fruitless months floated by.

What finally brought matters to a head was not the question of a constitution, but the prosaic need to settle the 1967–68 Estimates. These were due to be presented by 31 March. On this day Ojukwu, having received no answer from Gowon about how revenue-allocation was to be dealt with in the post-pogrom situation, and driven by pressing constraint to keep Eastern finances going, issued an edict ordering the payment to the Eastern Government of certain revenues of the former Federation whose collection took place in the East.

Gowon's reaction was sharp. He at once declared full-scale economic war, aimed at isolating the East both from the "Federation" and from the outside world. Thus through him the North, improperly arrogating to itself the style of a Federal Government, imposed a rapidly tightening blockade on the East, while the East continued to ease the constriction as best it could.

Early in May Gowon's long-drawn-out pretence of constitutional talks finally collapsed. The delegates from the West, the North, and Lagos severally and solemnly resigned from the Constitutional Committee, which never breathed again. Awolowo, speaking as a Western delegate, made his final protest. "The consensus of opinion," he said, "among the vast majority of people in Western Nigeria and Lagos is that Northern troops in the two territories constitute an army of occupation, and that their non-removal has virtually reduced the said territories to the status of a protectorate." A day or two later he told his supporters in Ibadan that, if the East were to stay outside the Federation, in his view the West and Lagos would have to stay out too.

In the same speech he gave perhaps his most striking testimony of the identity of Western and Eastern attitudes as against the North, when he declared, "It is my considered view that, whilst some of the demands of the East are excessive, within the context of a Nigerian union most of such demands are not only well founded, but are designed for smooth and healthy association among the various national units of Nigeria. If we are to live in harmony with one another as Nigerians, it is imperative that these demands and others which are related should be met."

By mid-May, in fact, there were distinct signs that a Southern front was seeking to establish itself for a final confrontation with the North. Its platform was a "temporary confederation" with a weak residual centre for the new Nigeria, as against the strong-centred Federation which the North was urging.

Ojukwu commented on the West's stand in the crisis. "This makes it quite clear," he said, "that the thing is not Ojukwu versus the rest of Nigeria. But it is and always has been a North versus South conflict in which the East has been in the van-guard of the struggle."

§9. *The Second Republic. 27 May to the July 1967*

An entente between Awolowo and Ojukwu would have been a serious obstacle to the North's plans for destroying the East, and might have necessitated a re-conquest of the West into the bargain. On 27 May, therefore, Gowon staged his one-man *coup d'état*, declaring a state of emergency throughout Nigeria, and simultaneously decreeing an outline constitution for the Second Republic.

The main constitutional points were (a) that full powers as Commander-in-Chief and Head of the Military Government were to be vested in Lieut.-Col. Gowon (or Major-General Gowon, to use the rank to which he at once promoted himself), (b) that Nigeria was to be divided into twelve "states" in place of the four regions of the First Republic.

A third point emerged a fortnight later. On 12 June Gowon in person swore in the members of a new Federal Executive Council, which included twelve civilians, one for each state. The civilian members were given full responsibility for Ministries and Departments, and were called Commissioners. Gowon was chairman of the Council, with Awolowo as his Vice-Chairman and Commissioner for Finance.

Gowon used the occasion of the swearing-in ceremony to declare publicly "I have taken the irrevocable decision to crush Ojukwu's rebellion, in order to re-unite Nigerians resident in the three Eastern states with their brothers and sisters in other parts of Nigeria as equal partners."[1]

Such, then, was the new "Federation of Nigeria" into which the North proposed to flog the East back. The main point of difference from the old was evidently the "states". In Gowon's propaganda the idea of the states was advanced as the definitive solution to the thorny problem of domination by one region over the rest. In particular, it was to reassure the East that the division of the Northern region into six states would render Northern domination permanently impossible.

Of the twelve new states six arose from a re-division of the Northern region, and three from a re-division of the Eastern region. The remaining three consisted of the old Western region, and old Mid-western region, and the old federal territory of Lagos, all virtually unchanged (three small areas were transferred from the West to Lagos which was to remain the seat of the Federal Government).

An air of unreality pervaded the whole scheme, because the powers of the states and their relationship with the federal

---

[1] The Nigerians to be thus happily re-united with their compatriots were precisely the people who just eight months earlier had been flung, with murderous violence, out of the North by their brothers and sisters and equal partners there. This kind of re-union, after a suitable dose of rebellion-crushing, is the process referred to above (§8) as flogging back in.

centre were not defined. On this crucial point all Gowon had
to say was that "representatives drawn from the new states
will be more able to work out the future constitution for this
country which can contain provisions to protect the powers of
the states to the fullest extent desired by the Nigerian people."
In short, apart from the very nominal creation of the twelve
states, the constitutional issue rested exactly where all the
abortive talks of the previous ten months had left it. All still
remained to be done.

The supposition presumably was that the states would
exercise in their areas the functions previously discharged by
the regions in theirs. But on this basis the creation of the states
would affect the real political situation of Nigeria only in a
minimal way. This was avowedly so in regard to the West,
the Mid-west, and Lagos, since there the new states *were* simply
the old regions (subject to minor re-delimitation of the West–
Lagos boundary). What of the six states in the North which
were to annul for ever the menace of Northern domination?
How would they modify the traditional power-structure[1] of the
immemorial North?

The answer is In no way. It is a tribute to Gowon's public
relations staff that anyone should ever have taken his amateur-
ish window-dressing seriously. In his re-drawn North all the old
Emirs and their non-Nigerian friends, all the politicians from
the pre-Ironsi régime, all the old civil servants constitute the
same solid bloc as before. To recreate in the six states as a
group the power the bloc always enjoyed in the old Northern
region would be the work of a few weeks, and in fact had
probably already been done before Gowon promulgated his
decree.

For the better consolidation of such work the decree actually
provides an "Interim Administrative Council" to ensure con-
tinuity and act as an umbrella for the Northern states until they
are established. The new Council is the old regional government re-christened. The interests represented on it are precisely
the interests which all along controlled the government of the

---

[1] Described in §7 above.

Northern region, and what is more significant, the Government of the Federation. The six states will be administered by precisely the same civil service personnel (there are no alternatives) who hitherto administered the Northern region. The difference will be that a few of them may have to move house from Kaduna to one or other of the state capitals.

There is no need to consider the effect of Gowon's decree as regards new states in the East, since it had none, and will have none, unless and until the East is defeated in war.

To sum up, then, Gowon's much-trumpeted new states are a characteristic piece of Northern eye-wash which leaves Nigeria's real dilemma quite unaltered. So much is clear. But what is still unclear is how the sudden *volte-face* of the West in its dealings with Gowon was brought about. Three weeks before Gowon's coup of 27 May the West, and for that matter the Mid-west as well, had declared their unwillingness to take part in the use of force against the East. Both regions had insistently renewed their pressure for the return of Northern troops to the North. Awolowo, as we saw, had even said that if the East were formally excluded from the Federation, the West would leave also.

What happened to Awolowo between 6 May (when he went with an unofficial mission to Enugu for discussions with Ojukwu) and 27 May (the day of Gowon's coup)? What arguments, threats, bribes did Gowon offer Awolowo to induce so abject a climb-down? Only two relevant points are known, (1) that Awolowo was offered the job of Gowon's Vice-Chairman on the new Federal Executive Council, (2) that the Supreme Military Council some time during the fourth week of May "decided" to withdraw Northern troops from the West. (In fact they were not withdrawn.)

These two points by themselves are nowhere near explanation enough. The missing factor, we may well surmise, is a threat from Gowon to turn Northern troops loose in the West, as they had been turned loose against Eastern residents in the North during October 1966. Be that as it may, the continued and increasingly menacing presence of Northern troops in

West, Mid-west, and Lagos is evidently the key to the whole situation in the second half of May.

Ojukwu had been saying ever since January that he would regard as a hostile act either a blockade of the East or the attempt to impose a new constitution on it without consultation. Gowon had presented him with the first after 31 March, and with the second on 27 May. On 30 May, accordingly, three days after Gowon's decree partitioning the East, Ojukwu issued a proclamation that the Eastern region would thenceforward be an independent sovereign state entitled the Republic of Biafra. The chief ground for this step was stated to be that the people of the East could no longer be protected in their lives and property by any government outside Eastern Nigeria. The proclamation expressed Biafra's readiness to enter into associa- with any sovereign state within the former Federal Republic of Nigeria or elsewhere on such terms and conditions as would best serve the common good.

Gowon the same day orders general mobilisation throughout his "Federation".

A day or two later we find him notifying O.A.U. that Ojuk- wu's independence declaration was "illegal, unconstitutional, and an act of rebellion. Any attempt at recognition would be regarded as an unfriendly act and direct interference in Nigerian affairs."

On 6 July Northern troops entered Biafra. Operation Over- kill had begun.

§10. *Why?*

It is not the purpose of these notes to trace the course of the war. Rather is it to seek true causes, and likely effects, of the calamity which has overtaken that Nigeria which nature has lavishly favoured, and which seems providentially designed for cultivating the arts of prosperous peace.

Nigeria's story since 1960 is a record of human disaster far more grievous than has befallen any other part of Africa in the modern era. Algeria, the Sudan, Rwanda-Burundi, the Congo—all these can boast their signal shames and terrors.

But the Nigerian débâcle belongs to an altogether different order of magnitude, both in scope of suffering and in pitiful betrayal.[1]

As we have seen, the débâcle has been the North's work. The question for the student is this: What motives could have been powerful and perverse enough to prompt such enormities? And the answer that imposes itself unchallengeably on the student's mind as he ploughs through the detailed events is *Fear*. The North's performance since the foundation of the First Republic has been in a real sense portentous. It exhibits brutality more savage, fraudulence more reckless, destruction more insensate than any human beings are wont to have recourse to, unless they are in the grip of hysterical panic.

Fear is readily admitted by the men of the North. If one presses them to say fear of what, equally readily comes the reply Fear of domination by the East. Asking further what sort of domination, one is told The oppressive intervention of people with better trained minds, who are therefore likely to be stronger candidates for the more important jobs.

Distaste for learning from others with fuller information and higher skill is marked in the North. (From whom else can one learn, however?) In regard to recruitment for the public service, for instance (and all this is mainly a civil servant's bogy) the North's motto has always been Northerners first, expatriates second, Westerners third, Easterners last. And the descending order of preference is also an ascending order of competence. Gowon himself found, when forming his new "states" in the North, that the only other ethnic group which any given ethnic group wanted to join up with was one where the school enrolment ratio was lower than its own.

The basic offence of the Easterners in Northern eyes is that they have discarded this guilty passion for ignorance, this relish for the inferior, and have taken up with the heresy that excellence is worthy of pursuit, at least in some areas of conduct. The heresy implies a profound revolution in traditional African

[1] Biafra alone has a population (14m.) as numerous as that of the entire Congo.

attitudes, a revolution which the North has not yet begun to approach.

A Rice Research Station in Sierra Leone recently carried out an investigation into the observed unwillingness of local peasants to sow a new type of high-yield rice. Three points were raised:

(1) Q. If one farmer gets a good yield of rice and his neighbour gets a poor one, how would people be likely to account for this?
A. They would say he (the successful one) took it (the unsuccessful one's crop) by witchcraft.

(2) Q. Are any farmers among you recognised as being particularly good at the job of growing rice?
A. We don't know. There is a rule that you ought not to go about scrutinising other people's crops. If you do, you will become a great suspect. At harvest time, should someone not reap a good crop, he would conclude that you are a witch, and have stolen his crop by witchcraft.

(3) Q. Would a farmer who had an exceptionally good crop, talk about it in the village?
A. If your crops are too good, people will hate you, witches will harm you. Even if they can't harm *you*, they will get at your children. So if you talk of a good crop, people would say you are a fool.

In this brief questionnaire the central dilemma of African modernisation is succinctly formulated. We see at once that the North v. East conflict in Nigeria is a revulsion of the anti-modernisers from the modernisers. From the North's standpoint, the men of the East are evil-doers who steal its crop by witchcraft. The above answers express beliefs and attitudes which are the chief spiritual treasure inherited by peasants anywhere in the continent. They form the foundation of African group-solidarity. They are therefore clung to with obdurate tenacity, and persons who openly reject them become objects of fear and hatred to the outraged group.

Plainly they are beliefs and attitudes which put an enormous premium on non-improvement. They ensure that every incentive within the system should point away from any kind of excellence. They make a virtue of subnormal performance, and call anathema down upon the supernormal.

They institute a form of kakistocracy. Themistocles used to praise the youth of Athens on the grounds that, when confronted with a higher and a lower alternative, they could be counted on to choose the higher. The African witchcraft syndrome exacts the opposite choice. The men of the North, still rigidly confined within that syndrome, hate and fear the East, because the East has escaped from it and begins to go Athenian.

This is why the North has wrecked the Federation, and now proposes to wipe Biafra off the map. But its way is far from clear. On the one hand, it has denied Biafrans contact with the rest of Nigeria. It wants desperately to be quit of them once for all. On the other hand, it covets no less desperately the natural and material resources of Biafran territory. It cannot drive the Biafrans out of Biafra, where indeed it has deliberately concentrated them, without spilling them all over the "Federation" once again. Therefore they must be liquidated within the four corners of Biafra.

But the liquidation of 14 million people, as Hitler could have explained, is not a simple matter. The North in its greedy rage has bitten off more than its primitive technology enables it to chew. The "final solution" is quite beyond its capacity. Even if it contrives to buy the instruments of biological warfare from the Western powers, whose substantial help in Operation Overkill has been unworthily pressed upon it, those instruments will be incompetently applied in the field. A modest decimation of the Biafran population will take the North many weary years.

The North may bring down the Republic of Biafra. Or again it may not. If it does, it will also have gone far towards ruining the nine "states" of its rump "Federation". In either case, it has already created a Biafran nation, which in one form or another form is being moulded into durability.

The North has rounded up in the East, and creamed off from

the other "states", the ablest brains and the freest minds in all Nigeria. In throwing them the supreme challenge of staying alive, it evokes in them an invincible motive. Their response will be more effective than the North's response to the challenge of putting them to death.

The Northern aggression is likely to do for the national spirit of Biafra what the Battle of Jena in 1806 did for that of Prussia.

APPENDIX D

		Page
§1.	Priority for Agriculture	280
§2.	Growth of the Commune	282
§3.	The Commune's Main Components	284
§4.	The Pillars of the System	288
§5.	Some Secondary Gains	290

CHINA STORY

§1. *Priority for agriculture*

In the body of the text, occasional mention has been made of the relevance for African contries of China's superhuman effort to find a concurrent solution for her agrarian and her demographic problems, especially since 1957. It is time to consider this relevance in rather more detail.

The scale of the Chinese effort has been rightly emphasised by René Dumont in his book *Chine Surpeuplée* (Editions du Seuil, Paris, 1965), which begins with the observation, "In the whole history of world agriculture, no peasant countryside has ever changed as much as that of Eastern China between 1955 and 1964." The purpose of the present sketch is to urge the need for strategists of African development to understand with an open mind the real nature of that change, the grounds on which it was carried through, the mistakes made during its execution, and the measure of its current and prospective success. No intelligent African who reaches that degree of understanding will find it difficult to draw such lessons as may be valid in the conditions of his continent.

In much of our contemporary world, especially in the west, of which this student happens to be a native and an inhabitant, it is regarded as a form of treason to speak of China except in terms of contumely. The attitude is a common one among the ruling cliques of Africa too. He is aware that he throws himself open to that charge in discussing Chinese affairs with politeness and objectivity. It is a risk that he is happy to run, if at the same time he can let in a little genuine light on the baffling problems of African re-birth. The world climax is too close upon us for grown men to allow themselves to be scared by childish bogies. He is comforted at finding himself in Dumont's company here, and proud to acknowledge his debt to Dumont's work.

China's independence came only about ten years ahead of Africa's. The country at that time had been ravaged by twenty years of war, and degraded by a century of colonialism. In point of economic development, the Chinese were among the most retarded nations of the world. China was already a land of endemic famine, sunk, in relation to its current productive capacity, in a terrifying slough of over-population. Its general situation was incalculably worse than that of any tropical African country since 1960, except the Belgian Congo.

The victory in the civil war had, however, been won by a well disciplined Communist Party. The Party leaders, who were also the political rulers, held the U.S.S.R. in warm regard as the father of practical communism, whose struggles and achievements afforded the only possible model for China to adopt. They showed no hesitation in stepping briskly out along the trail which the Bolsheviks had blazed over the previous thirty years. The key to Chinese development was to be urban industrialisation, with heavy industry as its base, plus the dictatorship of the proletariat.

Experience quickly showed that this pattern did not work in Chinese conditions. No rapid economic expansion took place. The Party, beginning to suspect that growth in China would have to be based on the peasantry, and not on industrial wage-earners, set out to re-think the whole problem of Chinese socialism. The end-result, after many years of intensive deliberation, was a new model which completely set aside the Soviet design. In accordance with Chinese custom, admission of this parting of the ways was a gradual process. It was not until 1964 that Chou En-lai openly and officially declared "the order of priority is agriculture, light industry, heavy industry".

By reducing the scope of heavy industry, the planners released large quantities of materials, equipment, and labour, and were therefore able to raise the proportion of investment earmarked for agriculture and for modes of production directly serving it, such as hydro-electric schemes, fertilisers, farm machinery, insecticides.

The People's Communes were originally conceived as the form of organisation for carrying out a great leap forward along the whole economic front including heavy industry. Their character and aims naturally shifted with the new primacy accorded to the rural interest. The constitution of the original type of Commune (it was christened Sputnik in honour of the U.S.S.R., rather ironically in view of later events) was published on 7 August 1958. There followed four years of radical experiment and re-adaptation, In 1962 the New Model Commune emerged in a fairly standardised form which gave effect to the special importance of the peasantry. It has undergone only minor structural alterations since.

The Commune, however, remains capable of indefinite organic evolution in harmony with changes in "the law of the situation". It is a mistake to suppose, as some enemies of China too readily do, that a phase of ossification is setting in. The official watchword of the future is continuous review, taking time by the forelock. Chen Yi declared in an interview on 12 May 1964: "At last we know precisely how to proceed. We have made and re-made the Communes, and if necessary we shall re-make them again until perfection is reached."[1] It is this fluent adaptability of structure, this ease of response to improved design, which should be of special interest in Africa.

§2. *Growth of the Commune*

The People's Commune did not spring fully armed from the brain of Chairman Mao. It grew naturally from objective and flexible attempts by peasants and Party alike to apply co-operative principles to farm production in Chinese conditions. In this early growth between 1952 and 1957 four main steps can be traced.

(1) *Mutual aid teams.* These were made up of anything from 6 to 15 households working together, at first on a seasonal basis, and chiefly on "public works" of an environmental rather than

[1] Quoted in Dumont, op. cit., p. 99.

a directly productive nature, e.g. roads, drainage, water supplies, conservation, etc. People found that it paid them to make such *ad hoc* arrangements permanent, and to extend them to many tasks of production. Such groups had long been known in China. The Party simply generalised them.

(2) *Agricultural producers' co-operatives (lower-grade)*. As the mutual aid teams became better organised and more universal, difficulties often arose in attempting to mix the collective character of the work with the private control of land, draught animals, implements, etc.

In the U.S.S.R. nationalisation of the land had been one of the very first steps taken by the revolution. In China, on the contrary, the development of the Communes has not so far called for such a policy, and the land is still unnationalised. Instead, the early producer co-ops met their problem by empowering their management committees to direct the utilisation of the land (still *owned* in private) in accordance with an agreed plan. All produce, furthermore, was treated as a unit for distribution. From it was taken first the tax, then the allocations for investment and welfare, the residue finally being apportioned among members according to the work and the land put in by each.

The reforms imparted a new development-momentum to the "lower-grade" co-op. Output increased significantly, and with it the earnings of members. The collective investments in turn, by constantly modernising the infrastructure, further improved the possibilities of production.

As the level rises in this way, new difficulties special to it crop up. Irrigation schemes, for instance, financed by collective investment and serving the holdings of many members, have to be installed on the privately owned land of one or a few. Or again a persistent tendency appears, in the distribution of earnings, for a member contributing more land and less labour to get a larger share than one contributing more labour and less land.

(3) *Agricultural producers' co-operatives (higher-grade)*. It is in resolving difficulties of this sort that the higher-grade co-ops (later to be called brigades) emerge. In them the land, together

with all other productive capital, becomes the collective property of the society as such. The element of land rent is eliminated from the calculation of members' earnings, which henceforward are distributed on the sole basis of work done (with adjustments for variations in the character of the land). At this stage, too, a new feature is introduced in the form of social assistance. "The five guarantees" are given to member-families who may fall into hardship—nourishment, clothing, shelter, education of children, and decent burial.

Members retain ownership of their houses, their small live-stock, and their private allotments (the aggregate of which, however, must not reach 10 per cent of the area worked by the co-op.).

The higher-grade co-op, like the lower-grade, settles its own production plan.

(4) *Non-agricultural organs*. Complementary to the higher-grade co-op, and essential for speeding up the rhythm of development, are co-ops for marketing, supply, credit and thrift, and crafts. In their beginnings these are really local agents, enjoying a considerable measure of autonomy, of the State Plan for sales and purchases. At a later stage they re-enter the scene as autonomous enterprises of the People's Commune. Between them they furnish the ground for a network of small rural business and industries which, as they grow, modernise themselves by whatever means are at hand.

§3. *The Commune's main components*

Such, in outline, was the position reached by agrarian policy in China by 1958, nine years after victory in the Civil War. In that year, as has been mentioned, the formal constitution of the People's Commune (Mark I) was for the first time made public. There immediately began a period of intensive growth and re-shaping of the prototype which lasted for four years. For an account of this complex series of difficulties, advances, retreats, successes, and failures the student is referred to pages 66–82 of Dumont's book, where details are impartially given. By 1962 the New Model commune, like a modern airliner, its development and its tests completed, was ready to go into commercial production.

The changes in design between Mark I and the New Model were made partly in response to the internal needs of the People's Commune considered as a social organism, partly in the light of larger events by which all China was affected. The four-year period includes the great leap forward, and the long black years of 1959–62 which shook the country to the core. It therefore includes the summer of 1960 when the Soviet experts and Soviet technical and financial aid were withdrawn. Thenceforward China was to live, albeit of choice as well as of necessity, by the motto "By ourselves alone", which applies to the People's Communes just as strictly as to the Chinese State.

By 1965 China completed the repayment of all her indebtedness to the U.S.S.R., including the cost of military supplies used in the Korean war. The Soviet offer, made in 1963, to reopen credits and renew the loan of experts was definitively refused, lest these things should be employed as instruments of political pressure.

The New Model commune has four basic components:

(1) *the work-teams.* These vary in number from one commune to another. There were 70 of them in one typical commune reported by Dumont (p. 136). Each work-team manages its own affairs by way of a general meeting of all members. Its day-to-day tasks are directed by its elected manager.

(2) *the brigades.* These consist of groups of work-teams. Each brigade is managed by a committee to which the work-teams nominate their delegates.

(3) *the commune.* The Council of the commune is constituted by representatives of the Brigade Committees chosen for two years. The Council meets twice yearly. Its General Purposes Committee, having elected a director and a deputy-director, meets once a week.

The director is assisted by various administrative sections, for example those concerned with accounts, purchases and sales, crop production, stock raising, works (i.e. buildings, irrigation, electricity), farm mechanisation, seed selection and testing.

(4) *the science team.* A further component part of some communes, though not yet of all—a feature of great interest and importance—is the science team. In the case of the commune *China-Cuba,* visited by Dumont in 1965, it was made up of 32 graduates, 43 technicians, and 360 peasant members, many of whom were undertaking evening courses of training. Twenty research scientists were testing various possibilities of technical progress.

The commune, for its part, through its personnel and installations, provides the science team with ample means of observation, experiment, and action.

The commune production plan forms, of course, an integral part of the State Plan, and is worked out, after a prolonged flow of two-way consultative traffic, at the level of the district; similarly the brigade production plan is worked out at the level of the commune; and the work-team production plan at the brigade level (though the means of executing the production plan agreed remain the responsibility of the work-team).

The production plan settles

(1) the kinds and amounts of output to be produced in the year;
(2) the amounts to be marketed, especially sales to the State;
(3) the gross income;
(4) members' earnings;
(5) allocations for investment.

In arriving at operative decisions on these matters, the *Three in One* rule is applied. In other words, on every important issue there must be unanimous agreement between the management (which includes the Party), the technicians, and the workpeople, especially the older peasants who represent an indispensable fund of local experience.

In point of size communes vary widely. Dumont reports that the smallest of the 22 communes which he visited had 10,000 inhabitants, and the largest had 75,000, though the latter was by no means typical because it was on the outskirts of the main town of the district.

Where a commune has a work-force of more than 3,000, it is usual to find it made up of 10–20 brigades, and a hundred or more work-teams.

The commune known as *China-Cuba* originated from 100 lower-grade co-ops, which merged in 1956 to form 3 higher-grade co-ops, thus regrouping 46 villages.

In 1965 *China-Cuba* consisted of 7,000 households, totalling 30,000 inhabitants. It had 3,600 hectares of land in cultivation. Of the inhabitants roughly a third were producers, a third were in school, and a third were housewives and elderly people. Of the producers a majority were women.

Dumont also throws light on the structure of earnings and costs from the case of the commune called *Han-Tcheun*. The table shows the heads of revenue and expenditure at work-team and brigade level. It does not take into account the various enterprises organised at commune level, namely poultry breeding, plant breeding, boat building, manufacture of farm implements, rice threshing, brick making, sugar refining, paper making.

REVENUE		EXPENDITURE	
Head	*per cent*	*Head*	*per cent*
sugar cane	24·0	investment	10·7
latania	14·5	workers' earnings	52·4
rice	40·6	welfare	1·2
groundnuts	5·1	running costs	29·7
other crops	7·1	land tax	6·0
(including fish and fruit)			
secondary occupations	8·7		
	100·0		100·0

Land tax is fixed at a rate which works out at 8–13 per cent of gross output in an average harvest. The 6 per cent rate in this example shows that the commune is more productive than the average.

§4. *The pillars of the system*

Even so brief an outline as the above affords some scope for assessing the first-order significance of the commune system. Four features appear to qualify for this description.

(a) China has founded its whole strategy on the farming domain as the crucial point of departure for all balanced social and economic development.

(b) Hence it endows the peasant unit of production with political and administrative powers. The commune management, merging as it does with the ground-level organs of the State administration, is responsible for all aspects of affairs within its area.

Dumont quotes (p. 83) the official definition: "The People's Commune is the basic unit of our socialist social structure, as also of the power structure of our socialist state. It brings together industry, agriculture, commerce, education, and military affairs."

This is an unusual, perhaps a unique, combination of competences to be entrusted to an organ of local government. The long-term consequences of its introduction seem likely to be important not only within China. Some observers, friendly and hostile alike, speak of it almost with bated breath, as if nothing in the world can henceforward be quite the same.

(c) China fuses together at all educational levels scholastic work with manual work. In this way a cultural cleavage between peasants and intelligentsia is sought to be avoided, officialdom to be prevented from hardening into a privileged caste, and the output of neo-mandarins from the school system to be radically curtailed. The Soviet weakness of arrogance among managers and the Cuban weakness of indiscipline among workpeople will both, it is hoped, be by-passed.

An enormous and constant effort of in-training is made, an unresting search for ways of upgrading the performance of workers on the job. Book-keepers, statisticians, "model-workers" stream through the agronomic institutes, refresher courses are arranged for those in authority, high or low.

Dumont's feeling is clearly that this intense preoccupation

with the means to an efficient social and economic order is matched by equal attention to the realm of ends. Every Chinese citizen is urged and helped to reflect as deeply as he can on the motives and the relationships of mutual aid, and on the requirements of the common good. This, in the party jargon, is called raising the level of socialist consciousness. It provides Chinese society, leaders and led, with what is altogether missing from African, a point to march on and to get its bearings by.

The outcome is the spread of an ascetic morality which seeks flexible sophistication in public affairs, yet holds to the child-state in private conduct. As all observers testify, it results in a marked reduction of corruption (in the African sense) in Chinese life. The resolve of Chinese leaders to *rester avec les pauvres* is always evident. *Puisse l'Afrique raisonner ainsi.*

(d) China has acknowledged the need to limit population growth, if economic expansion and social growth are to be speeded up. To be sure, there have been some fluctuations in the official line on this thorny issue. For the first six years of the revolution the issue was not faced at all, and was evidently not thought of as having high priority. In 1956–7 contraceptive practices were tentatively recommended by posters, etc., up and down the country. The year 1958 saw a complete *volte-face*, and all birth control steps were harshly condemned, at least in words.

The reversal, it seems, was based on the simplified view that every consumer is, or may be, also a producer. As the Chinese put it, each new mouth is accompanied by two new arms. The arms would increase the food supply in a measure satisfying to the mouth. The magnitude of the problem had been very faultily assessed.

The population growth-rate assumed in the first 5-year plan (1952–57) was 2·23 per cent a year. On a total population of 650 millions this would mean an annual increase of some 14 millions. It did not take the planners long to find out that any idea of feeding such numbers by stepping up Chinese agriculture was in the long term quite chimerical. Even at

650 millions, China was seriously overpopulated. The real need was to bring the growth-rate down below 1 per cent a year.

China always seeks to know the facts; and once they are known they are decisive. In 1963 the official line was corrected. Thenceforward the emphasis was on the paramount necessity of planned parenthood. Japan has cut its birth-rate by half in ten years, mainly by means of generalised abortion. China now discreetly does what it can to terminate unwanted pregnancies in the same way, subject to limits imposed by the distribution of doctors and rural clinics.

It also makes use of an ingenious variety of social and political pressures. The age of marriage is retarded by film propaganda. The allocation of housing is held up, often till the age of 30 for men and 25 for women. The private land-holdings of members of work-teams are limited to $\frac{1}{3}$ acre per head, with a maximum of 2 acres per household, so that parents cannot acquire an out-size plot by raising an out-size family.

Political discipline in China is such that the State and the Party can, as a serious practical measure, recommend not only the use of contraceptives, but also the observance of general continence. When Chairman Mao proclaims "It pays better to swat mosquitoes than to make love", he has some assurance that his powerful thoughts will indeed reduce the human as well as the insect population. Numbers of young people, devotees of the revolution, have responded by taking vows of permanent chastity, and their resolve has been warmly praised in public by Chou En-lai. *Puisse l'Afrique raisonner ainsi.*

§5. *Some secondary gains*

Such are the principles which form the main pillars of the commune system. If the New China is upheld by them, they may have a central significance for African modernisation also, as soon as African leaders come to study carefully their bearing on Africa's problems—which, after all, are in essence remarkably similar to China's. Indeed, it seems absurd that Africa should not benefit, and quickly, from the brilliant inventiveness of the Chinese experiments in social and economic organisation. Certainly the People's Commune is not a model that African countries can just copy word for word. But its organising principles can equally certainly be adapted to fit the material and the psycho-social conditions of Africa. For that, no more is needed that a sufficient proportion of Africans with the wit and the motive to grasp fully what those organising principles are all about.

When this adequate number of adequate Africans at length takes the field, they will be struck by the richness of second-order advantages that flow from the four cardinal points.

For example, the commune, by reason of its scale and scope, paves the way for an ever more sophisticated division of labour and an ever more varied pattern of land use within the farming process itself, by setting up, when occasion arises, special work-teams or brigades for fishing, fruit-growing, forestry, market-gardening, bee-keeping, poultry farming, pig production, dairying, industrial crops, etc. Equally important, it can provide economically a range of workshops and processing plants to service farm production. It can thus gradually bring about the measure of development in light industry that village life needs for full amenity, without allowing its perversion into the wasteful and psychologically perilous disorder of urbanism.

Industry introduced in this way to the heart of the village, even if it pauses temporarily at the craft stage (the level of "intermediate technology"), transforms the village mentality, deepens its belief in science and progress, diffuses among the rank and file the outlook of the estate manager and improver. At the same time, it offers a kind of preliminary training in the efficient use of tractors, engines, and power-machinery in general.

Again, the commune, in the readjusted and consolidated form now virtually universal in China, well appreciates the need to decentralise responsibility for the day-to-day running of farm work. The most important economic power, that which relates to the daily round and can take account of such vital details as rain or frost or settled sunny weather, is entrusted to the small units, usually the work-teams, sometimes the brigades, especially when "socialist consciousness" is well advanced in them.

With such necessary decentralisation the commune mixes a unified direction wherever it is desirable to maintain this, e.g. in settling of production plans, in planning large-scale construction, in arrangements for deliveries in kind to the State, in the disposal of local grain surpluses and of industrial crops. The mixture makes possible a constant dialogue between base and summit, which is a real exchange of views and not a mere transmission of orders from on high followed too late by remonstrances from below. As the Chinese put it, "the work-team within the commune is like a fish in water. As the fish, though it holds the initiative, is helpless without the water, so the team without the commune also is helpless." In economic terms, the work-team contributes the advantages of optimum location, the commune those of scale.

Another of the commune's claims is to have dealt successfully with that bugbear of Africa, the issue of rural investment. The commune is the channel for work-investment at all three levels, team, brigade, and commune itself, and such investment often approaches and sometimes exceeds 10 per cent of all days worked.

More specifically, Dumont lists all sources of investment internal to the commune and gives them a value:

(a) half the land tax   say 4·5 per cent of gross output
(b) the investment funds
    of work-teams,
    brigades and
    communes   say 7·0 ,,   ,,   ,,   ,,   ,,
(c) work-days earmarked
    for infrastructure
    work   say 5·0 ,,   ,,   ,,   ,,   ,,

Thus we get 15–20 per cent of farm output going into rural investment, a rate unknown in Europe before the industrial revolution, and unknown elsewhere in the Third World today.

Work-days earmarked by the communes as human investment have had remarkable effects on a vast scale all over China,
especially in connection with water-control. The Chinese used
to have a song

> No rain for three days and we're fighting drought;
> Two rainy days and the floods are out.

In many parts now they are close to the full mastery of water,
by means of electric pumping-stations (used for both drainage
and irrigation), together with dams and reservoirs which work
by gravity. Dumont sums up : The enormous mass of investment
has issued in a profound transformation of the countryside,
above all in the way of water storage and control, the reclamation and levelling of land, afforestation, and anti-erosion
works.

The Chinese evidence is proof, which Africa must surely one
day heed, that the sole factor which cannot be dispensed with in
social development is an unshakeable reliance on self-help. If
that is absent, foreign aid is useless; if that is present, foreign
aid is, if not otiose, at least very secondary.

Self-help, among many other things, involves putting the
whole rural population to productive work the whole year
round, as the only possible way of reaching that high rate of
productive investment which is everywhere and always the vital
fulcrum of generalised growth. Among African peasant farmers,
working the whole year round is something that has never
and nowhere been known.

Finally, over and above the investment question, the commune system displays an economic sophistication which may
well prove decisive for human relations in industry. It has shown
how to avoid the more serious defects of agricultural organisation in the U.S.S.R. and Cuba, namely too large work-teams,
tax-liability which rises with productivity, and earnings not
geared to output.

In consequence, it is well on the way to solving the big
problem of socialism during the phase of struggle to establish
itself alongside a predominant capitalism. This is the problem

of working out an incomes policy which, while being fair as between persons and grades, is at the same time the most effective in encouraging individual endeavour within the framework of the collective task.

INDEX

A.A.L.A. countries: rural and peasant nature of, 49–50; and China, 50–3; detachment of Latin America, 53–4; and the U.N., 54–5; urbanisation in, 106, 107, 112

A.A.L.A. Gap, 13, 19, 21, 35–7, 40, 41, 44–6, 50, 54, 106, 188, 189, 210, 212, 213, 216, 223–5

Abidjan, Ivory Coast: riots in, 154; population, 182

Accra, Ghana, 110, 159

Action Group. *See* A.G.

Adaji, Alhaji Hasim, 260

Addis Ababa, Ethiopia, Conference of African States at (1961), 244

Addo, N. O., *Demographic Aspects of Urban Development in Ghana in the 20th Century*, 104, 111

Ademulegun, Brigadier Sam, 258–9

African Independence Party for Guinea and the Cape Verdes. *See* P.A.I.G.C.

African Socialism in its Application to Planning in Kenya (Kenya White Paper), 81–2

Afrifa, Brigadier, 155n.

A.G. (Action Group; Nigeria), 254, 255, 257, 260

Agriculture: subsistence farming, 74, 77–8, 121; land allocation and land use, 87–9; full-time profitable farming, 89–96; planning and execution of development programmes, 97–8; introduction of the industrial factor, 98–101; organisation and improvement of community life, 101–5; and education, 119–20; in the Ivory Coast, 172–6; in Guinea (Conakry), 199–202; in Rhodesia, 239–40, 245; in China, 280–2, 283–7

Akintola, Chief Samuel Ladoke, 257–9

Akoliufu Farm Project, Nigeria, 87–89, 110

Algeria, 179, 186, 267, 274

All Peoples Congress (Sierra Leone), 165

Amin, Samir, 169

Aristophanes, 191

Arusha declaration, Nyerere's, 208

Asians, 135, 143–8, 149

Attwood, William, 184n, 185, 196

Australia, 50

Awolowo, Chief Obafemi, 257, 263, 269–71, 273

Balewa, Sir Abubakar Tafala (Federal Prime Minister, Nigeria) 259

Bananas, 170, 173, 174, 202

Banks (foreign), possible nationalisation of, 165–6

Bauxite, 193

Beadwork, 100

Bello, Air Ahmadu, 258, 259, 266

Benin City, Nigeria, 16–17, 258n.

Biafra, 207, 238, 274, 277–8; population, 275n.

Bilharzia, 103

Birth-rate: necessity of reduction, 79–81; family planning, 81–3; possible results of a population policy, 83–4
See also Population problem

Bismarck, Otto von, 36

Blohorn, firm of, 170

Boké, Guinea, 195
B.P.N. (Bureau Politique, Guinea), 187, 189
Brazzaville Conference (1944), 177
Brazzaville group of states, 179
Britain. *See* United Kingdom
Bulawayo African Township (Rhodesia), Sculpture Centre in, 249
Bureau Politique National. *See* B.P.N.
Burundi, 60

Cabral, Amilcar, 162
Cameroon, 60; output per head, 28; French influence, 207; statistics of, 234
Caradon, Lord, 31
Cavour, Count, 36
Central African Federation, 133, 238
Central African Republic, 60
Ceramics, 100
Chad, 60, 153; output per head, 28; statistics of, 234
Chad Basin Commission, 157
Chaka, 17–18
Charbonneau, René, 176
Charity, old and new concepts of, 213–15
Chen Yi, 282
Chiang Kai-shek, 52
Child welfare, 78
Chile, 81
China, 34, 39, 81, 189; seeks leadership of A.A.L.A. group, 50–2; industrialisation, 50–1, 281, 282; quarrel with U.S.S.R., 51; plan for struggle with N.A.T.O. powers 52–3; and the U.N., 54; and the anti-N.A.T.O. front in Africa, 151; aid to Guinea, 196, 197; development strategy, 221; agriculture, 280–2; growth of the Commune, 282–4; main components of the Commune, 284–7; results of Commune system, 288–294

Chou En-lai, 281, 290
Class struggle, Guinean concept of, 187–8
Cocoa, 31, 44, 170, 173, 174
Coconut-palm, 174
Coffee, 170, 173, 174, 200, 201–2
Collèges d'Enseignement Rural, in Guinea, 201
Colonial system, 24
Common Market. *See* European Economic Community; West African Common Market
Commune system. *See* China
Communist Party, Chinese, 281
Community development, in Rhodesia, 239–41
Community life, organisation and improvement of, 101–5
Community principle, 114–15
Conakry, Guinea, 193, 194; conference at (1957), 190
Confectionery, 100
Congo, River, 27
Congo Basin treaty, 20
Congo Brazzaville, 60, 117
Congo-Kinshasha, 11, 147, 179, 222, 274; political disunity, 60
Conservative Government (U.K.; 1951–5), 238
Contraception, 82–3, 289
See also Birth-rate; Population problem
Co-operative Bank of Eastern Nigeria, 90
Copper, 45
Cotton, 174
Cuba, 221, 288, 293
Cultural improvement, related to genetic improvement, 76
Currency question, in Guinea, 202–203
Czechoslovakia, 197

Dahomey, 60, 62, 154n,; expenditure on public salaries, 61; poverty and tribalism in, 115–16; joins U.D.O.A., 155; statistics of, 235
Daily Times (Lagos), 262, 263

David, Kingsley, 106-9, 113
Death-rate. *See* Mortality rate
Débrouillage, 57-8, 228
Decentralisation, in China, 291-2
Déséquilibre ville-campagne. See Town and country disequilibrium problem
Development Decade. *See* United Nations
Dia, Mamadou, 164
Diamonds, 45, 200
Diawara, Mahomed, 180, 182-3
Dingana, 17
Dressmaking, 100
Dual Mandate, Lugard's, 21
Dumont, René, 223; *Chine Surpeuplée*, 280-1, 284-6, 288, 292-3

East Africa, strength of independence in, 207
East African Federation project, 152
East Cameroon, agriculture in, 85
East Germany, 197
E.C.A. (Economic Commission for Africa), 159-60
Education: in Tanzania, 73; the rural and urban elites, 117; schooling for the peasantry, 117-118; reform of the system, 118-120; and tribalism, 120-1; the goal of universal education, 121-124; failure to draw peasantry into main stream, 124-5; teaching of rural science, 125-6; literacy training and selection for postprimary schooling, 126-8; pace of advance, 128-9; distortion in the system, 129-30; necessity to eliminate waste, 130-1; in Rhodesia, 244-5
Egypt. *See* United Arab Republic
Ejoh, Lieut.-Col., 260
Electrical appliances, 100
Embroidery, 100
Entente States, 154
Enugu, Nigeria, 273; University of, 266
Esua, E. E., 258

European Economic Community, 161, 212
Evolution, progress of, 76-7
Expectation of life, 24
Export markets, the race for, 34

Fajuyi, Lieut.-Col., 26*n.*, 260, 263
Family planning, 81-3, 192; in China, 289
See also Population problem
Fanon, Frantz, 150*n.*, 217, 222-3
Farming. *See* Agriculture
Foreign aid, African attitude to, 23-4
Foreign domination, ill-effects of, 19-21
Foulah, 190
France, 33, 195; and the Franco-African Community, 152-5; and the Ivory Coast, 169, 177-8; and Guinea, 184-6, 197; influence in Senegal, Ivory Coast and Cameroon, 207
Franco-African Community, 152-5
French Somaliland, 9
French Union, 152
F.R.I.A., firm of, 195

Gabon, 60, 117; output per head, 28
Gambia, 54, 60, 164
Gaulle, General de, 152-3, 117, 184-6, 202-3, 207*n.*
G.C.F. (Great Colonial France), 177, 179, 183
Genetic improvement, related to cultural improvement, 76-7
George, Henry, 212
Germany, 34
Ghana, 9, 22-3, 60, 61, 121, 196, 207*n.*, 208,; output per head, 28; danger of bankruptcy, 37; growth of G.N.P., 85-6; urbanisation in, 107, 109; Volta River Resettlement Scheme, 109-11; Seven-Year Plan, 111; separatism in, 155; statistics of, 234
Gladstone, W. E., 264
Gold, 45

Gouina, Mali, 158, 159
Gowon, Major-General Y., 261, 262n., 263, 265–6, 269–75
Graduate output, 130
Great Colonial France. See G.C.F.
Gross National Product, estimated for next 20 years, 84
Groundnuts, 202
Guerrilla fighters, 150, 239
Guinea (Bissau), 9, 162, 164; precariously held by Portuguese, 163
Guinea (Conakry), 60, 122, 159, 162, 167, 207, 210, 212, 216n.; joins W.A.F.T.A., 156; and the Senegal Basin Scheme, 157; possible political development in, 163; first nine years of independence, 184–5; declines to join French Community, 185–6; the P.D.G. and the class struggle, 186–9; Touré takes control, 189–90; tribal reforms, 190–1; enfranchisement of women, 191–2; attempt to suppress polygamy, 191–2; best organised state in West Africa, 192–3; natural resources, 193; precarious economy, 193–4; state of the economy, 194–196; foreign aid to, 196–7; industry, 197–9; agriculture, 199–202; currency question, 202–3; harshness of habitat, 203–4; seeks commercial and financial independence, 211; statistics of, 235

Hausa-Fulani people, 255
Health services, 78–80
Henderson Research Station, Mazoe (Rhodesia), 119
Hitler, Adolf, 277
Hospital services, segregation is abolished in Kenya, 137
Houphouët-Boigny, M. (President of the Ivory Coast), 28, 153–4, 177, 179, 185
Human capacity, waste of, 69–71
Hydro-electricity, 27, 39, 110
Hygiene, 103

Ibadan University (Nigeria), First African Population Conference at, 208, 256n.
Ibo people, 255, 264
Incomes policy, 294
Independence: problems of, 29–32; more prized in East than in West Africa, 207; lack of preparation for, 208; cardinal issues arising from, 208
India, 20, 34, 81, 147; urbanisation in, 108, 220
Indigent countries: economic stagnation in, 30; Patel's blueprint for Africa, 30; advance in 1964, 31; average annual rate growth since 1960, 31; factors against development, 31–2; exploitation of, 34–5; affluence of overdeveloped nations related to indigence of under-developed, 35–6; international development aid, 36–9, the Onitri Gap, 39–42
See also Third World
Indo-China, 53
Indonesia, 54, 264
Industrial Growth in Africa (U.N. publication), 71
Industry: increase of urban industry 71–2; equipment of light industries in relation to agriculture, 98–101; in Ivory Coast, 167–9,; in Guinea, 197–9; in Rhodesia, 241–4, 246, 247; in China, 281, 282
Inefficiency, 69–70
Integrated rural development, 97
Intellectuals: expatriate, 217; native, and the peasantry, 217–18
International Development Aid, 36–39, 213–14
Ironsi, Major-General Aguiyi-, 26n., 259n., 260–3, 269
Irrigation schemes, in China, 283
Italy, 33, 34
Ivory Coast, 60, 117; output per head, 28; and the Franco-African Community, 153, 154; joins

U.D.O.A. and W.A.F.T.A., 155–156; economic expansion 1960–65 167–9; European job-holders in, 170–1; African labour market, 171–2; the peasantry, 172–6; expansion without growth, 176–8; hopeful signs, 178–81; strategy of national development, 181–3, 208, 211–13; French influence, 207; attitude to the Third World, 212; public and private sector investments, 214; statistics of, 235

Jackson, Dr. L. N., 69
Japan, 33, 34, 49, 83, 84; decline in birth-rate, 290
Jeune Afrique, 185
Jewellery, 100
Johnson, President Lyndon, 223
Journal of Modern African Studies, 30
Jugoslavia, 196

Kaduna, Nigeria, 273
Kaldor, Nicholas, 38
Kano, Nigeria, disorders in, 254
Katsina, Major Hassan, 260
Kent, Colonel John, 96
Kenya, 24, 60, 83, 84, 210, 216n.; output per head, 28; pioneer in family planning, 81–2; Million-acre Scheme, 91–4, 97; Development Plan 1964–70, 94; and the white settlers, 94–6; Central Land Board, 96, 97; Department of Settlement, 97, 102; Surveys Department, 97; Agriculture Department, 97; race issue, 133–138, 147; statistics of, 234
Kenya Plantation and Agricultural Workers' Union, 95
Kinangop, Nigeria, 96
Korean war, 285
Ku Chawe Inn, Malawi, 47

Lagos, Nigeria, 265, 269, 271, 272, 274
Land problem: land tenure, 59;

fragmentation of holdings, 59–61; Land Apportionment Act (Southern Rhodesia), 243, 250n.; in China, 283, 287
See also Agriculture
Latin America, 49, 59
Leadership, inadequacies of, 29
Lenin, 29, 188
Liberation movement, 36
Liberia, 60, 168, 176, 193, 200; joins W.A.F.T.A., 156; the privileged settler minority, 207; statistics of, 234
Lincoln, Abraham, 36
Literacy training, 127
Living standards, comparative. *See* A.A.L.A. Gap
Lugard, Lord, 21

Madagascar, 153
Magic, 121
Magwende Commission, Rhodesia, 246
Malawi, 60, 238; output per head, 28; and the Ivory Coast, 212; statistics of, 234
Maldives, 54
Mali, 60, 162, 197, 207n., 216n.; output per head, 28; 'aid' to, 38; joins U.D.O.A., 155; and the Senegal Basin Scheme, 157, 159, 163,; struggles towards socialist development, 163; statistics of, 235
Mali Federation, 160
Malinke, 190
Mao Tse-tung, 52, 282, 290
Margai, Sir Albert, 196
Market towns, project for, 103–4
Marx, Karl, 188
Mauritania, 60, 164; output per head, 28; joins U.D.O.A., 155; and the Senegal Basin scheme, 157; signs Common Market agreement, 159; statistics of, 235
Mazoe. *See* Henderson Research Station
Metal-work, 100

Million-acre Scheme, Kenya, 91–4, 97, 110
Mineral resources, 27
Mining, increase of, 71–2
Modernisation, definition of, 167
Monde, Le, 214
Monrovia, Liberia, 193
Morocco, 81, 196
Mortality rate, 24–5; social effects of reduction of, 79–80
Multi-racialism, 146

Nairobi, Kenya: Central Land Board in, 96, 97; secondary schools in, 136–7
National Council of Nigeria and Cameroon. *See* N.C.N.C.
National Family Programmes: a Guide (U.S. Population Council), 82
Nationalisation of banks, 165–6
N.A.T.O. countries, 36, 41, 43–6, 50, 59, 129, 188, 189, 212, 225, 228; and the U.N., 54–5; future prospects, 55–6; urbanism in, 107, 108, 113, 219, 220; revolt of the Third World against, 150–1, 210–11, 215, 223
N.C.N.C. (National Council of Nigeria and Cameroon), 254, 260
Neo-colonialism, 24, 37, 63, 77
New Nigerian (Kaduna), 263
New Zealand, 50
Niger, 60, 117, 154; output per head, 28; joins U.D.O.A., 155; statistics of, 235
Niger, River, 27
Niger expedition, 20
Nigeria, 11, 36, 61, 83, 147, 222; execution of Ironsi, 26*n.*; output per head, 28; political disunity, 60; agriculture, 87–90; number of persons employed in education, 128; separatism in, 155; signs Common Market agreement, 159; Moslem political control, 207; statistics of, 234; division into three regions, and the political

parties, 254; constitution of October 1954, 254–5; becomes independent, 255; dominance of the North, 255–6; Federal Government takes over the Western region, 256–8; the Army take-over of January 1966, 258–60; the Ironsi regime, 260–1; the North takes revenge, 261–4; end of the First Republic, 264–7; the North attempts to liquidate the East, 267–70, 277–8; the Second Republic, 270–4; Northern fear and hatred of the East, 274–8
Nigerian National Democratic Party. *See* N.N.D.P.
Nile, River, 27
Nkrumah, Kwame, 28, 180, 196
N.N.D.P. (Nigerian National Democratic Party), 257, 258, 260
Non-racialism, 146
North Africa, attendance at schools in, 129
Northern People's Congress, *See* N.P.C.
Northern Rhodesia. *See* Zambia
Nouakchott, Mauritania, conference at, 157
N.P.C. (Northern People's Congress; Nigeria), 254–7, 260, 262, 264, 266
Nsukka, University of (Nigeria), 266
Nyasaland. *See* Malawi
Nyerere, Julius, 141, 142, 152, 165, 208
Nzeogwu, Major Chukwuma, 259, 262

O.A.U. (Organisation for African Unity), 20, 179, 267*n.*; Summit Conference (1963), 161
O.C.A.M. (Organisation Commune Africaine et Malgache), 179
Ojukwu, Lieut.-Col., 260, 263, 265, 268–71, 274
Okotie-Eboh, Chief Festus, 259
Oligarchies, 62
Onitri, Dr. H.M.A., 39–40

Onitri Gap, 39–42, 59–60, 62, 77, 85, 93, 112, 188, 126–17
Organisation Commune Africaine et Malgache. *See* O.C.A.M.
Organisation for African Unity. *See* O.A.U.
Orizu, Dr. Nwafor, 259
Outgrowers, 175
Output per head, 28
Owerri (Nigeria), Industrial Development Centre in, 100

P.A.I.G.C. (African Independence Party for Guinea and the Cape Verdes), 163
Pakistan, 81
Palestine, 239
Palm oil, 170, 174, 175, 202
Pan-African monetary zone, proposed, 171
Parti Démocratique de Guinée. *See* P.D.G.
Partition of Africa, 34
Patel, Surendra J., 30, 39
P.D.G. (Parti Démocratique de Guinée), 185–9, 191–2, 200, 202–203
Peasantry, the: and education, 124–125; the problem in the Ivory Coast, 172–6; and the intellectuals, 217–18; of Africa the prototype of all peasantry, 229–31
Petroleum, 45
Pineapples, 170, 174, 175, 202
Plastics, 100, 198
Pléven, René, 177, 178
Political fragmentation, 60–1
Polygamy, attempt to suppress it in Guinea, 191–2
Population problem, 69*ff.*, 192, 208–10; in China, 289–90
See also Family planning; Town and country disequilibrium problem
Portugal, 12
Portuguese: alliance with Rhodesia and South Africa, 150; precarious hold in Guinea, 163

Portuguese Guinea. *See* Guinea (Bissau)
Positive Policy, 20, 21, 40; social planning, 58–9; and fragmentation of land-holdings, 59–60; and political fragmentation, 60–1; obliged to mark time, 62; and neo-colonialism, 63; and the leadership, 63–5; and waste of human capacity, 69–72; and training of manpower reserves, 72; and population increase, 72–5, 77–84; and a general productivity policy, 75–6, 77–9; and evolutionary processes, 76–7; and educational aspects, 114
Primary schools, 105; percentage attending, 73, 129; high costs, 131; in Rhodesia, 244–5
Productivity policy, need of, 75–9
Public sector, overstaffing of, 71

Race relations: removal of colour bar, 132–8; improvement in relations, 138–43; the Asians, 143–8; a new era in, 148–50; factors making for violence, 150–1; in Rhodesia, 245, 247–51
Rhodes, Cecil, 69, 248
Rhodesia, 12, 64; output per head, 28; race issue, 133, 138, 143; 247–51; alliance with the Portuguese and South Africa, 150; the privileged settler minority, 207; statistics of, 234; and the Central African Federation, 238; declares independence, 238–9; development of African tribal areas, 239–241; industrial labour, 241–4; African education, 244–5; social and economic results, 245–7
Rice, 174, 210; Research Station, Sierra Leone, 276
Rubber, 170, 174, 175
Russia, her export markets in 19th century, 34
See also U.S.S.R.
Rwanda, Rwanda-Burundi, 60, 274

Salisbury (Rhodesia, Rhodes National Gallery in), 249
Sanitation, 103
Schacht, Hjalmar, 45
Secondary schools: percentage attending, 73, 129; high costs, 131; in Nairobi, 136–7; in Rhodesia, 244
Self-modernisation, 24
Senegal, 60, 153, 200, 202, 203; output per head, 20; school enrolment in, 122–3; and the Senegal Basin scheme, 157; supports P.A.I.G.C., 163; political struggles in, 163–4; French influence, 207; statistics of, 235
Senegal River Basin scheme, 157–9, 161–3, 164
Senghor, President, 122, 153, 158, 164
Separatism, 152, 154–5, 165
Sierra Leone, 60, 162, 200; joins W.A.F.T.A., 156; political struggles in, 165; statistics of, 235
Simpson, J. T., 10
Singapore, 54
Slavery, slave trade, 19–20, 24
Smallwood, Major-General G. R., 80n.
S.M.D.R. (Sociétés Mutuelles de Développement Rural; Guinea), 190
Smith, Ian, 171
Smuggling, in Guinea, 200–1
Sociétés Mutuelles de Développement Rural. See S.M.D.R.
S.O.D.E.P.A.L.M. (Société pour le développement du palmier a huile), 175–6
Soil erosion, 72
Soussou, 190
South Africa, 12, 28, 50, 53, 207; alliance with the Portuguese and Rhodesia, 150
Southern Rhodesia. See Rhodesia
Spanish Guinea, 9
Spanish Sahara, 9
Stevens, Siaka, 162

Subsistence farming, 74, 77–8, 121, 172
See also Agriculture
Sudan, 9, 147, 222, 264, 274
Sugar, 174, 175
Sweden, 107

Tanzania, 60, 207, 212, 216n.; output per head, 28; results of population growth, 73–4; agricultural exports, 78; model village layouts, 102; race issue, 132, statistics of, 234
Teacher training programme, 129
Thant, U, 32
Themistocles, 277
Third World: in revolt against N.A.T.O. countries, 150–1, 188–189, 210–11, 215, 223; struggle of Portuguese Guinea, 163; attitude of African stages to, 212; and Rhodesia, 239
Timber, 170, 174
Timbuktu, Mali, 204
Tin, 45
Togo, 60, 154n.; statistics of, 28, 235
Touré, Sékou, 153, 180, 184–92, 196, 200, 202–3
Town and country disequilibrium problem, 39–42, 59–60, 62, 77, 85, 93, 106–13, 192, 208, 210, 216–21
See also Agriculture; Land problem; Peasantry; Population problem; Urbanisation
Tracheomycose, 202
Trade Unions, and separatism, 155
Trans-Saharan Transport, Committee on, 157
Tribalism: in Dahomey, 115–16; divisive effect, 120–1; and race relations, 151; and separatism, 155; suppression of chiefs and town tribal organisations in Guinea, 190; development of tribal areas in Rhodesia, 239–41
Tshombe, Moise, 28, 179, 268
Tubman, President, 171, 185
Tunisia, 81

Turkey, 81

U.A.M. (Union Africaine et Malgache), 179
U.D.E.A.O. (Union Douanière des Etats de l'Afrique de l'Ouest), 155–6, 161
U.D.O.A. (Union Douanière Ouest-Africaine), 155–6
Uganda, 10, 60, 83, 175; output per head, 28; education in, 130; statistics of, 234
U.N.C.T.A.D. conferences, 42–3, 211n.
Underdeveloped countries. See Indigent countries
Unemployment, 100
U.N.E.S.C.O., 121, 129n., 131
Union Africaine et Malgache. See U.A.M.
Union Douanière des Etats de l'Afrique de l'Ouest. See U.D.E.A.O.
Union Douanière Ouest-Africaine. See U.D.O.A.
United Arab Republic, 11, 81, 196, 266–7
United Kingdom, 31, 33; export markets in 19th century, 34; and Ghana, 37; urbanisation in, 106, 107, 220; and the Asians, 147; and the Central African Federation, 238; and Rhodesia, 239; and Nigeria, 254
United Nations, 31, 208, 239, 267n.,; Development Decade, 31, 35, 38, 74, 75; and the A.A.L.A. group, 54–5; and the colour bar, 132, 133; and the Senegal Basin scheme, 159
United Nations Conference on Trade and Development. See U.N.C.T.A.D.
United People's Party. See U.P.P.
United States, 33; export markets in 19th century, 34; crime increase in, 46; and Latin America, 53;

urbanisation in, 107, 108; and Guinea, 195, 196
Universities, 131, 265
U.P.G.A. (United Progressive Grand Alliance; Nigeria), 256n., 257
Upholstery, 100
U.P.P. (United People's Party, later Nigerian National Democratic Party—See N.N.D.P.), 257
Upper Volta, 60, 62, 154n.; output per head, 28; revolt in, 61; economic planning in, 70–1; joins U.D.O.A., 155; statistics of, 235
U.P.S. (ruling party in Senegal), 164
Urban industry. See Industry
Urbanisation: the dilemma, 106; world growth of, 106–7; in relation to rural development, 107–12
U.S.S.R., 49, 54, 189, 221, 281, 288, 293; quarrel with China, 51; and the anti-N.A.T.O. front in the Arab sector, 150–1; aid to Guinea, 196, 197; urbanisation in, 220; nationalisation of land, 283

Village life. See Community life
Ville-campagne, la question. See Town and country disequilibrium problem
Volta River Resettlement Scheme, 109–11

W.A.E.C. (West African Economic Community), 160, 162
W.A.F.T.A. (West African Free Trade Area), 156, 161
Water supply, 103
West Africa: reorganisation of community life in, 102; attendance at primary and secondary schools, 129; and the colour bar, 132; fragmentation of, 152; and the Franco-African Community, 153–154; vested interests in separatism, 154–5; attempts at a customs union, 155–6; association through

West Africa—*cont.*
common geographical and ecological features, 156–9; plan for an economic community, 159–61; the struggles of the various states, 161–5; chances of a West African axis, 156–6; attitude to independence, 207
West African Common Market, 159–60
See also W.A.E.C.
West African Economic Community *See* W.A.E.C.
West African Free Trade Area. *See* W.A.F.T.A.
West African Interim Organisation for Economic Co-operation, 156

West Germany, 168, 196
Witchcraft, witch-doctors, 25, 121, 277
Women: industriousness of, 69; enfranchised in Guinea, 190–1
World Food Panel, 223

Yoruba people, 255, 263, 264n.

Zambia, 60, 216n., 238; output per head, 28; race issue, 132–3, 138; alliance against, 150; statistics of, 234
Zambesi, River, 27
Zanzibar, 147; statistics of, 234